NOTHING

SPECIAL

The boundary to
what we can
accept is the boundary
to our freedom

NOTHING

SPECIAL

Living
Zen

_____

CHARLOTTE JOKO BECK
EDITED BY STEVE SMITH

HarperOne
An Imprint of HarperCollinsPublishers

HarperOne

HarperCollins Web site: http://www.harpercollins.com

HarperCollins®, ♣®, and HarperOne™ are trademarks of HarperCollins Publishers.

FIRST HARPERCOLLINS PAPERBACK EDITION PUBLISHED IN 1995

Library of Congress Cataloging-in-Publication Data
Beck, Charlotte Joko.
    Nothing special : living Zen / Charlotte Joko Beck.—1st ed.
      p. cm.
    Includes biobliographical references.
    ISBN: 978–0–06–251117–1
    1. Religious life—Zen Buddhism. I. Title.
BQ9286.2.B44   1993   92–56131
294.3'444—dc20

11 12 RRD(H) 40 39 38 37 36 35 34 33

Zen is not some fancy, special art of living. Our teaching is just to live, always in reality, in its exact sense.

Shunryu Suzuki,
Zen Mind, Beginner's Mind

CONTENTS

Preface

Living Zen is nothing special: life as it is. Zen is life itself, nothing added. "Put no head above your own," declared Master Rinzai. When we seek from Zen (or from any spiritual path) the fulfillment of our fantasies, we separate from the earth and sky, from our loved ones, from our aching backs and hearts, from the very soles of our feet. Such fantasies insulate us for a time; yet in ten thousand ways reality intrudes, and our lives become anxious scurrying, quiet desperation, confusing melodrama. Distracted and obsessed, striving for something special, we seek another place and time: *not* here, *not* now, *not* this. Anything but this ordinary life, this . . . nothing special.

Living Zen means reversing our flight from nothingness, opening to the emptiness of here and now. Slowly, painfully, we reconcile to life. The heart sinks; hope dies. "Things are always just as they are," observes Joko. This empty tautology is no counsel of despair, however, but an invitation to joy. Dying to ego-dreams, no longer straining for effect, we return to a simple mind. In the garden of everyday experience, we uncover unexpected treasures. Ingenuous, living from what we are, we move from a self-centered toward a reality-centered life—and open to wonder. Abandoning magical thought, awakening to the magic of this moment, we realize in dynamic emptiness the grace of nothing special . . . living Zen.

In her life and teaching, in her very presence, Joko Beck manifests the remarkable absence that is living Zen. As Lenore Friedman observes, "In her absolute plainness, Joko embodies the Zen quality of 'Nothing Special.' She is simply there, in each bare moment."* Joko's blunt clarity carries far. Her

---

*Sources for quotations are listed at the end of the book.

thought has touched a resonant chord in countless readers around the world. *Everyday Zen: Love and Work* brought the insights of Zen to ordinary life in a form that is attuned to the rhythms of contemporary Western experience. *Nothing Special: Living Zen* extends and enlarges Joko's teaching. Its heightened maturity and closer attention to actual practice make this book useful not only for those who wish better understanding of Zen in the West, but also for those who are determined to transform their lives.

Like its predecessor, this book is the fruit not only of Joko's thought, but also of generous support from many of her devoted students and friends. Some will find talks here that they first transcribed or suggested for inclusion. Without their help, the book might not have come into being. John Loudon, senior editor at HarperSanFrancisco, guided the project with encouragement and wisdom. I am grateful for his stewardship and good judgment. Few authors and editors can be more fortunate than I in their secretarial support: with unflagging good humor, Pat Padilla has worked quickly and accurately with my often messy revisions. Once again, collaborating with Joko has been the greatest joy of all. Through compassion seasoned by wisdom, she continues to serve every life she touches.

Steve Smith
Claremont, California
February 1993

I

STRUGGLE

Whirlpools and Stagnant Waters

We are rather like whirlpools in the river of life. In flowing forward, a river or stream may hit rocks, branches, or irregularities in the ground, causing whirlpools to spring up spontaneously here and there. Water entering one whirlpool quickly passes through and rejoins the river, eventually joining another whirlpool and moving on. Though for short periods it seems to be distinguishable as a separate event, the water in the whirlpools is just the river itself. The stability of a whirlpool is only temporary. The energy of the river of life forms living things—a human being, a cat or dog, trees and plants— then what held the whirlpool in place is itself altered, and the whirlpool is swept away, reentering the larger flow. The energy that was a particular whirlpool fades out and the water passes on, perhaps to be caught again and turned for a moment into another whirlpool.

We'd rather not think of our lives in this way, however. We don't want to see ourselves as simply a temporary formation, a whirlpool in the river of life. The fact is, we take form for a while; then when conditions are appropriate, we fade out. There's nothing wrong with fading out; it's a natural part of the process. However, we want to think that this little whirlpool that we are isn't part of the stream. We want to see ourselves as permanent and stable. Our whole energy goes into trying to protect our supposed separateness. To protect the separateness, we set up artificial, fixed boundaries; as a consequence, we accumulate excess baggage, stuff that slips into our whirlpool and can't flow out again. So things clog up our whirlpool and the process gets messy. The stream needs to flow naturally and freely. If our particular whirlpool is all bogged down, we also impair the energy of the stream itself. It can't go anywhere. Neighboring whirlpools may get less water because of our frantic holding on. What we can best do for ourselves and for life is to keep the water in our whirlpool rushing and clear so that it is just flowing in and flowing out. When it gets all clogged up, we create troubles—mental, physical, spiritual.

We serve other whirlpools best if the water that enters ours is free to rush through and move on easily and quickly to whatever else needs to be stirred. The energy of life seeks rapid transformation. If we can see life this way and not cling to anything, life simply comes and goes. When debris flows into our little whirlpool, if the flow is even and strong, the debris rushes around for a while and then goes on its way. Yet that's not how we live our lives. Not seeing that we are simply a whirlpool in the river of the universe, we view ourselves as separate entities, needing to protect our boundaries. The very judgment "I feel hurt" establishes a boundary, by naming an "I" that demands to be protected. Whenever trash floats into our whirlpool, we make great efforts to avoid it, to expel it, or to somehow control it.

Ninety percent of a typical human life is spent trying to put boundaries around the whirlpool. We're constantly on guard: "He might hurt me." "This might go wrong." "I don't like him anyway." This is a complete misuse of our life function; yet we all do it to some degree.

Financial worries reflect our struggle to maintain fixed boundaries. "What if my investment doesn't work out? I might lose all of my money." We don't want anything to threaten our money supply. We all think that would be a terrible thing. By being protective and anxious, clinging to our assets, we clog up our lives. Water that should be rushing in and out, so it can serve, becomes stagnant. A whirlpool that puts up a dam around itself and shuts itself off from the river becomes stagnant and loses its vitality. Practice is about no longer being caught in the particular, and instead seeing it for what it is—a part of the whole. Yet we spend most of our energies creating stagnant water. That's what living in fear will do. The fear exists because the whirlpool doesn't understand what it is—none other than the stream itself. Until we get an inkling of that truth, all of our energies go in the wrong direction. We create many stagnant pools, which breed contamination and disease. Pools seeking to dam themselves for protection begin to contend with one another. "You're smelly. I don't like you." Stagnant pools cause a lot of trouble. The freshness of life is gone.

Zen practice helps us to see how we have created stagnation in our lives. "Have I always been so angry, and just never noticed it?" So our first discovery in practice is to recognize our own stagnation, created by our self-centered thoughts. The biggest problems are created by attitudes we cannot see in ourselves. Unacknowledged depression, fear, and anger create rigidity. When we recognize the rigidity and stagnation, the water begins to flow again, bit by bit. So the most vital part of practice is to be willing to be life itself—which is simply the incoming sensations—that which creates our whirlpool.

Over the years, we have trained ourselves to do the opposite: to create stagnant pools. This is our false accomplishment. Out of this ongoing effort come all of our troubles and our separation from life. We don't know how to be intimate, to be the stream of life. A stagnant whirlpool with defended boundaries isn't close to anything. Caught in a self-centered dream, we suffer, as one of our daily Zen Center vows states. Practice is the slow reversal of that. With most students, this reversal is the work of a lifetime. The change is often painful, especially at first. When we are used to the rigidity and controlled stiffness of a defended life, we don't want to allow fresh currents into awareness, however refreshing they may truly be.

The truth is, we don't like fresh air very much. We don't like fresh water very much. It takes a long time before we can see our defensiveness and manipulation of life in our daily activities. Practice helps us to see these maneuvers more clearly, and such recognition is always unpleasant. Still, it's essential that we see what we are doing. The longer we practice, the more readily we can recognize our defensive patterns. The process is never easy or painless, however, and those who are hoping to find a quick and easy place of rest should not undertake it.

That's why I am uneasy with the growth of the Zen Center of San Diego. Too many seekers are looking for easy, painless solutions to their difficulties. I prefer a smaller center, limited to those who are ready and willing to do the work. Of course, I don't expect from beginners the same thing I expect from experienced students. We all learn as we go. Still, the bigger the center, the more difficult it is to keep the teaching clean and rigorous. It's not important how many students we attract to the center; what is important is maintaining strong practice. So increasingly I am tightening up the teaching. This is not a place to be if one is seeking an artificial peace or bliss or some other special state.

What we do get out of practice is being more awake. Being more alive. Knowing our own mischievous tendencies so well that we don't need to visit them on others. We learn that it's never okay to yell at somebody just because we feel upset. Practice helps us to realize where our life is stagnant. Unlike rushing mountain streams, with wonderful water flowing in and flowing out, we may be brought to a dead halt by "I don't like it. . . . He really hurt my feelings," or "I have such a hard life." In truth, there is only the ongoing rush of the water. What we call our life is nothing but a little detour, a whirlpool that springs up, then fades away. Sometimes the detours are tiny and very brief: life swirls for a year or two in one place, then is wiped away. People wonder why some babies die when they are young. Who knows? We don't know why. It is part of this endless rushing of energy. When we can join this, we're at peace. When all of our efforts go in the opposite direction, we are not at peace.

STUDENT: In our individual lives, is it a good idea to choose some specific direction and set our sights on that, or is it better just to take things as they come? Setting up specific goals can block the flow of life, right?

JOKO: The problem lies not in having goals, but in how we relate to them. We need to have some goals. For example, parents typically set certain goals for themselves, such as planning ahead to provide for their children's education. People with natural talents may have the goal of developing them. Nothing wrong with that. Having goals is part of being human. It's the way we do it that creates the trouble.

STUDENT: The best way is to have goals but not cling to the end result?

JOKO: That's right. One simply does what is required to reach the goal. Anyone who seeks an educational degree needs to register in an educational program and take the courses, for example. The point is to promote the goal by accomplishing it in the present: doing this, doing that, doing this, as it becomes necessary, right here, right now. At some point, we get the degree or whatever. On the other hand, if we only dream of the goal and neglect to pay attention to the present, we will probably fail to get on with our lives—and become stagnant.

Whatever choice we make, the outcome will provide us with a lesson. If we are attentive and aware, we will learn what we need to do next. In this sense, there is no wrong decision. The minute we make a decision, we are confronted with our next teacher. We may make decisions that make us very uncomfortable. We may be sorry that we did what we did—and we learn from that. There is, for example, no ideal person to marry or ideal way to live one's life. The minute we marry somebody, we have a fresh set of opportunities for learning, fuel for practice. That's true not only of marriage, but of any relationship. Insofar as we practice with what comes up, the outcome will nearly always be rewarding and worthwhile.

STUDENT: When I set a goal for myself I tend to go into a "fast forward" mode and ignore the flow of the river.

JOKO: When the whirlpool tries to become independent of the river, like a tornado spinning out of control, it can cause a lot of damage. Even though we think of the goal as some future state to achieve, the real goal is always the life of this moment, this moment, this moment. There's no way to push the river aside. Even if we have created a dam around ourselves and become a stagnant pool, something will turn up that we have not anticipated. Perhaps a friend invites herself and her four children to visit for a week. Or someone dies; or our work suddenly changes. Life seems to present us with whatever it takes to stir up the pool.

STUDENT: In terms of the analogy of the whirlpools and the river, what is the difference between life and death?

JOKO: A whirlpool is a vortex, with a center around which the water spins. As one's life goes on, that center gradually gets weaker and weaker. When it weakens enough, it flattens out and the water simply becomes part of the river again.

STUDENT: From that point of view, wouldn't it be better to always be just part of the river?

JOKO: We are always part of the river, whether or not we are a whirlpool. We can't avoid being part of the river. We don't know that, however, because we have a distinct form and do not see beyond it.

STUDENT: So it's a delusion that life is different from death?

JOKO: That's true in an absolute sense, though from our human point of view they are distinct. On different levels, each is true: there is no life and death *and* there is life and death. When we know only the latter, we cling to life and fear death. When we see both, the sting of death is largely mitigated.

If we wait long enough, every whirlpool will eventually flatten out. Change is inevitable. Having lived in San Diego for a long time, I have watched the cliffs of La Jolla for many years. They're changing. The shoreline that now exists is not the same shoreline that I saw thirty years ago. Likewise with whirlpools; they also change and eventually just weaken. Something gives way and the water rushes on—and that's fine.

STUDENT: When we do die, do we retain anything of what we were or is it all gone?

JOKO: I'm not going to answer that. Your practice will give you some insight into that question.

STUDENT: You have sometimes described the energy of life as a native intelligence that we are. Does that intelligence have any boundaries?

JOKO: No. Intelligence is not a thing; it is not a person. It doesn't have boundaries. The minute we give something boundaries, we've put it back into the phenomenal sphere of things, like a whirlpool that sees itself as separate from the river.

STUDENT: Another of our regular Zen Center vows speaks of a "boundless field of benefaction." Is that the same as the river, the native intelligence that we are?

JOKO: Yes. Human life is simply a temporary form taken by this energy.

STUDENT: Yet in our lives there do need to be boundaries. I have a lot of difficulty reconciling this with what you're saying.

JOKO: Some boundaries are simply inherent in what we are; for example, each of us has a limited amount of energy and time. We need to recognize our limitations in this sense. This doesn't mean that we have to establish artificial, defensive boundaries that block our life. Even as small whirlpools, we can recognize that we are part of the river—and not become stagnant.

The Cocoon of Pain

When we bow in the zendo, what are we honoring? One way to answer this question is to ask what we actually honor in our lives, as shown by what we think and do. And the truth of the matter is that in our lives we do not honor buddha nature, nor the God that encompasses everything, including life and death, good and evil, all the opposites. The truth is, we're not interested in that. We certainly don't want to honor death, or pain, or loss. What we do is erect a false god. The Bible says, "Thou shalt have no other gods before me." But we do just that.

What is the god that we erect? What do we actually honor and pay attention to moment by moment? We might call it the god of comfort and pleasantness and security. In worshiping that god, we destroy our lives. In worshiping the god of comfort and pleasantness, people literally kill themselves—with drugs, alcohol, high speeds, recklessness, anger. Nations worship this god on a much larger, more destructive scale. Until we honestly see that this is what our lives are about, we will be unable to discover who we really are.

We have many ways to cope with life, many ways to worship comfort and pleasantness. All are based on the same thing: the fear of encountering any kind of unpleasantness. If we must have absolute order and control, it's because we're trying to avoid any unpleasantness. If we can have things our way, and get angry if they're not, then we think we can survive and shut out our anxiety about death. If we can please everyone, then we imagine no unpleasantness will enter our life. We hope that if we can be the star of the show, shining and wonderful and efficient, we can have such an admiring audience that we won't have to feel anything. If we can withdraw from the world and just entertain ourselves with our own dreams and fantasies and emotional upheavals, we think we can escape unpleasantness. If we can figure everything out, if we can be so smart that we can fit everything into some sort of a plan or order, a complete intellectual understanding, then perhaps we won't be threatened. If we can submit to an authority, have it tell us what to do, then we can give someone else the responsibility for our lives and we don't have to carry it anymore. We don't have to feel the anxiety of making a decision. If we pursue life madly, going after any pleasant sensation, any excitement, any entertainment, perhaps we won't have to feel any pain. If we can tell others what to do, keep them well under control, under our foot, maybe they can't hurt us. If we can "bliss out," if we can be a mindless "buddha" just relaxing in the sun, we don't have to assume any responsibility for the world's unpleasantness. We can just be happy.

All these are versions of the god we actually worship. It is the god of no discomfort and no unpleasantness. Without exception, every being on earth pursues it to some degree. As we pursue it, we lose touch with what really is. As we lose touch, our life spirals downward. And the very unpleasantness that we sought to avoid can overwhelm us.

This has been the problem of human life since the beginning of time. All philosophies and all religions are varying attempts to deal with this basic fear. Only when such attempts fail us are we ready to begin serious practice. And they do fail. Because the systems we adopt are not based upon reality; they can't work, despite all of our feverish efforts. Sooner or later, we come to realize that something is amiss.

Unfortunately, we often merely compound our error by trying harder, or by plastering over our old faulty system with a new faulty system. It's seductive, for example, to give ourselves over to some false authority or guru who will run our lives for us as we attempt to find something or someone outside of ourselves to take care of our fear.

Yesterday a butterfly flew through my open door and fluttered about in my room. Someone caught it and released it outside. It made me think about the life of a butterfly. A butterfly begins as a worm, which moves slowly and can't see very far.

Eventually the worm builds itself a cocoon, and in that dark, quiet space it stays for a long time. Finally, after what must seem like an eternity of darkness, it emerges as a butterfly.

The life history of a butterfly is similar to our practice. We have some misconceptions about both, however. We may imagine, for example, that because butterflies are pretty, their life in the cocoon before they emerge is also pretty. We don't realize all that the worm must go through in order to become a butterfly. Similarly, when we begin to practice, we don't realize the long and difficult transformation required of us. We have to see through our pursuit of outward things, the false gods of pleasure and security. We have to stop gobbling this and pursuing that in our shortsighted way, and simply relax into the cocoon, into the darkness of the pain that is our life.

Such practice requires years of our lives. Unlike the butterfly, we don't emerge once and for all. As we spin within the cocoon of pain, we may have momentary glimpses of life as a butterfly, fluttering in the sun. At such times we sense the absolute wonder of what our life is—something we never know as a busy little worm, preoccupied with itself. We begin to know the world of the butterfly only by contacting our own pain, which means no longer worshiping the god of comfort and pleasantness. We have to give up our slavish obedience to whatever system of pain avoidance we have devised and realize that we can't escape discomfort simply by running faster and trying harder. The faster we run from our pain, the more our pain overtakes us. When what we depended on to give our life meaning doesn't work any more, what are we going to do?

Some people never give up this false pursuit. Eventually they may die of an overdose, literally or figuratively. In the struggle to gain control we go faster, we strain, we try harder, we squeeze people tighter, we squeeze ourselves tighter. Yet life can never really be brought under control. As we flee from reality, the pain increases. This pain is our teacher.

Sitting is not about finding a happy, blissful state. The states may occur in sitting, when we've really experienced our pain over and over, so that finally there's just letting go. That surrender and opening into something fresh and new is the consequence of experiencing pain, not a consequence of finding a place where we can shut the pain out.

Sitting sesshin* and everyday practice are a matter of wrapping ourselves in that cocoon of pain. We don't do this unwillingly. First, we may be willing to have only one little strand wrapped around us, and then we'll break away. Again we'll wrap it around us and again break away. Eventually we become willing to sit with that portion of our pain for a while. Then perhaps we become willing to tolerate two or three strands. As our vision gets clearer, we can just sit within our cocoon and find it's the only peaceful space we've ever been in. And when we're perfectly willing to be there—in other words, when we're willing for life to be as it is, embracing both life and death, pleasure and pain, good and bad, comfortable in being both—then the cocoon begins to dissolve.

Unlike the butterfly, we alternate between the cocoon and the butterfly many times. This process continues through our life. Each time we uncover unresolved areas of our life we have to build another cocoon and rest quietly in it until the learning period completes itself. Each time our cocoon bursts and we take a little step, we are freer.

The first, essential step in becoming a butterfly is to recognize that we can't make it as a worm. We have to see through our pursuit of the false god of comfort and pleasure. We have to get a clear picture of that god. We have to relinquish our sense of entitlement—our sense that life owes us this and that. For example, we have to abandon the notion that we can compel others to love us by doing things for them. We have to recognize that we cannot manipulate life to satisfy ourselves, and that finding fault with ourselves or others is not an effective way of helping anyone. We slowly abandon our basic arrogance.

---

*An intensive Zen meditation retreat.

The truth is, life inside the cocoon is frustrating and heart-breaking, and it's never totally behind us. I don't mean that from morning to night we feel, "I am wrapped in pain." I mean that we're waking up constantly to what we're about, what we're really doing in our lives. And the fact is, that's painful. But there's no possibility of freedom without this pain.

I recently heard a quotation from a professional athlete: "Love is not shared pleasure. It is shared pain." That's a good insight. We can certainly enjoy going out with our partner, for example, and having dinner together. I'm not questioning the value of shared enjoyment. But if we want a relationship to be closer and more genuine, we need to share with our partner that which is most scary for us to share with anybody. When we do that, then the other person has freedom to do the same thing. Instead, we want to keep our image, particularly with somebody we're trying to impress.

Sharing our pain does not mean telling our partners how they irritate us. That's a way of saying, "I'm angry with you." It does not help us break down our false idol and open us to life as a butterfly. What does open us is sharing our vulnerabilities. Sometimes we see a couple who has done this difficult work over a lifetime. In the process, they have grown old together. We can sense the enormous comfort, the shared quality of ease between these people. It's beautiful, and very rare. Without this quality of openness and vulnerability, partners don't really know each other; they are one image living with another image.

We may seek to avoid the cocoon of pain by drifting into a hazy, unfocused state, a vaguely pleasant drifting that can last for hours. When we realize that's what's happening, what is a good question to ask?

STUDENT: "What am I avoiding?"

STUDENT: I might ask, "What am I experiencing right now?"

JOKO: Those are both good questions to ask. The curious thing is, we say that we want to know reality and see our life as it is; yet when we begin to practice, or attend sesshin, we immediately find ways to avoid reality by retreating into this hazy, dreamy state. That's just another form of worshiping the false god of comfort and pleasure.

STUDENT: Isn't there a flaw in seeking out suffering and focusing on it?

JOKO: We don't have to seek it; it's already there in our lives. Every five minutes, we're in trouble in some way. All of our "seeking" is to escape it. There are countless ways people try to escape, or to put a safe shell around themselves. Despite our efforts, the shell does get broken. Then we get more frantic and try harder. We go to work and find that the boss has had a bad night, or our child calls about getting in trouble at school. The shell is constantly under assault. There's no way we can be sure of keeping it in place. Our lives break down because we can't stand any opposition to the way we want things to be.

Pain is constantly in our lives. We feel not only our own pain, but the pain of people around us. We try to build our wall thicker, or we avoid people in distress; yet it's always present, nonetheless.

STUDENT: Supposing I'm sitting, and I'm not in pain. I'm actually rather comfortable. Is it useful to remember painful times in my life, to go back to unresolved situations and try to deal with them?

JOKO: That's not necessary. If we're alert to what's going on in our thoughts and our body in this moment, we'll have plenty to work with.

When we are fully awake in this moment, sitting can be pleasurable, too. But we shouldn't seek that out and try to escape the pain; then we bring into practice the false god and refuse to be awake to what is.

STUDENT: Over time, I find that what begins to come up in sitting is not so much pleasure or pain or something in between, but just interest. Experience can be looked on with a kind of curiosity.

JOKO: Yes, good point.

STUDENT: Are we talking about the difference between the absolute and the relative? Can we say that the absolute is paying attention to everything and that the relative is pursuing only pleasure and comfort? Is relaxing into the cocoon of pain a means to arriving at the absolute?

JOKO: I wouldn't say it's "a means to arriving at the absolute," since we're always there. But we choose not to notice we're there and to shut out part of our experience. The absolute always embraces pain and pleasure. There's nothing wrong with pain per se; we just don't like it. There isn't something called the absolute that is greater than the relative. There are just two sides of the same coin. The phenomenal world of people, trees, and rugs, and the absolute world of pure unknowable nothing, of energy, are the same thing. Rather than pursuing a one-sided ideal, we need to bow to the absolute in the relative, as well as the relative in the absolute. We need to honor everything.

Sisyphus and the Burden of Life

Greek mythology tells the story of Sisyphus, king of Corinth, condemned by the gods to Hades and eternal punishment. Endlessly he had to roll an enormously heavy boulder up a hill—and when it reached the top, it would roll down again. He struggled to bring the boulder to the top of the hill, only to watch it roll back down, over and over again, for eternity.

Like all myths, this story contains a teaching. How do you see the myth? What is it about? Like a koan, it has many aspects.

STUDENT: The myth suggests to me that life is a cycle. There is a beginning, a middle, and an end, and then it starts all over.

STUDENT: It reminds me of practice as polishing the mirror, polishing the mirror, polishing the mirror. We have to do this until we give up and simply live in the moment.

STUDENT: Sisyphus's punishment is awful only if he hopes for an end to it.

STUDENT: The myth reminds me of obsessive action, when I am trapped in a repetitive cycle of behaviors and thoughts.

STUDENT: Sisyphus sounds like a person who is struggling with life and its burdens, trying to get free from them.

STUDENT: The story sounds like our practice. If we live each moment, without a thought of a goal or getting somewhere or finally achieving something, then we just live. We do what's next: pushing, the rock falling back, then pushing again.

STUDENT: I think the story of Sisyphus represents the idea that there is no hope.

STUDENT: The nature of my mind is not to be satisfied with my own accomplishments and to be more interested in the challenge of getting somewhere. Once I have accomplished something, it doesn't mean much to me.

STUDENT: Sisyphus is who I am. We are all Sisyphus, trying to do something with our lives, and saying "I can't." The boulder itself is "I can't."

JOKO: A question I'd like to pose is, what does it mean to do evil? It's interesting that somebody judged Sisyphus for doing evil, and that he was condemned to a special place called Hades. But setting such questions aside, if we can see that there is just this moment, then pushing the rock up the hill or watching it roll back down are in a way the same thing. Our ordinary interpretation is that Sisyphus's task is difficult and unpleasant. Yet all that happens is simply pushing the rock and watching it roll back, moment by moment. Like Sisyphus, we are all just doing what we're doing moment by moment. But to that activity we add judgments, ideas. Hell lies not in pushing the rock, but in thinking about it, in creating ideas of hope and disappointment, in wondering if we will finally get the rock to stay at the top. "I've worked so hard! Maybe this time the boulder will stay."

Our efforts do make things happen, and in making things happen, we get to the next second. Perhaps the boulder *will* stay at the top for a while; perhaps it won't. Neither event is in itself good or bad. The weight of the boulder, the burden, is the thought that our life is a struggle, that it should be other than it is. When we judge our burden to be unpleasant, we look for ways to escape. Perhaps one person gets drunk to forget about pushing the boulder. Another manipulates people into helping push it. Often we try to shift the burden onto someone else so we can escape the work.

What would be the enlightened state for King Sisyphus? If he pushes the rock a few thousand years, what may he finally realize?

STUDENT: To be one with pushing in each moment.

JOKO: Just to push the rock and to have abandoned hope that his life will be other than it is. Most of us imagine that the enlightened state will feel much better than pushing a rock! Have you ever awakened in the morning and muttered, "I don't even want to think about all the things I have to do today"? But life *is* as it is. And our practice is not about having life feel good, even though that's a very human hope. We all like things that make us feel good. We especially like partners who make us feel good. If our partner doesn't make us feel good, we assume that things have to be changed, that he or she needs to change! Because we are human, we think that feeling good is the aim of life. But if we simply push our current boulder and practice being aware of what goes on with us as we push, we slowly transform. What does it mean to transform?

STUDENT: More acceptance, less judgment, more relaxation with life, an openness to life.

JOKO: *Openness to life* and *acceptance* are a bit off, though it's hard to find words that are exactly right.

STUDENT: Enlightenment has something to do with coming to zero, to "no place."

JOKO: But what does "no place" for a human being mean? What is that "no place"?

STUDENT: Right now.

JOKO: Yes, but how do we live it? Suppose I get up in the morning with a headache and have a heavy schedule before me. We all have days like this. What does it mean to "be a zero" with that?

STUDENT: It means simply to be here with all of my feelings and all of my thoughts—just being here, not adding anything extra to what is.

JOKO: Yes, and even if we do add something extra, that is also part of the package, part of life as it is at this moment. Part of the package is, "I just don't want to do this day." When that thought is what I acknowledge as being present, then I am just pushing my boulder. I go through the difficult day and I go to bed, and what do I get to do the next day? Somehow the boulder slipped back down the hill while I was asleep, so here I go again: push, push, push. "I hate this . . . yes, I know I hate it. I wish there were some way out, but there isn't, or at least I don't see a way out right now." Perfect in being as it is.

When we truly live each moment, what happens to the burden of life? What happens to our boulder? If we are totally what we are, in every second, we begin to experience life as joy. Standing between us and a life of joy are our thoughts, our ideas, our expectations, and our hopes and fears. It's not that we have to be totally willing to push the rock. We can be unwilling, so long as we acknowledge our unwillingness and simply feel it. Unwillingness is fine. A major part of any serious practice is "I don't want to do it." And we don't. But when our unwillingness drifts into efforts to escape, that's another matter. "Well, I'll have another piece of chocolate cake. I think there's one left." "I'll call up my friends; we'll talk about how terrible things are." "I'll creep into a corner so I can really worry about how bad my life is and feel sorry for myself." What are some other ways to escape?

STUDENT: To be very busy and tire myself out.

STUDENT: To procrastinate.

STUDENT: To make plans and then redo them over and over again.

STUDENT: My way is to become temporarily ill.

JOKO: Yes, we often do that: we catch a cold, sprain an ankle, get the flu.

When we label our thoughts, we become aware of how we escape. We begin to see the thousand and one ways we try to escape from living this moment, from pushing our rock. From the time we get up in the morning to the time we go to sleep, we are doing something; we are pushing our boulder all day long. It's our judgment about what we're doing that is the cause of our unhappiness. We may judge ourselves to be victims: "It's the way they are treating me." "I'm working with somebody who is unfair to me." "I can't defend myself."

Our practice is to see that we are just pushing—to get that basic fact. Nobody realizes this all the time; I certainly don't. But I notice that people who have been practicing for some time begin to have a sense of humor about their burden. After all, the thought that life is a burden is only a concept. We're simply doing what we're doing, second by second by second. The measure of fruitful practice is that we feel life less as a burden and more as a joy. That does not mean there is no sadness, but the experience of sadness is exactly the joy. If we don't find such a shift happening over time, then we haven't yet understood what practice is; the shift is a very reliable barometer.

Burdens are always turning up in our lives. For example, suppose I have to spend some time with somebody I don't like, and that feels like a burden. Or I have a tough week coming up, and I'm discouraged by it. Or the classes I'm teaching this semester have unprepared students in them. Raising kids can make us feel burdened. Illness, accidents, whatever difficulties we meet can be felt to be burdens. We cannot live as human beings without meeting difficulties, which we can choose to call "burdens." Life then becomes heavy, heavy, heavy.

STUDENT: I was just reminded of a concept from psychology of "the beloved burden."

JOKO: Yes, though "the beloved burden" cannot remain merely in our heads; it must transform into our being. There are many wonderful concepts and ideals, but if they don't become who we are, they can be the most fiendish burdens. Understanding something intellectually is not enough; sometimes it is worse than not understanding at all.

STUDENT: I'm having trouble with the idea that we're always pushing the boulder up the hill. Maybe it's because right now everything seems to be going my way.

JOKO: That could be. Sometimes things *do* go our way. We may be in the middle of a wonderful new relationship. The new job is still exciting. But there is a difference between things going our way and true joy. Suppose we are in the middle of one of those nice periods when we have a good relationship or a good job, and it's just great. What's the difference between that good feeling, which is based on circumstances, and joy? How would we know?

STUDENT: We have a fear that it will end.

JOKO: And how will that fear express itself?

STUDENT: In some body tension.

JOKO: Body tension will always be present if our good feeling is just ordinary, self-centered happiness. Joy has no tension in it, because joy accepts whatever is as it is. Sometimes in pushing the heavy rock we will even have a nice period. How does joy accept that good feeling?

STUDENT: Simply as it is.

JOKO: Yes. By all means if we are in a nice period of our lives, enjoy it—but without clinging to it. We tend to worry that we will lose it and try to hold on.

STUDENT: Yes, I notice that while I'm just living and enjoying it, I'm fine. It's when I stop and think, "This is great," that I begin to worry, "How long is this going to last?"

JOKO: None of us would choose to be Sisyphus; yet in a sense, we all are.

STUDENT: We have rocks in our heads.

JOKO: Yes. When we entertain the rock in our heads, the rock of life seems heavy. Otherwise our lives are just whatever we are doing. The way we become more content to just live our life as it is, just lifting the burden each day, is by being the experience of lifting, lifting, lifting. That's experiential knowledge, and intellectual understanding may evolve from it.

STUDENT: If I knew that the rock was going to come down each time, I would think, "Well, let me see how fast I can get it up this time. Maybe I can improve my time." I'd turn it into a game, or somehow create some significance in my mind.

JOKO: But if we are doing this through eternity, or even over a lifetime, what will happen to the significance we create? Such a creation is purely conceptual; sooner or later, it will collapse. That's the problem with "positive thinking" and affirmations: we can't keep them up forever. Such efforts are never the path to freedom. In truth, we are already free. Sisyphus was not a prisoner in Hades, living out eternal punishment. He was already free, because he was just doing what he was doing.

Responding to Pressure

Before service we recite the verse of the *Kesa:* "Vast is the robe of liberation, a formless field of benefaction. I wear the universal teaching, saving all sentient beings." The phrase "a formless field of benefaction" is particularly evocative; it calls forth who we are, which is the function of a religious service. The point of Zen practice is to be who we are—a formless field of benefaction. Such words sound very nice, but living them in our own lives is difficult and confusing.

Let's look at how we handle pressure or stress. What is pressure for one person may not be pressure for someone else. For a person who is shy, pressure might be walking into a crowded party. For another, pressure might be being alone, or meeting deadlines. For another, pressure might mean having a slow, dull life without any deadlines. Pressure could be a new baby, a new lover, a new friend. It might be success. Some people do well with failure but can't handle success. Pressure is what makes us tighten up, what arouses our anxiety.

We have different strategies for responding to pressure. Gurdjieff, an interpreter of Sufi mysticism, called our strategy our "chief feature." We need to learn what our chief feature is—the primary way we handle pressure. When the pressure's on, one person tends to withdraw; another struggles harder to be perfect, or to be even more of a star. Some respond to pressure by working harder, others by working less. Some evade, others try to dominate. Some get busy and talk a lot; others become quieter than usual.

We discover our chief feature by watching ourselves under pressure. Each morning when we get up, there is probably something in the day ahead that will cause pressure for us. When things are going badly, there's just nothing but pressure in our lives. At other times there's very little pressure, and we think things are going well. But life always pressures us to some degree.

Our typical pattern for responding to pressure is created early in our lives. When we meet difficulties as children, the smooth fabric of life begins to pucker. It's as if that puckering forms a little sack that we pull together to hide our fear. The way we hide our fear—the little sack that is our coping strategy—is our chief feature. Until we handle the "chief feature" and experience our fear, we can't be that seamless whole, the "formless field of benefaction." Instead we are puckered, full of bumps.

Over a lifetime of practice one's chief feature shifts almost completely. For instance, I used to be so shy that if I had to enter a room with ten or fifteen people—say, a small cocktail party—it would take me fifteen minutes of pacing outside before I could get up my courage to enter the room. Now, however, though I don't prefer big parties, I'm comfortable with them. There's a big difference between being so scared one can hardly walk into a room and being comfortable. I don't mean to say that one's basic personality changes. I will never be "the life of the party," even if I live to be one hundred and ten. I like to watch others at parties, and talk to a few people; that's my way.

We often make the mistake of supposing that we can simply retrain ourselves through effort and self-analysis. We may think of Zen practice as studying ourselves so that we can learn to think differently, in the sense that we might study chess or cooking or French. But that's not it. Zen practice isn't like learning ancient history or math or gourmet cooking. These kinds of learning have their places, of course, but when it comes to our chief feature—the way we tend to cope with pressure—it is our misuse of our individual minds that has created the emotional contraction. We can't use it to correct itself; we can't use our little mind to correct the little mind. It's a formidable problem: the very thing we're investigating is also our means or tool for investigating it. The distortion in how we think distorts our efforts to correct the distortion.

We don't know how to attack the problem. We know that something's not right with us because we're not at peace; we tend to try all sorts of false solutions. One such "solution" is training ourselves to do positive thinking. That's simply a maneuver of the little mind. In programming ourselves for positive thinking, we haven't really understood ourselves at all, and so we continue to get into difficulties. If we criticize our minds and say to ourselves, "You don't think very well, so I'll force you not to think" or "You've thought all those destructive thoughts; now you must think nice thoughts, positive thoughts," we're still using our minds to treat our minds. This point is particularly hard for intellectuals to absorb, since they have spent a lifetime using their minds to solve problems and naturally approach Zen practice in the same way. (No one knows this better than I do!) The strategy has never worked, and it never will.

There's only one way to escape this closed loop and to see ourselves clearly: we have to step outside of the little mind and observe it. That which observes is not thinking, because the observer can observe thinking. We have to observe the mind and notice what it's doing. We have to notice how the mind produces these swarms of self-centered thoughts, thus creating tension in the body. The process of stepping back is not complicated, but if we're not used to it, it seems new and strange, and perhaps scary. With persistence, it becomes easier.

Suppose we lose our job. Floods of thoughts come up, creating various emotions. Our chief feature springs in, covering our fear so that we don't deal with it directly. If we lose our job, the only thing to do is to go about finding another one, assuming we need the money. But that's often not what we do. Or, if we do look for another job, we may not do it effectively because we're so busy being upset by the activity of our chief feature.

Suppose we've been criticized by somebody in our daily life. Suddenly we feel pressure. How do we handle it? Our chief feature jumps right in. We use any mental trick we can find: worrying, justifying, blaming. We may try to evade the problem by thinking about something useless or irrelevant. We may take some sort of drug to shut it out.

The more we observe our thoughts and actions, the more our chief feature will tend to fade. The more it fades, the more we are willing to experience the fear that created it in the first place. For many years, practice is about strengthening the observer. Eventually, we're willing to do what comes up next, without resistance, and the observer fades. We don't need the observer anymore; we can be life itself. When that process is complete, one is fully realized, a buddha—though I haven't met anyone for whom the process is complete.

Sitting is like our daily lives: what comes up as we sit will be the thinking that we want to cling to, our chief feature. If we like to evade life, we'll find some way in sitting to evade our sitting. If we like to worry, we'll worry. If we like to fantasize, we'll fantasize. Whatever we do in our sitting is like a microcosm of the rest of our lives. Our sitting shows us what we're doing with our lives, and our lives show us what we do when we sit.

Transformation doesn't begin with saying to ourselves, "I should be different." Transformation begins with the realization expressed in the verse of the *Kesa:* "Vast is the field of liberation." Our very lives themselves are a vast field of liberation, a formless field of benefaction. When we wear the teachings of life, observing our thoughts, experiencing the sensory input we receive in each second, then we are engaged in saving ourselves and all sentient beings, just by being who we are.

STUDENT: My "chief feature" seems to change according to the situation. Under pressure I am usually controlling, domineering, and angry. In another situation, however, I might become withdrawn and quiet.

JOKO: Still, for any person, different behaviors in responding to pressure come from the same basic approach to handling fear, though they may look different. There is an underlying pattern that's being expressed.

STUDENT: When I feel pressured—especially when I feel criticized—I work hard and try to do well; I try not to just react, but to sit with the anxiety and fear. In the last year, however, I've come to realize that when I feel criticized, underlying my efforts to perform well is rage. I really want to attack; I'm a killer shark.

JOKO: The rage has been there the whole time; being a nice person and a fine performer is your cover. There's a killer shark in everybody. And the killer shark is unexperienced fear. Your way of covering it up is to look so nice and do so much and be so wonderful that nobody can possibly see who you really are—which is someone who is scared to death. As we uncover these layers of rage, it's important not to act out; we shouldn't inflict our rage on others. In genuine practice, our rage is simply a stage that passes. But for a time, we are more uncomfortable than when we started. That's inevitable; we're becoming more honest, and our false surface style is beginning to dissolve. The process doesn't go on forever, but it certainly can be most uncomfortable while it lasts. Occasionally we may explode, but that's better than evading or covering our reaction.

STUDENT: Often I can see other people's patterns much more quickly than my own. When I care about them, I'm tempted to set them straight. I feel like I'm seeing a friend drowning and not throwing a lifesaver. When I do intervene, however, it often feels like I'm butting into their lives when it is not my business at all.

JOKO: That's an important point. What does it mean to be a formless field of benefaction? We all see people doing things that obviously harm them. What should we do?

STUDENT: Isn't it enough to be aware and be present to them?

JOKO: Yes, that is generally the best response. Occasionally people will ask us for help. If they are sincere in asking, it's fine to respond. But we can be too quick to jump in and give advice. Many of us are fixers. An old Zen rule of thumb is not to answer until one has been asked three times. If people really want your opinion, they'll insist on having it. But we are quick to give our opinion when nobody wants it. I know; I've done it.

The observer has no emotions. It's like a mirror. Everything just passes in front of it. The mirror makes no judgment. Whenever we judge, we've added another thought that needs to be labeled. The observer is not critical. Judging is not something the observer does. The observer simply watches or reflects, like a mirror. If garbage passes in front of it, it reflects garbage. If roses pass in front of it, it reflects roses. The mirror remains a mirror, an empty mirror. The observer doesn't even accept; it just observes.

STUDENT: Isn't the observer really part of the little mind?

JOKO: No. The observer is a function of awareness that only arises when we have an object come up in our experience in the phenomenal world. If there's no object coming up (for example, in deep sleep), the observer is not there. The observer finally dies when we are *just* awareness and no longer need the observer.

We can never find the observer, no matter how long we look for it. Still, though we can never locate it, it is obvious that we can observe. We could say that the observer is a different dimension of mind but not an aspect of the little mind, which is on the ordinary linear level. Who we are is awareness. Nobody has ever observed awareness; yet that's who we are—a "formless field of benefaction."

STUDENT: It seems that an unpleasant sensation can anchor me in the present and focus my attention here and now.

JOKO: There's an old saying to the effect that human extremity is God's opportunity. When things are pleasant, we try to hold on to the pleasantness. In trying to cling to pleasure, we destroy it. When we are sitting and are truly still, however, the discomfort and pain draw us back to the present. Sitting makes more obvious our desire to escape or evade. When we are sitting well, there's no place to go. We tend not to learn that unless we're uncomfortable. The more unconscious we are of our discomfort and our efforts to escape, the more mayhem is created within phenomenal life—from war between nations down to personal arguments between individuals, to arguments within ourselves; all such problems arise because we separate ourselves from our experience. The discomfort and pain are not the cause of our problems; the cause is that we don't know what to do about them.

STUDENT: Even pleasure has an element of discomfort to it. For example, it's a pleasure to have some peace and quiet, but then I have an uncomfortable feeling that the noise and racket might start up again.

JOKO: Pleasure and pain are simply opposite poles. Joy is being willing for things to be as they are. With joy, there's no polarity. If the noise starts, it starts. If it stops, it stops. Both are joy. Because we want to cling to pleasure and push away pain, however, we develop an escape strategy. When something unpleasant happens to us as children, we develop a system—a chief feature for coping with unpleasantness—and live our life out of that instead of seeing it as it is.

The Baseboard

In ordinary life we all carry around what we can call an imaginary baseboard: an electrical baseboard that jolts us whenever we encounter what feels like a problem. We can imagine it with millions of outlets, all within our reach. Whenever we feel threatened or upset, we plug ourselves into it and react to the situation. The baseboard represents our fundamental decision about how we have to be in order to survive and get what we want in life. As young children we discovered that life wasn't always the way we wanted it to be, and things often went wrong from our personal point of view. We didn't want anyone to oppose us, we didn't want to experience unpleasantness, and so we created a defensive reaction to block the possible misery. That defensive reaction is our baseboard. We're always plugged into it, but we especially notice it at times of stress and threat. We have made a decision that ordinary life—life as it actually is—is unacceptable to us. And we try to counter what's happening.

All of this is inevitable. Our parents were not totally enlightened beings or buddhas, but other beings and events contributed, too. As young children we were not mature enough to handle them wisely. So we plugged into our baseboards and had a tantrum, "freaked out," or perhaps withdrew. From that time on, life was not lived for the sake of living life, but for the sake of our baseboard. It sounds silly; yet that's what we do.

Once the baseboard is established, whenever something unpleasant happens to us—even if somebody looks at us a little crossly—we plug into our baseboard. The baseboard we have constructed can take an indefinite number of plugs, and during the day we may plug into it a thousand times. As a result, we develop a very strange view of our life. For example, suppose that Gloria has said something snippy to me. The bare facts are simply that she's said something. She and I may have a little issue to discuss, but the truth of the matter is, she has simply said something. Immediately, however, I feel separated from Gloria. As far as I'm concerned, there is something wrong with her. "After all, look at what she did! She's really a most unpleasant person." Now I have it in for Gloria. The truth is, however, that my issue is not with Gloria; she has nothing to do with it. While it's true that she has said something, my upset comes not from her but from plugging into my baseboard. I experience my baseboard as a type of tension, which is unpleasant. I don't want to have anything to do with such a feeling, so I go to war with Gloria. But it's my baseboard that is causing me distress.

If the incident is minor, in a relatively short time I forget about it and plug something else into my baseboard. If the incident is major, however, I may take drastic action. I remember a friend of the family during the Great Depression who was fired from a job he had held for forty years. He raced up to the rooftop and jumped off, killing himself. He didn't understand his life. Something had happened, it's true, but it didn't merit committing suicide. He had plugged into his baseboard, however, and his suffering was so strong that he couldn't stand it.

Whenever something major happens in our lives, we get a sharp shock from our baseboard. We don't know what to do with that shock. Though the shock comes from inside us, we assume it comes from outside, "over there." Someone or something has treated us badly; we're victims. With Gloria, it feels obvious to me: the problem is Gloria. "Who else would it be? No one else has insulted me today. It has to be her!" In reacting, I start plotting: "How can I get back at her? Maybe I'll never speak to her again. If she's going to act like that I don't want her for a friend. I've got enough troubles. I don't need

Gloria." In fact, the real source of my distress is not Gloria. She did something I didn't like, but her behavior is not the source of my pain. The source of the pain is my fictional baseboard.

In sitting, we gradually become more aware of our body, and we find that it is contracted all the time. Usually the contraction is very fine and subtle, and not visible to other people. When we get really upset, the contraction strengthens. Some people are contracted so strongly that this is obvious to others. It depends on one's particular history. Even if a person has had a relatively happy and easy life, the contraction is constantly there as a marginal tension.

What can we do about this contraction? The first thing is to be aware that it exists. This usually takes a number of years of sitting. In the first years of sitting, we are usually dealing with the gross thoughts that we cook up out of the seeming troubles that we have with the universe. These thoughts mask the underlying contraction. We have to deal with them, and settle our lives down to the point that our emotional reactions are not so obstreperous. When our lives become somewhat more settled and normal, we become aware of the underlying marginal contraction that has been present all of the time. We can then become aware of the contraction more strongly when something goes wrong from our point of view.

Practice is not about the passing events of our life. Practice is about the baseboard. The baseboard will register these passing events. Depending on the events and how our baseboard registers them, we call our reactions upset, anger, depression. The distress is caused not by the events, but by our baseboard. For example, if a marital couple is quarreling, they think they are quarreling with each other; yet the quarrel is not actually with each other, but with each person's baseboard. A quarrel happens when each person plugs into his or her own baseboard in reaction to the other. So when we try to resolve a quarrel by dealing with our partner, we don't get anywhere; our partner isn't the source of the problem.

Another thing that adds to the confusion is that we like our baseboard. It gives us self-importance. When I don't understand my baseboard, then I can demand a lot of attention by quarreling with Gloria, getting even with her so that she knows the score. When I do this, I maintain my baseboard, which I see as my protection from the world. I have relied upon it since I was very small, and I don't want to get rid of it. If I were to drop my baseboard, I would have to face my terror; instead, I'd much rather fight with Gloria. That's what sitting is: to face the terror and to be the tension—marginal or major—in the body. We don't want to do this. We want to deal with our problems through our baseboard.

Years ago I worked for a large company. I was the assistant to the boss of my section, the scientific research lab. I was assigned a parking spot close to the entrance to the lab. That was nice; when it rained, I could jump from my car into the building without getting very wet. A problem developed around my parking space, however, because the door also led directly to the vice president's office. So the vice president's secretary decided that I had the best parking spot. She raised a fuss, and memos began to fly. She sent memos to the personnel office, to my boss, to her boss, and to a few other places. She was upset because on paper she outranked me, yet I had the best parking spot. I thought, "She's trying to take away my parking spot. I've always had that parking spot. It's legally mine." My boss, who was head of the scientific research laboratory, identified with me and started to fight with the vice president. Their egos became involved. Who was more important? There wasn't a clear answer. So now, instead of simply the two of us quarreling, our bosses were battling also. Every night when I pulled out of my parking spot, I *knew* I was right!

The battle went on for months. The memos would die down, then—whenever the secretary saw me—they would start to fly again. Finally one night at an intersection as I sat in my car waiting for the light to change, I realized, "I'm not married to that parking spot. If she wants it, let her have it." So the next day, I got my own memos going. With permission from personnel, I gave her my parking spot. My boss was furious with me. Since it wasn't a big issue, however, he got used to it. A week later, the secretary called me and invited me to lunch. We never became close friends, but we had a cordial relationship.

The real issue wasn't between that secretary and me. The parking spot was a symbol for other kinds of struggles. I don't mean to imply that one should always give up one's parking spot. In this case, however, the issue was trivial: I had to walk maybe forty or fifty feet instead of seven feet. Once or twice a winter, I got a bit wetter. Yet until the controversy was resolved, it kept many people busy for many months.

Our issues are not ever with others, but with our own baseboard. If we have a baseboard with many outlets just asking to be plugged into, almost anything will serve. We like our baseboard; without it we would feel terrified, as we felt when we were children.

The point of practice is to become friendly with the baseboard. We're not going to get rid of it all at once; we're too fond of it for that. But as the mind truly quiets and becomes less interested in fighting with the world, when we give up our position in some pointless battle, when we don't have to do all of that fighting because we come to see it for what it is, then our ability to just sit increases. At that point, we begin to sense what the real problem is: that ancient creation made of grief—a little child's grief that life isn't what we want it to be. The grief is layered with anger, fear, and other such feelings. There's no escape from the dilemma except to go back the way we came and just experience these feelings. We're not interested in doing this, however; that's what makes sitting difficult.

When we go back to the body, it's not that we uncover some great melodrama going on inside of us. For most of us most of the time, the contraction is so marginal that we can hardly tell it's there. Yet it is. When we just sit and keep getting closer to feeling this contraction, we learn to rest in it for longer and longer periods: five seconds, ten seconds, and eventually thirty minutes or more. Because the baseboard is our creation and has no fundamental reality, it begins to resolve a bit, here and there. After sesshin for a time we may find that it's gone. Then it may be back. If we understand our practice, over years of sitting the baseboard becomes thinner and less dominating. Momentary openings in it may occur. In themselves, such openings are unimportant, since the baseboard usually goes right back into operation as soon as we have another unpleasant encounter with somebody. I'm not particularly interested in creating openings in the baseboard; the real work lies in slowly dissolving it altogether. We know that the baseboard is functioning when we're upset with somebody or something. Undoubtedly we do have issues in the outside world to resolve, some of them very difficult. But such issues are not what upsets us. What upsets us is being plugged into our baseboard. When that happens, there is no serenity, no peace.

This kind of practice—working directly with the baseboard, our underlying contraction—can be harder than koan practice. With koan practice,* one always has a little incentive or reward to pass the next koan. There's nothing wrong with this, and I sometimes work on koans with my students. Still, this approach is not as fundamental as the baseboard, which is present in each one of us. Are we aware of it? Do we know what it means to practice? How seriously do we take our difficulties with other people or with life? When we are plugged in, life is so hopeless. We're all plugged in to varying degrees, including myself. Over the years, I have become better able to recognize when I'm plugged in. I don't miss much anymore. We can catch ourselves being plugged in by watching how we talk to ourselves and others: "There is something wrong with him. It's his fault. He should be different." "I should be better." "Life's just unfair to me." "I am truly hopeless."

---

*Koan: a traditional paradoxical question not amenable to rational analysis, used to deepen meditation.

When we play these sentences through our minds without questioning them, then we're waging a false fight and we end up where any false fight leads: nowhere, or into more trouble. We have to wage the real fight: to stay with that which we do not want to stay with. Practice takes courage. The courage builds with practice, but there is no quick, easy fix. Even after much sitting, when we become angry we have an impulse to attack another. We look for ways to punish others for what they have done. Such activity is not experiencing our anger, but avoiding it through drama.

Many schools of therapy encourage the client to express hostility. When we express our hostility, however, our attention goes outward, toward another person or thing, and not on the real problem. Expressing our feelings is natural, and not a terrible thing in itself. But it often creates problems for us. When truly experienced, anger is very quiet. It has a certain dignity. There's no display, no acting out. It's just being with that fundamental contraction that I have called the baseboard. When we truly stay with anger, then the personal and self-centered thoughts separate out and we're left with pure energy, which can be used in a compassionate way.

That's the whole story of practice. A person who can do this with great consistency is a person we call enlightened. Having a momentary experience of being without the baseboard is not true enlightenment. A truly enlightened person is one who can transform the energy nearly all of the time. It's not that the energy no longer arises; the question is, what do we do with it? If somebody bashes into the side of our car without paying attention, we're not just going to smile sweetly. We'll have a reaction: "Damn it!" But then what? How long do we stay with that reaction? Most of us prolong the reaction and enlarge upon it. An example is our propensity for lawsuits. I'm not saying that a suit is never justified; it may sometimes be necessary to resolve an issue. But many lawsuits are about something else and are counterproductive. If I express my anger at Gloria, Gloria in some way will direct it back at me. My friendship with Gloria may be over. When the personal element—how I feel about her—is removed, then there is just energy. When we sit with great dignity with this energy, though it is painful at first, it turns into the place of great rest. A phrase from a Bach chorale comes back to me: "In Thine arms I rest me." That means resting in who I truly am. "Those who would molest me cannot find me here." Why can't they find me here? Because there is no one home. There is no one here. When I am pure energy, I am no longer me. I am a functioning for good. That transformation is why we're sitting. It's not easy. And it doesn't happen overnight. But if we sit well, over time we become less and less engaged in interpersonal mischief, harming ourselves and others. Sitting burns up the self-centered element and leaves us with the energy of our emotions, without the destructiveness.

Sesshins, regular sitting, and life practice are the best ways to bring about this transformation. Bit by bit, there is a shift in our energy, and more of the baseboard is burned out. As our self-centered preoccupations drop away, we can't go back to the way we were. A fundamental transformation has taken place.

"In Thine arms I rest me." There is real peace when we rest within that fundamental contraction, just experiencing the body as it is. As Hubert Benoit says in his wonderful book *The Supreme Doctrine,* when I am in real despair, at least let me rest on that icy couch. If I truly rest on it, my body conforms to it, and there is no separation. At that point, something shifts. How do I feel about Gloria now? Oh, we had a little disagreement, so we'll take a nice walk today and talk about it. No problem.

II

SACRIFICE

Sacrifice and Victims

As I listen to many people talk about their lives, I am struck that the first layer we encounter in sitting practice is our feeling of being a victim—our feeling that we have been sacrificed to others. We *have* been sacrificed to others' greed, anger, and ignorance, to their lack of knowledge of who they are. Often this victimization comes from our parents. Nobody has two buddhas for parents. Instead of buddhas, we have parents for parents: flawed, confused, angry, self-centered—like all of us. I was mistreated by my parents, and I certainly mistreated my children at times. Even the very best of parents sometimes mistreat their children, because they're human.

In practice we become aware of having been sacrificed, and we are upset about this fact. We feel that we have been hurt, that we have been misused, that somebody has not treated us the way we should have been treated—and this is true. Though inevitable, it's still true, and it hurts, or seems to.

The first stage is simply to become aware of the fact of having been sacrificed. The second stage is working with the feelings that come out of that awareness: our anger, our desire to get even, our desire to hurt those who have hurt us. These desires vary greatly in intensity: some are mild, some are powerful and persistent. Many therapies deal with unearthing our experiences of victimization; they differ in what to do about such experiences. In politics we seem to think we have to fight back. We can fight back, or we can do something else. But what would that be?

As we practice, we become aware of our anger about events, our desire to get even, our confusion and withdrawal and coldness; if we continue to practice (maintaining awareness, labeling our thoughts), then something different—though also painful—begins to arise in our consciousness. We begin to see not only how we have been sacrificed, but also how we have sacrificed others. This can be even more painful than our first realization. Especially when we act on our anger and resentment and try to get even, it begins to dawn on us that we are now sacrificing others, just as we have been sacrificed. As the Bible says, the evil is visited upon generation after generation. When our sorrow begins to be as great for what we do to others as for what has been done to us, our practice is maturing.

If we are committed to healing, we want to atone. What does the word *atone* mean? It means to be "at one." We can't wipe out what we have done in the past; we've done it. Feeling guilty about it is a way of sacrificing ourselves now because we have sacrificed others in the past. Guilt doesn't help. Saying that one is sorry—apologizing—is not always atonement, either. Though it may be necessary, it may not be enough. Religious practice is about atonement, practicing with our lives, seeing our desire to sacrifice others because we are angry. We need to see these desires but not act on them.

The process of atonement goes on for a lifetime. That's what human life is: endless atonement. In contrast, feeling guilty is an expression of the ego: we can feel sorry for ourselves (and a bit noble) if we get lost in our guilt. In true atonement, instead of focusing upon our guilt, we learn to focus more upon our sisters and brothers, upon our children, upon anyone who is suffering. Such efforts can be genuine, however, only if we first deal with the initial layer—which is to become aware of all our thoughts, our feelings, and our anger about what our life has been. Then we have to develop a sharp eye and a sharp sense of our present desire to sacrifice others. This is much more important: not what has been done to us, but what we are doing to others. *Somebody* has to stop the process. How do we stop it? We stop it when we move out of our bitter thoughts about the past and future and just begin to be here with what is, doing the best we can, noticing what we do. Once this process becomes clear, there is only one thing that we really want to do: to break that chain, to ease the suffering of the world. If one person in ten in the world were to break the chain, the whole cycle would collapse; it would not have enough strength to maintain itself.

What does this have to do with oneness and enlightenment? An enlightened person would be willing, second by second by second, to be the sacrifice that's necessary to break the cycle of suffering. Being willing to be sacrificed doesn't mean being "holier than thou"; that's merely ego. The willingness to be sacrificed is simpler and more basic. As we sit, as our knowledge of ourselves and our lives increases, we get a choice about what we are going to do: we get to choose whether to sacrifice another person. For example, we get to choose whether to snap at somebody. This may seem like a little thing, but it's not. We get to choose how we relate to the people we are close to. It's not that we become martyrs; choosing to be a martyr is actually quite self-centered. And it's not that we give up fun in life. (We certainly don't want to be around people who never have fun.) The main point is, to become aware of our feelings of having been sacrificed and then to begin to see how we sacrifice others. This stage has to be clear. I often hear, "Why shouldn't I strike back? Look at what has been done to me!"

STUDENT: Sometimes when I feel guilty, I get into a mode of self-punishment. How can I get out of that mode?

JOKO: Self-flagellation is simply thinking. We can be aware of this thinking and sense the body tension that goes with it. We can ask ourselves what we accomplish by punishing ourselves over and over. In a way, we like self-flagellation because it is self-centered: it makes us the center of things. A guilt trip is a very self-centered activity.

STUDENT: What about being with people whom I used to be close to and don't like anymore? Anger comes up, like a shadow. When I think of them, I have a sinking feeling.

JOKO: Just be aware of your feelings; notice what you are thinking. If there is an appropriate time when you need to be with these people, see what that is like. And don't avoid people who bring up that anger. I'm not suggesting that you necessarily seek them out, but at least don't avoid them.

STUDENT: I frequently feel guilty that I'm not spending enough quality time with my parents. I have watched myself do this over and over again; yet I keep doing it.

JOKO: You are measuring yourself against a mental ideal. When you are with your parents, just be with them and see what comes up. That's all. The rest is a fantasy about how you should be. Who knows how you should be? We simply do our best, over and over and over. In time, we lose all interest in our past.

The Promise That Is Never Kept

Our human trouble arises from desire. Not all desires generate problems, however. There are two kinds of desires: demands ("I have to have it") and preferences. Preferences are harmless; we can have as many as we want. Desire that *demands* to be satisfied is the problem. It's as if we feel constantly thirsty, and to quench our thirst, we try to attach a hose to a faucet in the wall of life. We keep thinking that from this or that faucet, we will get the water we demand. As I listen to my students, everyone seems thirsty for something. We may get a bit of water here and there, but it only tantalizes us. Being really thirsty is not fun.

What are some of the faucets we try to attach ourselves to, in order to quench our thirst? One might be a job we feel that we must have. Another might be "the right partner," or "a child who behaves as he or she should." Fixing a personal relationship may seem to be the way to get that drink. Many of us also believe that we will finally quench our thirst if we can only fix ourselves. It makes no sense for the self to fix the self, but we persist in trying to do it. What we regard as ourselves is never quite acceptable to us. "I don't get enough done." "I'm not sufficiently successful." "I'm always angry, so I'm worthless." "I'm a poor student." We demand countless things of ourselves and the world; almost anything can be seen as desirable, a socket we can attach ourselves to, so that we can finally get the drink we believe we need. Bookstores are full of self-help books, proclaiming various remedies for our thirst: *How to Make Your Husband Love You,* or *How to Build Self-Esteem,* and so on. Whether or not we seem to be self-assured, underneath it all we feel that there is something lacking. We feel we have to fix our life, to quench our thirst. We've got to get that connection, to hook up our hose to the faucet and draw that water to drink.

The problem is that nothing actually works. We begin to discover that the promise we hold out to ourselves—that somehow, somewhere, our thirst will be quenched—is never kept. I don't mean that we never enjoy life. Much in life can be greatly enjoyed: certain relationships, certain work, certain activities. But what we want is something absolute. We want to quench our thirst *permanently,* so that we have all the water we want, all the time. That promise of complete satisfaction is never kept. It can't be kept. The minute we get something we have desired, we are momentarily satisfied—and then our dissatisfaction rises again.

If we have been trying for years to attach our hose to this or that faucet, and each time have discovered that it wasn't enough, there will come a moment of profound discouragement. We begin to sense that the problem is not with our failure to connect with something out there, but that nothing external can ever satisfy the thirst. This is when we are more likely to begin a serious practice. This can be an awful moment—to realize that nothing is ever going to satisfy. Perhaps we have a good job, a good relationship or family, yet we're still thirsty—and it dawns on us that nothing really can fulfill our demands. We may even realize that changing our life—rearranging the furniture—isn't going to work, either. That moment of despair is in fact a blessing, the real beginning.

A strange thing happens when we let go of all our expectations. We catch a glimpse of yet another faucet, one that has been invisible. We attach our hose to it and discover to our delight that water is gushing forth. We think, "I've got it now! I've got it!" And what happens? Once again, the water dries up. We have brought our demands into practice itself, and we are once again thirsty.

Practice has to be a process of endless disappointment. We have to see that everything we demand (and even get) eventually disappoints us. This discovery is our teacher. It's why we should be careful with friends who are in trouble, not to give them sympathy by holding out false hopes and reassurances. This kind of sympathy—which is not true compassion—simply delays their learning. In a sense, the best help we can give to anybody is to hasten their disappointment. Though that sounds harsh, it's not in fact unkind. We help others and ourselves when we begin to see that all of our usual demands are misguided. Eventually we get smart enough to anticipate our next disappointment, to know that our next effort to quench our thirst will also fail. The promise is never kept. Even with long practice, we'll sometimes seek false solutions, but as we pursue them, we recognize their futility much more rapidly. When this acceleration occurs, our practice is bearing fruit. Good sitting inevitably promotes such acceleration. We must notice the promise that we wish to exact from other people and abandon the dream that they can quench our thirst. We must realize that such an enterprise is hopeless.

Christians call this realization the "dark night of the soul." We've worn out everything we can do, and we don't see what to do next. And so we suffer. Though it feels miserable at the time, that suffering is the turning point. Practice brings us to such fruitful suffering, and helps us to stay with it. When we do, at some point the suffering begins to transform itself, and the water begins to flow. In order for that to happen, however, all of our pretty dreams about life and practice have to go, including the belief that good practice—or indeed, anything at all—should make us happy. The promise that is never kept is based on belief systems, personally centered thoughts that keep us stuck and thirsty. We have thousands of them. It's impossible to eliminate them all; we don't live long enough for that. Practice does not require that we get rid of them, but simply that we see through them and recognize them as empty, as invalid.

We throw these belief systems around like rice at a wedding party. They turn up everywhere. For example, as the Christmas season approaches, we may have expectations that it will be pleasant and fun, a nice time of year. Then when the season doesn't meet our expectations, we're depressed and upset. In fact, Christmas will be what it will be, whether our expectations are met or not. Likewise, when we discover Zen practice, we may hold out a hope that it is going to solve our problems and make our life perfect. But Zen practice simply returns us to life as it is. Being our lives more and more is what Zen practice is about. Our lives are simply what they are, and Zen helps us to recognize that fact. The thought "If I do this practice patiently enough, everything will be different" is simply another belief system, another version of the promise that is never kept. What are some other belief systems?

STUDENT: If I work hard, I'll make it.

JOKO: Yes, that's a good American belief system.

STUDENT: If I'm nice to people, they won't hurt my feelings.

JOKO: Yes, that one often disappoints us. People will be as they will be, that's all. No guarantees.

STUDENT: I have a belief that we're all doing the best we can.

JOKO: That's a belief system I share.

STUDENT: If I exercise daily, I'll be healthy.

JOKO: I just heard of a fellow who exercises regularly who tripped and shattered his hip.

STUDENT: If I lived elsewhere, I would enjoy life more.

STUDENT: If I help other people, I'm a good person.

JOKO: That's a real pitfall, a seductive belief system that will get us in trouble. Of course, we should do what's appropriate and necessary; in a deeper sense, however, we can't help another person.

STUDENT: I've been sitting for so long, I shouldn't be angry anymore.

JOKO: If you're angry, you're angry.

STUDENT: If my car starts right away, my day will go smoothly.

STUDENT: If I work for a worthy cause, the world will be a better place.

STUDENT: The pain that I experience should make me a better person.

JOKO: You're already fine as you are.

It's useful to review our belief systems in this way, because there's always one that we don't see. In each belief system we hide a promise. As for Zen practice: the only promise we can count upon is that when we wake up to our lives, we'll be freer persons. If we wake up to the way we see life and deal with it, we will slowly be freer—not necessarily happier or better, but freer.

Every unhappy person I've ever seen has been caught in a belief system that holds out some promise, a promise that has not been kept. Persons who have practiced well for some time are different only in the fact that they recognize this mechanism that generates unhappiness and are learning to maintain awareness of it—which is very different from trying to change it or fix it. In itself, the process is as simple as it can be; yet we human beings find it extremely difficult. We have absolutely no interest in maintaining our awareness. We want to be thinking about something else, anything else. And so our lives give us endless discouragement, the perfect gift.

When people hear this, they want to get up and leave. Yet life pursues them; their belief systems keep making them miserable. We want to hold onto our belief systems; but if we do, we suffer. In a sense, everything works perfectly. I never care whether anyone leaves practice or enters practice, it doesn't make any difference; inevitably, the process goes on. It's true that some people in their entire lifetime never seem to learn anything about this process. We all know some people like this. Still, the process goes on, even when they ignore it. Practice lessens our ability to ignore it; after a certain amount of practice, even if we say, "Well, I'm not going to do this practice, it's too hard," we can't avoid it. After a while we just practice. Once the awareness is awakened, we can't stuff it back in the box.

The basic concepts of practice are really quite simple. But to do the practice and to gain a genuine understanding of it takes time. Many suppose within the first two years that they clearly understand it. In fact, if we get practice straight in ten or fifteen years, we're doing pretty well. For most, twenty years is what it takes. That's when a practice is reasonably clear and we're doing it as much as we can from the time we wake up in the morning to the time we go to bed at night. Then, practice even goes on all night in one's sleep. So there's no "quick fix." As we continue to practice, however, it becomes more enjoyable, even fun. Our knees may ache, we may face all sorts of problems in our lives, but practice can be fun, even while it is difficult, painful, frustrating.

STUDENT: At times, it's exhilarating. Whenever I become pain-free in practice, I start to laugh.

JOKO: Because you see something you haven't seen before?

STUDENT: Yes, of course.

STUDENT: You suggested that in a sense, there's no such thing as Zen practice. Could you explain?

JOKO: There's a practice of maintaining awareness; in that sense, Zen practice exists. But so long as we're alive, there's the question of awareness. We can't avoid it. In that sense, there's no way to avoid practice, or even to do it. It's just being alive. Though there are certain formal activities that assist us in waking up (which we can call Zen practice if we want), real "Zen practice" is just being here right now and not adding anything to this.

STUDENT: Back to the analogy of the wall with little faucets on it: when we find a faucet and attach ourselves to it, we do get some water out, don't we?

JOKO: Yes, for a while we quench our thirst slightly. For example, suppose for six months you have wanted to take a girl out on a date, and finally you get up the courage to ask her and she says yes. For a brief moment there's tremendous elation. We could call that getting water, though whether you are truly satisfied is another question. Sooner or later, the elation subsides, and life again seems to present us with new problems. I'm talking about a way of living in which life itself is no problem. We *have* problems, but there's no problem in dealing with them. Everyone probably has a glimpse of that now and then.

In a sense, Zen is a religious practice. *Religion* really means to rejoin that which seems to be separate. Zen practice helps us to do that. But it's not a religion in the sense that there's something outside of ourselves that's going to take care of us. A lot of people who practice Zen have no formal religious affiliation. I have nothing against formal religion; in all religions there are some remarkable people who truly practice and know what they're doing. But there are also people who have no connection with formal religion whatsoever, yet who practice just as well. In the end there is no practice except what we're doing each second.

Because true practice and religion help us to rejoin what seems to be separate, all practice has to be about anger. Anger is the emotion that separates us. It cuts everything right in two.

STUDENT: Is not this practice very difficult to do entirely by oneself? When one of my belief systems breaks down, I feel betrayed and need some support from others.

JOKO: "I feel betrayed" is, of course, just another thought. It is more difficult to practice alone, but it's not impossible. It's useful to come to a Zen center to get a foundation, then maintain some contact long distance and come to sit with others when one can. When one practices alone, it's like swimming against the current. In a community of persons practicing together, we have a mutual language and common understanding of what practice is. Still, I have some excellent students who live far from Zen centers and who talk with me on the phone. Some of them are doing very well. And for some, the struggle of a practice done with such minimal support may be the most useful thing.

Justice

As we become increasingly sensitive to ourselves and the transitory experiences of our lives—our thoughts, emotions, sensations—it becomes obvious to us that the underlying stratum of our lives is anger. When someone insists, "I am never angry," I am incredulous.

Since anger and its subsets—depression, resentment, jealousy, backbiting, gossip, and so on—dominate our lives, we need to investigate the whole problem of anger with care. For a life free of anger would be the promised land of milk and honey, nirvana, an existence in which our own worth and that of others is a blessedly confirmed reality.

For the psychologically mature person, the ills and injustices of life are handled by counteraggression, in which one makes an effort to eliminate the injustice and create justice. Often such efforts are dictatorial, full of anger and self-righteousness.

In spiritual maturity, the opposite of injustice is not justice, but compassion. Not me against you, not me straightening out the present ill, fighting to gain a just result for myself and others, but compassion, a life that goes against nothing and fulfills everything.

All anger is based upon judgments, whether of ourselves or others. The idea that our anger must be expressed for us to be healthy is no more than a fantasy. We need to let these judgmental, angry thoughts pass before our witnessing, impersonal self. We gain nothing by expressing them. It is a mistake to suppose that our unexpressed anger hurts us and that we must express it and thereby hurt others.

The best answer to injustice is not justice, but compassion, or love. You ask, "But what *am* I to do in this difficult situation? I must do something!" Yes, but what? Always our practice must

be the basis for our actions. An appropriate and compassionate response does not come from a fight for justice, but from
that radical dimension of practice that "passeth all understanding." It's not easy. Perhaps we must go through agonized
weeks or months of sitting. But the resolution will come. No
person can provide this resolution for us; it can be provided
only by our true self—if we open wide the gates of practice.

Let us not adopt some facile, narrowly psychological view
of our lives. The radical dimension I speak of demands everything we are and have. Joy, not happiness, is its fruit.

Forgiveness

Perfect love means to love the one through whom one became unhappy.

Søren Kierkegaard

Who is it that you cannot forgive? Each of us has a list, which may include ourselves (often the hardest one to forgive), as well as events, institutions, and groups.

Isn't it natural that we should feel this way about a person or event that has injured us—perhaps severely and irrevocably? From the ordinary standpoint, the answer is yes. From a practice standpoint, the answer is no. We need to vow: I *will* forgive even if it takes me a lifetime of practice. Why such a strong statement?

The quality of our whole life is on the line. Failing to grasp the importance of forgiveness is always part of any failing relationship and a factor in our anxieties, depressions, and illnesses—in all our troubles. Our failure to know joy is a direct reflection of our inability to forgive.

So why don't we just do it? If it were easy, we would all be realized buddhas. But it is not easy. There is no use in saying, "I should forgive, I should, I should, I should. . . ." Such desperate thoughts help very little. Analysis and intellectual efforts can produce some softening of the rigidity of nonforgiveness. But true or complete forgiveness lies on a different plane.

Nonforgiveness is rooted in our habit of thinking self-centered thoughts. When we believe in such thoughts, they are like a drop of poison in our glass of water. The first, formidable task is to label and observe these thoughts until the poison can

evaporate. Then the major work can be done: the active experiencing as a bodily physical sensation of the anger's residue in the body, without any clinging to self-centered thoughts. The transformation to forgiveness, which is closely related to compassion, can take place because the dualistic world of the small mind and its thoughts has been deserted for the nondual, nonpersonal experiencing that alone can lead us out of our hellhole of nonforgiveness.

Only an acute realization of the critical need for such practice will enable us to do it with strength and determination over the years. A maturing practice knows there is no other choice.

So, who is it you cannot forgive?

The Talk Nobody Wants to Hear

If we're honest, we have to admit that what we really want from practice—especially at the beginning, but always to some degree—is greater comfort in our lives. We hope that with sufficient practice, what bothers us now will not bother us anymore. There are really two viewpoints from which we can approach practice, which need to be spelled out. The first viewpoint is what most of us *think* practice is (whether we admit it or not), and the second is what practice actually is. As we practice over time, we gradually shift from one viewpoint toward the other, though we never completely abandon the first. We're all somewhere on this continuum.

Operating from the first viewpoint, our basic attitude is that we will undertake this demanding and difficult practice because we hope to get certain personal benefits from it. We may not expect them all at once. We may have some limited patience, but after a few months of practice, we may begin to feel cheated if our life has not improved. We enter practice with an expectation or demand that it will somehow take care of our problems. Our basic demands are that we be comfortable and happy, that we be more peaceful and serene. We expect that we won't have those awful feelings of upset, and we will get what we want. We expect that instead of being unfulfilling, our life will become more rewarding. We hope to be healthier, more at ease. We hope to be more in control of our life. We imagine that we will be able to be nice to others without it being inconvenient.

From practice we demand that we become secure and increasingly achieve what we want: if not money and fame, at least something close. Though we might not want to admit it, we demand that someone take care of us and that the people

close to us function for our benefit. We expect to be able to create life conditions that are pleasing to us, such as the right relationship, the right job, or the best course of study. For those with whom we identify, we want to be able to fix up their lives.

There is nothing wrong with wanting any of these things, but if we think that achieving them is what practice is about, then we still don't understand practice. The demands are all about what *we* want: we want to be enlightened, we want peace, we want serenity, we want help, we want control over things, we want everything to be wonderful.

The second viewpoint is quite different: more and more, we want to be able to create harmony and growth for everyone. We are included in this growth, but we are not the center of it; we're just part of the picture. As the second viewpoint strengthens in us, we begin to enjoy serving others and are less interested in whether serving others interferes with our own personal welfare. We begin to search for life conditions—such as a job, health, a partner—that are most fruitful for such service. They may not always be pleasing for us; what is more important to us is that they teach us to serve life well. A difficult relationship can be extremely fruitful, for example.

As we increasingly adopt the second viewpoint, we learn to serve everyone, not just people we like. Increasingly, we have an interest in being responsible for life, and we're not so concerned whether others feel responsible for us. In fact we even become willing to be responsible for people who mistreat us. Though we may not prefer it, we become more willing to experience trying situations in order to learn.

As we move toward the second viewpoint, we will probably retain the preferences that defined the first viewpoint. We will continue to prefer to be happy, to be comfortable, to be peaceful, to get what we want, to be healthy, to have some control of things. Practice does not cause us to lose our preferences. But when a preference is in conflict with what is most fruitful, then we are willing to give up the preference. In other words, the center of our life is shifting from a preoccupation with our-

selves to life itself. Life includes us, of course; we haven't been eliminated in the second viewpoint. But we're no longer the center.

Practice is about moving from the first to the second viewpoint. There is a pitfall inherent in practice, however: if we practice well, many of the demands of the first viewpoint may be satisfied. We are likely to feel better, to be more comfortable. We may feel more at ease with ourselves. Because we're not punishing our bodies with as much tension, we tend to be healthier. These changes can confirm in us the misconception that the first viewpoint is correct: that practice is about making life better for ourselves. In fact, the benefits to ourselves are incidental. The real point of practice is to serve life as fully and fruitfully as we can. And that's very hard for us to understand, especially at first. "You mean that I should take care of someone who has just been cruel to me? That's crazy!" "You mean that I have to give up my own convenience to serve someone who doesn't even like me?"

Our ego-centered attitudes are deep-rooted, and it takes years and years of hard practice to loosen these roots a bit. And we're convinced that practice is about the first viewpoint, that we are going to get something from it that's wonderful for ourselves.

True practice, however, is much more about seeing how we hurt ourselves and others with deluded thinking and actions. It is seeing how we hurt people, perhaps simply because we are so lost in our own concerns that we can't see them. I don't think we really want to hurt others; it's just that we don't quite see what we are doing. I can tell how well someone's practice is going by whether he or she is developing greater concern for others, concern that extends beyond merely what *I* want, what's hurting *me*, how bad life is, and so on. This is the mark of a practice that's moving along. Practice is always a battle between what we want and what life wants.

It's natural to be selfish, to want what we want, and we are inevitably selfish until we see an alternative. The function of

teaching in a center like this is to help us see the alternative and to disturb us in our selfishness. So long as we are caught in the first viewpoint, governed by wanting to feel good or blissful or enlightened, we *need* to be disturbed. We *need* to be upset. A good center and a good teacher assist that. Enlightenment is, after all, simply an absence of any concern for self. Don't come to this center to feel better; that's not what this place is about. What I want are lives that get bigger so that they can take care of more things, more people.

This morning I had a call from a former student who has lung cancer. In an earlier operation, three-quarters of his lungs were removed, and he's devoting himself to sitting and practice. Some time after the operation, he began to have troubles with his vision and with severe headaches. Tests revealed two brain tumors: the cancer had spread. He's back in the hospital for treatment. We talked about the treatment and how he's doing. I told him, "I'm really very sorry this has happened for you. I just want you to be comfortable. I hope things will go well." He replied, "That's not what I want from you. I want you to rejoice. This is it for me—and it's wonderful. I see what my life is." He went on to say, "It doesn't mean I don't get angry and frightened and climb the walls. All those things are going on, *and* now I know what my life is. I don't want anything from you except that you share in my rejoicing. I wish everyone could feel the way I do."

He is living from the second viewpoint, the one in which we embrace those life conditions—our job, our health, our partner—that will be most fruitful to all. He's got it. Whether he lives two months, two years, or a long time, in a sense it does not matter. I'm not suggesting that he's a saint. He will have days of extreme difficulty: pain, anger, rebellion. These things are going on now for him; yet that wasn't what he wanted to talk about. If he were to recover, he would still have all the struggles and difficulties that everyone else does, the demands and dreams of the ego. These things never really go away, but how we hold them can change.

The shift from the first to the second viewpoint is hard for us to comprehend, especially at first. I have noticed in talking with people who are new to practice that often my words simply don't register. Like a cat on a hot tin roof or drops of water in a hot frying pan, the words touch momentarily and then jump off and vanish. Over time, however, the words don't bounce off so quickly. Something begins to sink in. We can hold the truth longer about how life is as opposed to how we think it might be or should be. Over time the ability simply to sit with what life really is increases.

The shift does not happen overnight; we are much too stubborn for that. It may be accelerated by a major illness or disappointment, by a profound loss or other problem. Though I don't wish such crises on anyone, they often bring about needed learning. Zen practice is difficult largely because it creates discomfort and brings us face-to-face with problems in our lives. We don't want to do this, though it helps us to learn, and prods us toward the second viewpoint. To sit quietly when we're upset and would really like to be doing something else is a lesson that sinks in little by little. As we recognize the value of practice, our motivation to practice increases. We begin to sense something. We gain strength to sit day after day, to participate in an all-day sitting, to do a sesshin. The desire to do this hard practice increases. We slowly begin to comprehend what my former student meant when he said, "Now I know what my life is." We're mistaken if we feel sorry for him; perhaps he is one of the lucky ones.

STUDENT: You say that from the second viewpoint, we demand that our lives be more fruitful. Do you mean fruitful to one's practice, or what?

JOKO: Fruitful for life. Fruitful for life overall, including as much of life as possible. That sounds very general, but when it happens in our life, we understand it. For example, perhaps we might go and help a friend to move, even when we're really tired and don't want to do it. We put ourselves out, we

inconvenience ourselves, not to be noble but just because it's needed.

STUDENT: When I hear stories like that, I immediately want to start making plans to do fruitful things.

JOKO: Yes, we can make anything into an ideal to pursue. If we do this, however, we quickly encounter our own resistance—which gives us something to work with. It's all grist for the mill.

We don't have to push ourselves to the point where we fall apart. We shouldn't set ourselves up as a martyr; that's just another ideal, an image of how we should be as opposed to how we really are.

STUDENT: When I plan how I can make my life more secure and comfortable, I imagine that it will make me happy at last. But then a question arises: "Will I really be happy?" I notice in myself an anxious grabbing after security and happiness, and behind that ideal is a feeling of dissatisfaction, because somehow I know that's not going to be it, either.

JOKO: There's some value for us in chasing after such dreams, because when we've achieved what we thought we wanted, we can see more clearly that this doesn't give us the satisfaction we craved. That's how we learn. Practice is not about changing what we do so much as being very observant and experiencing what's going on with us.

STUDENT: That process of chasing dreams seems endless. Does it ever fade?

JOKO: It does fade, but only after years and years of practice. For years, I began every sesshin with a sense of resistance: "I don't want to do this because I know how tired I'll be at the end." Who wants to be tired? That resistance has faded for me, now. When sesshin starts, it starts. If we're practicing, ego agendas slowly fade. We shouldn't make that fading yet an-

other agenda item, however. We shouldn't think of practice as a way to get somewhere else. There's nowhere to get to.

STUDENT: In my life right now, I'm making a lot of new friends and contacts. It's exciting. I don't know who's helping whom—whether I'm giving to them, or they to me. Is that related to practice?

JOKO: Practice changes patterns of friendship away from calculating costs and benefits for oneself toward simply being more genuine. In a sense, we can't help others; we can't know what's best for them. Practicing with our own lives is the only way we can help others; we naturally serve others by becoming more who we are.

STUDENT: If we want to operate from the second viewpoint and do what is most fruitful for life, how do we know what to do? How can we tell whether this job or that relationship is the right one?

JOKO: Living from the second viewpoint, we don't bring in ideals or agendas; it's more a matter of seeing clearly what is before us. We act without turning the question over and over in our mind.

Sitting with the issue helps; as we pay attention to our thoughts and the tension in our body, we begin to see more clearly how to act. The actual practice of sitting is always somewhat murky. If we keep sitting long enough, however, slowly over time things get clearer. There's a continuum, and to sit is to move along that continuum. It's not that we get somewhere; more and more we just get ourselves. I don't mean only sitting on a cushion. If we're practicing well, we're doing zazen all the time.

STUDENT: We dream that we're going to know the right thing to do, when in fact at some point we just take a course of action and then, whatever it is, we learn from it. If we make mistakes

and hurt people, we apologize. When I watch my mind and stay with my body, out of that comes some course of action. It may be a very confused course of action. If I'm staying with my practice, however, in some way I will learn from it, and that's the best I can do. I can't hope always to know what's best for life. I can only do what I can do.

JOKO: Yes. The thought that there should come a time when we absolutely know what to do is part of the first viewpoint. On the way to the second viewpoint, we say, "I'll practice, I'll do my best, and I'll learn from the results."

STUDENT: On the question of helping others, I think that as we see increasingly well our feelings and our tendencies to manipulate a situation, to that extent we're going to be acting more in harmony, or at least creating less havoc. So we don't have to go far to help people. Simply seeing what we're doing as we interact tends to help people naturally without our even really trying.

JOKO: Yes. In contrast, if we view someone outside ourselves as being someone to help, we can be sure we've got a problem. As we just sit over time with our own confusions and limitations, without trying to do anything we do something.

STUDENT: Sometimes what's valuable is not what we do for other people, but what we don't do to them.

JOKO: Right. Often the right course of action is just to let people be. For example, it would be a mistake for me to try to do something for my former student who has cancer. I can only listen to him and be myself. He is living through his situation; that's his learning. I can't do anything about that.

STUDENT: In myself lately I have discovered a greater availability. I seem to be less self-conscious, and more open-ended and available to others. Part of it is simply being more relaxed. People come to me with their concerns. It's not that they're asking for help; usually they just want someone to listen. All I

have to do is just be myself and be available, say, to someone at the other end of the telephone line who says, "I want to share something with you. . . ."

JOKO: Yes.

STUDENT: Joko, you seem to be available all of the time in that way.

JOKO: Not always; I turn off the phone sometimes.

STUDENT: I think you don't do it enough for your own good. There are some people who really take advantage of you.

JOKO: But that's my job. And, remember, no one can "take advantage" of me.

STUDENT: Are you saying that whenever somebody cries out to you, "I need help, I need help, I need help!" you must always respond? What do you do with people who call up and complain the whole time?

JOKO: I say something like "I hear what you're saying. Maybe you could practice with this. How would you practice with this?"

I don't mind if somebody complains; we're all complaining, though we may not admit it. We all like to complain. I do mind, however, if people just want to tell their story endlessly, without any space for reflection on what they might do to deal with their life. I have no place in that. They may have to suffer until they are willing to wake up a little.

STUDENT: I was very touched by your story of your former student with cancer. I have tremendous resistance to acknowledging that amount of suffering as okay.

JOKO: It's not for us to say that the suffering is okay. I don't want him to suffer either. But it's what he says that matters.

Life presents us with lessons all the time. It's better if we can learn each one, including the small ones. But we don't want to

learn them. We want to blame a problem on somebody else, just brush it aside, or block it out. When we refuse to learn from the smaller problems, we're forced to confront bigger ones. Practice is about learning from each thing as it comes up, so that when bigger issues confront us, we're more able to handle them.

STUDENT: I recently got reacquainted with the fact that when I start moving away from the rut I've been traveling in and moving more in the direction that I need to be going, it will occasion all kinds of chaos. It's not going to feel good.

JOKO: Right. As we begin serious practice, and for some time thereafter, life often feels worse, not better. That's another part of the talk nobody wants to hear.

The Eye of the Hurricane

Security is mostly a superstition. It does not exist in nature,
nor do the children of men as a whole experience it. Avoiding
danger is no safer in the long run than outright exposure. Life
is either a daring adventure, or nothing.

Helen Keller

Some students here work on koans, though not all. While there
is much to be learned from koan study, I believe that to rely on
koan study exclusively can be limited. If we understand our
lives, we understand koans. And working directly with our
lives is more valuable and more difficult. Those who work
with koans for a time may begin to get a knack for seeing what
the koan's about, but seeing isn't necessarily the same as
being. Though koan practice is based on the idea that if we see
what is true, we'll be it, that's not always the case. Still, koans
can be very useful. Let's begin with one from the *Gateless Gate*,
Kyogun's Man up a Tree: Master Kyogun said, "It's like a man
up a tree hanging from a branch with his mouth; his hands
cannot grasp a bough, his feet won't reach one. Suppose there
is another man under the tree who asks him, 'What is the
meaning of Bodhidharma's coming from the West?' If he does
not respond, he goes against the wish of the questioner. If he
answers, he will lose his life. At such a time, how should he respond?" We might restate the koan as asking, "What is the
meaning of life?" Not to respond is to fail in our responsibility;
to answer is to lose our lives.

To approach this koan, I'll tell another story. Many years ago
I was living in Providence, Rhode Island. A severe hurricane
came up the coast and battered New England. I moved the crib

of my baby against the wall and covered the crib so that if windows were broken the glass wouldn't hit the baby, and we made other appropriate preparations. But we were directly in the path of the hurricane, and it was fierce. In front of the house we could see enormous old trees cracking and falling over. The winds were one hundred thirty to one hundred forty miles an hour.

Then after three or four hours, within a matter of minutes, it became quiet. The sun came out, and the birds started to sing. The wind ceased. We were in the eye of the hurricane. In another hour or so, the eye had moved on, the winds began again, and we went through the other side of the whirling mass of winds. Though not as bad as the first side, it was also fierce. Eventually we were left with a huge mess to clean up. I learned later that sometimes pilots are accidentally caught in hurricanes, subjecting the plane and themselves to terrible stresses. When this happens, they often try to fly into the center, the eye of the hurricane, to give themselves a little chance to recover.

Most of us are like the man up the tree or the pilot in the plane, just holding on, hoping we'll make it out of the storm. We feel ourselves caught up in the buffetings of life. These may be natural occurrences, such as severe illness. They may be difficulties in relationships, which can seem quite unfair. From birth to death, we're caught in this swirling of winds, which is really what life is: an enormous energy, moving and changing. Our aim is like that of the pilot: to protect ourselves and our plane. We don't want to stay where we are. So we do everything possible to preserve our own lives and the structure of our plane so that we can escape the hurricane. There is this enormously powerful thing we call our life, and we're somewhere sitting in the middle of it in our little plane, hoping to make our way through without being hurt.

Suppose that instead of being in a plane, we were in a glider in the middle of the hurricane, without the control and power that an engine provides. We're caught in the sweeping winds.

If we have any idea that we're going to get out alive, we're foolish. Still, as long as we live within that enormous mass of wind, we have a good ride. Even with the fear and terror, it can be exhilarating and joyful—like riding a roller coaster.

The man up the tree, holding on for dear life, is like the pilot in the plane, desperately hoping he can save himself from the buffetings of life. And then he is asked, "What is the meaning of life?" How does he answer? How do *we* answer? As we live our lives, and as we do zazen, we're trying to protect ourselves. This mind that thinks, pictures, gets excited, gets emotional, blames other people, and feels like a victim is like the pilot in the airplane who's trying desperately to make his way through the hurricane. In such a life of tension and constriction, it takes everything we have just to survive. All of our attention is on ourselves and our control panel; in trying to save ourselves, we don't notice anything else. But the man in the glider can enjoy everything—the lightning, the warm rain, the scream of the wind. He can have a great time. What will happen at the end? Both men die, of course. But which one knows the meaning of life? Who knows joy?

Like the first pilot, we spend our lives trying to protect ourselves. The more intent we are upon protecting ourselves from the buffeting of our current situation, the more stress we feel, the more miserable we are, and the less we truly experience our lives. We must ignore most of the landscape if we're obsessed with our control panels, which will fail us sooner or later in any case.

As we do zazen, we can watch our protective mechanisms by watching our minds. We can notice how we try to explain our pain away by blaming our troubles on someone else. We can see our ruthless and fruitless attempts to save ourselves. Our efforts don't work, of course. The harder we try, the more tense and upset we get.

Only one thing finally solves the problem, but nobody wants to hear about it. Think about the man in the glider. Would we really want to be up there? From the very beginning, he doesn't

have a chance. He's just there for the ride—the greatest ride in the world. Our own lives are like a ride, which inevitably ends in our death. We're trying to do the impossible, to save ourselves. We can't do that; in fact, we're all dying right now. How many minutes do we have? Like the glider, perhaps we have just one minute, perhaps a hundred minutes. It doesn't matter which; in the end, we're going down. But the one who can answer "What is the meaning of life?" is the glider pilot, not the airplane pilot. The glider pilot will know before he crashes, and he will probably crash with "Wow!"

We come to sesshin hoping that within the hurricane of our own turmoil, we're going to find the little eye, the little nirvana. We think: "It must be somewhere. Where is it? Where is it?" Sometimes we hit a little spot of quiet, of good feelings. Then we try to cling to it. But we can't hold onto the eye of a hurricane. The hurricane is racing on. Nirvana is not finding that little calm space where we're sheltered and protected by something and someone. That's an illusion. Nothing in the world will ever protect us: not our partner, not our life circumstances, not our children. After all, other people are busy protecting themselves. If we spend our life looking for the eye of the hurricane, we live a life that is fruitless. We die without having really lived.

I don't feel sorry for the pilot in the glider. When he dies, at least he has lived. I feel sorry for those who so blind themselves with their protective endeavors that they never live. When we're with them, we can sense the fear and futility. In sesshin we can see the mistake more clearly: we're not trying to live our life; we're trying to find the eye of the hurricane, the place where we'll be safe at last.

No one can know what life is. But we can experience life directly. Only that is given to us as human beings. But we don't accept the gift; we don't experience our lives directly. Instead, we spend our lives protecting ourselves. When our protective systems break down, then we blame ourselves or others. We have systems to cover up our problems; we're unwilling to

face the pain of life directly. In fact, when we face it directly, life is a great ride.

Of course it's fine to buy life insurance and make sure the brakes work on our car. But in the end, even these don't save us; sooner or later, all of our protective mechanisms will fail. No one can solve the koan of life completely—though we imagine that the other guy maybe has done it. We blame other people because we think they should have life all figured out. We don't, but we still think others should never be sloppy about how they live. In fact, we're all sloppy, because we're all immersed in this game of self-protection instead of the real game of life. Life is not a safe space. It never was, and it never will be. If we've hit the eye of the hurricane for a year or two, it still cannot be counted on. There is no safe space, not for our money, not for ourselves, not for those we love. And it's not our business to worry about that.

Until we see through the game that doesn't work, we don't play the real game. Some people never see through it and die without ever having lived. And that's too bad. We can spend our life blaming other people, circumstances, or our bad luck and thinking about the way life should have been. We can die that way if we want. That's our privilege, but it's not much fun. We have to open up to the enormous game going on that we're part of. Our practice must be careful, meticulous, patient. We have to face everything.

III

Separation and

Connection

Can Anything Hurt Us?

A Zen student called me recently to complain about my emphasis on the difficulty of practice. She said, "I think you make a mistake in urging your students to take their practice so seriously. Life should be about enjoying ourselves and having a good time." I asked her, "Has that approach ever worked for you?" She said, "Well, not really . . . yet. But I have hope."

I understand her attitude, and I sympathize with anyone who feels that practice is really hard work. It is. But I also feel sad for those who are not yet willing to do this kind of serious work, because they will suffer most. Still, people have to make their own choices, and some are just not ready for serious practice. I said to the Zen student, "Just do your practice or not according to your own lights, and I'll support you in doing that." Whatever people are doing, I want to support them—because that's where they are, and that's fine.

The fact is that for most of us, our lives are *not* working well. Until we engage in a serious practice, our basic view of life usually remains pretty much untouched. In fact, life continues to aggravate us, and even gets worse. Serious practice is needed if we are to see into the fallacy that is at the bottom of almost all human action, thinking, and emotion.

As human beings we see life by means of a certain sensory apparatus and because people and objects seem external to us, we experience much misery. Our misery stems from the misconception that we are separate. Certainly it *looks* as though I am separate from other people and from all else in the phenomenal world. This misconception that we're separate creates all the difficulties of human life.

As long as we think we're separate, we're going to suffer. If we feel separate we're going to feel that we have to defend ourselves, that we have to try to be happy, that we have to find

something in the world around us that's going to make us happy.

Now the truth of the matter is that we're not separate. We are all expressions or emanations of a central point—call it multidimensional energy. We can't picture this; the central point or energy has no size, no space, no time. I'm speaking metaphorically about what can't really be spoken of in ordinary terms.

Following this metaphor, it's as though this central point radiates out in billions of rays, each thinking that it's separate from all others. In truth, each of us is always that center, and that center is us. Because everything is connected in that center, we're all just one thing.

We don't see that unity, however. Perhaps if we know enough contemporary theoretical physics, we can see the point intellectually. As we practice over the years, however, some inkling of this truth begins to creep into our experience here and there: we don't feel so separate from others. As we begin to feel less separate, life as it happens around us isn't as upsetting. Situations, people, and difficulties begin to land on us a little more lightly. A subtle shift is taking place. Over a lifetime of sitting this process slowly strengthens. There may be brief moments when we flash into who we really are, though by themselves, such moments are not terribly important. More important is the slowly growing realization that we're not separate. In ordinary terms, we still appear to exist separately, but we don't feel as separate. Consequently, we don't struggle with life as much: we don't have to fight it, we don't have to please it, we don't have to worry about it. This is the path of practice.

If we don't struggle with life, does this mean that life can't hurt us? Is there anything outside of ourselves that can hurt us? Being Zen students, we may have learned to say—intellectually at least—that the answer is no. But what do we really think? Is there any person or situation that can hurt us?

Of course, we all think there is. In working with my students, I hear countless stories of being hurt or upset. They are all versions of "This happened to me." Our partners, our par-

ents, our children, our pets—"This happened, and it upset me." We all do this, without exception. That's what our life is. Perhaps things go fairly smoothly for a time, and then suddenly something happens to upset us. In other words, we're a victim. Now that's our usual human view of living. It's ingrained, almost inborn.

When we feel victimized by the world, we look for something outside of ourselves that will take away our hurt. It could be a person, it could be getting something we want, it could be some change in our job status, some recognition, perhaps. Since we don't know where to look, and we hurt, we seek comfort somewhere.

Until we truly see that we're not separate from anything, we're going to struggle with our lives. When we struggle, we have trouble. We either do foolish things or we feel upset or we feel unfulfilled or we feel as though something's missing. It's as though life presents us with a series of questions that can't be answered. And as a matter of fact, they can't. Why?

Because they're false questions. They're not based on reality. Feeling that something is wrong and seeking ways to fix it— when we begin to see the error in this pattern, serious practice begins. The young woman who called me hasn't reached this point. She still imagines that something external will make her happy. Maybe a million dollars?

With people who practice, on the other hand, there's a little chink in the armor, a little insight. We may not want to recognize this insight. Still, we do begin to comprehend that there's another way to live beyond feeling assaulted by life and then trying to find a remedy.

From the very beginning, there's nothing wrong. There is no separation: it's all one radiant whole. Nobody believes this, and until we have practiced a long time it's hard to get. Even with six months of intelligent practice, however, there begins to be a little shake in the false structure of our beliefs. The structure begins to fall apart here and there. As we practice over the years, the structure weakens. The enlightened state exists when it falls apart completely.

Yes, we do have to be serious about our practice. If you're not ready to be serious, that's fine. Just go live your life. You need to be kicked around for a while. That's okay. People shouldn't be at a Zen center until they feel there's nothing else they can do: that's the time to show up.

Let's return to our question: can something or someone hurt us? Let's take up some real disasters. Suppose I've lost my job and I'm seriously ill. Suppose all my friends have left me. Suppose an earthquake has destroyed my house. Can I be hurt by all that? Of course I think that I can. And it would be terrible for such things to happen. But can we truly be hurt by such events? Practice helps us to see that the answer is no.

It's not that the point of practice is to avoid feeling hurt. What we call "hurt" still happens: I may lose my job; an earthquake may destroy my house. But practice helps me to handle crises, to take them in stride. So long as we are immersed in our hurt, we'll be a bundle of woe that is of little use to anybody. If we're not wrapped up in our melodrama of pain, on the other hand, even during a crisis we can be of use.

So what happens if we truly practice? Why does the feeling that life can hurt us begin to soften over time? What takes place?

Only a self-centered self, a self that is attached to mind and body, can be hurt. That self is really a concept formed of thoughts we believe in; for example, "If I don't get that, I'll be miserable," or "If this doesn't work out for me, it's just terrible," or "If I don't have a house to live in, that's *really* terrible." What we call the self is no more than a series of thoughts that we're attached to. When we're engrossed in our small selves, reality— the basic energy of the universe—is hardly noticed at all.

Suppose I feel I have no friends, and I'm very lonely. What happens if I sit with that? I begin to see that my feelings of loneliness are really just thoughts. As a matter of fact, I'm simply sitting here. Maybe I'm sitting alone in my room, without a date. Nobody has called me, and I feel lonely. In fact, however, I'm simply sitting. The loneliness and the misery are simply my thoughts, my judgments that things should be other than

what they are. I haven't seen through them; I haven't recognized that my misery is manufactured by me. The truth of the matter is, I'm simply sitting in my room. It takes time before we can see that just to sit there is okay, just fine. I cling to the thought that if I don't have pleasant and supportive company, I am miserable.

I'm not recommending a life in which we cut ourselves off in order to be free of attachment. Attachment concerns not what we have, but our opinions about what we have. There's nothing wrong with having a fair amount of money, for example. Attachment is when we can't envision life without it. Likewise, I'm not saying to give up being with people. Being with people is immensely enjoyable. Sometimes, however, we're in situations where we have to be alone. For example, one might have to spend six months doing a research project somewhere in the middle of a desert. For most of us, that would be very hard. But if I'm doing research in the middle of nowhere for six months, the truth of the matter is, that's just the way it is; that's just what I'm doing.

The difficult, slow change of practice grounds our life and makes it genuinely more peaceful. Without striving to be peaceful, we find that more and more, the storms of life hit us lightly. We're beginning to release our attachment to the thoughts we think are ourselves. That self is simply a concept that weakens with practice.

The truth is that nothing can hurt us. But we certainly can *think* we're being hurt, and we certainly can struggle to remedy the thoughts of hurt in ways that can be quite unfruitful. We try to remedy a false problem with a false solution, and of course that creates mayhem. Wars, damage to the environment—all come out of this ignorance.

If we refuse to do this work—and we won't do it until we're ready—to some degree we suffer, and everything around us suffers. Whether one practices is not a matter of good or bad, right or wrong. We have to be ready. But when we don't practice, a sad price is paid.

Of course, the original oneness—that center of multidimensional energy—remains undisturbed. There's no way that we can disturb it. It always just *is*, and that's what we are. From the standpoint of the phenomenal life we live, however, there's a price that is paid.

I'm not trying to create guilty feelings in anyone. Such feelings are themselves merely thoughts. I'm not criticizing the young woman who didn't want to take practice seriously. That's just exactly where she's at, and that's perfect for her. As we practice, however, our resistance to practice diminishes. It does take time.

STUDENT: I can see how we can be one with other people, but it's hard for me to understand what it means to be one with a table or something like that.

JOKO: One with a table? I think the table is a lot easier than people! I haven't had anyone complain to me about conflict with a table. Our troubles nearly always are with people, either individually or in groups.

STUDENT: Maybe I don't understand what you mean by being "one with."

JOKO: "One with" is an absence of anything that divides.

STUDENT: But I just don't feel like a table.

JOKO: You don't have to feel like a table. By "being one with the table," I mean that there's no sense of opposition between you and the table. It's not a question of some special feeling, it's a lack or an absence of feeling separated in an emotional way. Tables usually do not arouse emotion. That's why we don't have any trouble with them.

STUDENT: If someone has, say, arthritis, and is in pain all the time, do you say that that doesn't hurt?

JOKO: No. If we have persistent pain, we should of course do what we can to deal with it. But finally if there's still a residue

of pain, all we can do is experience that residue. It doesn't help to add onto the pain judgments, such as "This is terrible! Poor me; why is it like this?" The pain just *is*. Taken in this way, the pain is a teaching. In my experience, most people who have had a serious illness and who have learned how to use it have found it the best thing that ever happened to them.

STUDENT: If someone can't hurt us, and we can't hurt someone else, that doesn't necessarily give us license to speak our mind because we can't hurt anybody.

JOKO: That's right. If we misinterpret the point and say, "I can tell you off because I can't hurt you," already that's a separation. We don't attack others unless we feel separate from them. All serious practice presumes a devotion to basic moral precepts, moral grounds.

STUDENT: What about the historical samurai ethic in Japan? For example, a samurai warrior might say, "Since I'm one with everything, when I slice off the head of an innocent person, there's no killing: that person is me."

JOKO: In an absolute sense, there isn't any killing, since we're all—"alive" or "dead"—just manifestations of that central energy that is everything. But in practical terms, I don't agree with the samurai ethic. If we see that we're not separated from other people, we simply won't attack. The samurai warriors were confusing the absolute and the relative. Absolutely, of course, there is no one who kills and no one to be killed. But in the life that we live, yes, there is. And so we don't do it.

STUDENT: In other words, if we confuse the absolute and the relative, we might use the absolute to justify what we do in the relative?

JOKO: Yes, but only if we live in our heads. If we take practice to be about a philosophical position, we can get really confused. If we know the truth of practice in our very bones—without even thinking about it—we won't make that mistake.

STUDENT: Before I started sitting I didn't think things could hurt me either, because I didn't feel them.

JOKO: That's quite different. You're talking about a psychological numbness. When we're numb, we're not one with the pain; we're pretending it's not there.

STUDENT: When I finally tune in and feel how much I'm hurting myself in different ways, it becomes much easier to stop the counterproductive behavior. Until that time, as you said, we're going to do what we're going to do. If we're going to screw things up, that's what we're going to do.

JOKO: That's right. And I don't mean never to object to others' behavior. If someone has done something to me—perhaps stolen all my money for groceries—I may need to object and take some action. If others mistreat us or cause us pain, they may need to know about it. But if we speak to them with anger, they'll never learn what they need to learn. They won't even hear us.

The underlying attitude or knowledge that we're not separate creates a fundamental shift in our emotional life. That knowledge means that whatever happens, we're not especially disturbed by it. Having the knowledge doesn't mean we don't take care of problems as they arise; however, we no longer inwardly say, "Oh, this is awful; nobody else has the troubles I have." It's as if our understanding cancels out such reactions.

STUDENT: So feeling hurt is just our thoughts about the situation?

JOKO: Yes. When we no longer identify with such thoughts, we simply handle the situation and do not get caught emotionally by it.

STUDENT: But one can *feel* hurt.

JOKO: Yes. And I don't mean to deny that feeling. In practice, we work with the complex of physical sensation and thought

that is "I feel hurt." If we totally experience the sensations and thought, then the "feeling hurt" evaporates. I never would say that we shouldn't feel what we feel.

STUDENT: You're saying to give up the attachment to the hurt?

JOKO: No. We can't force ourselves to give up an attachment. Attachment is thought, but we can't just say, "I'm going to give it up." That doesn't work. We have to understand what attachment is. We have to experience the fear—the bodily sensation—that underlies the attachment. Then the attachment will just wither away. A common error in Zen teaching is that we have to "let go." We can't force ourselves to "let go." We have to experience the underlying fear.

Experiencing the attachment or feeling also does not mean dramatizing it. When we dramatize our emotions, we just cover them up.

STUDENT: Are you saying that if we really experience our sadness, for example, we wouldn't need to cry?

JOKO: We might cry. Still, there's a difference between just crying and dramatizing our sadness, or our fear or anger. The dramatizing is quite often a cover. For instance, people who get in fights and throw things and yell and scream are not yet in touch with their anger.

STUDENT: Back to the young woman who thought practice should be less serious and who didn't want to come here to sit: are you equating serious practice with sitting regularly in a Zen center?

JOKO: No, though such regular sitting is immensely useful. I have some students living at a distance who have very strong practices; still, they find some way to get here once in a while. The young woman just isn't ready yet to be doing that. And she's the one who suffers, which is the sad part.

The Subject-Object Problem

Our basic problem as humans is the subject-object relationship. When I first heard this stated years and years ago, it seemed abstract and irrelevant to my life. Yet all of our disharmony and difficulty come from not knowing what to do about the subject-object relationship. In everyday terms, the world is divided into subjects and objects: I look at you, I go to work, I sit on a chair. In each of these cases, I think of myself as a subject relating to an object: you, my work, the chair. Yet intuitively we know that we are not separate from the world and that the subject-object division is an illusion. To gain that intuitive knowledge is why we practice.

Not understanding subject-object dualism, we see the objects in our world as the source of our problems: *you are* my problem, my *work* is my problem, my *chair* is my problem. (When I see *myself* as the problem, I have made myself into an object.) So we run from objects we perceive as problems, and seek objects we perceive as nonproblems. From this point of view, the world consists of me, and things that please or don't please me.

Historically, Zen practice and most other meditative disciplines have sought to resolve the subject-object dualism by emptying the object of all content. For example, working on Mu* or major koans empties the object of the conditioning we attach to it. As the object becomes increasingly transparent, we are a subject contemplating a virtually empty object. Such a state is sometimes called samadhi. Such a state is blissful be-

---

*Mu—literally "no" or "nothing"—is often assigned to beginning students as a means of focusing attention.

cause the empty object is no longer troublesome to us. When we have achieved this state, we tend to congratulate ourselves on how much progress we have made.

But this state of samadhi is still dualistic. When we achieve it, an inner voice says, "This must be it!" or "Now I'm really doing well!" A hidden subject remains, observing a virtually blank object, in what amounts to a subject-object separation. When we realize this separation, we try to turn on the subject as well and empty it of content. In doing so, we turn the subject into yet another object, with an even more subtle subject viewing it. We are creating an infinite regression of subjects.

Such states of samadhi are not true enlightenment precursors, because a thinly veiled subject is separated from a virtually blank object. When we return to daily life, the blissful feeling dissipates and we're again at sea in a world of subjects and objects. Practice and life do not come together.

A clearer practice does not try to get rid of the object, but rather to see the object for what it is. We slowly learn about *being* or *experiencing* in which there is no subject or object at all. We do not eliminate anything, but rather bring things together. There's still me, and there's still you, but when I am just my experience of you, I don't feel separate from you. I'm one with you.

This kind of practice is much slower, because instead of concentrating on one object, we work with everything in our life. Anything that annoys or upsets us (which, if we're honest, includes almost everything) becomes grist for the mill of practice. Working with everything leads to a practice that is alive in every second of our life.

When anger arises, for example, much of traditional Zen practice would have us blot out the anger and concentrate on something, such as the breath. Though we've pushed the anger aside, it will return whenever we are criticized or threatened in some way. In contrast, our practice is to become the anger itself, to experience it fully, without separation or rejection. When we work this way, our lives settle down. Slowly, we learn to relate to troublesome objects in a different way.

Our emotional reactions gradually wear themselves out; for example, objects we have feared gradually lose their power over us, and we can approach them more readily. It's fascinating to watch that change take place; I see it happening in others, and in myself as well. The process is never completed: yet we are increasingly aware and free.

STUDENT: How is what you describe different from traditional shikantaza practice?*

JOKO: It's very close to shikantaza, correctly understood. Even in shikantaza, however, there is a tendency to blank out the mind. It's possible to get into a kind of shimmering experience in which the subject is not included. This is simply another form of false samadhi. Thought processes have been excluded from awareness, and we blank out our sensory experience as we might some other object of awareness.

STUDENT: You say that the true purpose of practice is to experience our oneness with all things, or rather just to be our own experience, so that, for example, we're just totally hammering some nails, if that's what we're doing. But isn't there a paradox in trying to achieve even that?

JOKO: I agree with you: we can't *try* to be one with the hammering. In trying to become it, we separate ourselves from it. The very effort defeats itself. There is something we *can* do, however: we can notice the thoughts that separate us from our activity. We can be aware that we're not fully doing what we're doing. That's not so difficult. Labeling our thoughts helps us to do this. Instead of saying, "I'm going to be one with the hammering," which is dualistic—thinking about the activity rather than just doing it—we can always notice when we're *not* doing it. That's all that's necessary.

---

*Shikantaza—"just sitting": a pure form of sitting meditation, without the aid of breath counting or koan practice, in which the mind maintains highly concentrated and alert yet unhurried awareness of the present.

Practice is not about having experiences, not about having giant realizations, not about getting somewhere or becoming something. We are perfect as we are. By "perfect" I mean simply that this is it. Practice is simply maintaining awareness—of our activities and also of the thoughts that separate us from our activities. As we hammer nails or sit, we simply hammer nails or sit. Since our senses are open, we hear and feel other things as well: sounds, smells, and so on. When thoughts arise, we notice them, and return to our direct experience.

Awareness is our true self; it's what we are. So we don't have to try to develop awareness; we simply need to notice how we block awareness, with our thoughts, our fantasies, our opinions, and our judgments. We're either in awareness, which is our natural state, or we're doing something else. The mark of mature students is that most of the time, they don't do something else. They're just here, living their life. Nothing special.

When we become open awareness, our ability to do necessary thinking gets sharper, and our whole sensory input becomes brighter, clearer. After a certain amount of sitting, the world looks brighter, sounds are sharper, and there's a richness of sensory input, which is just our natural state if we are not blocking out experience with our tense, worrying minds.

When we begin to practice, we can maintain awareness only very briefly, and then we drift away from the present. Caught up in our thoughts, we don't notice we are drifting. Then we catch ourselves and pick up our sitting again. Practice includes both awareness of our sitting and awareness of our drifting. After years of practice, the drifting diminishes until it's almost gone, though it never completely disappears.

STUDENT: Sounds and smells and also our emotions and thoughts are all part of our sitting?

JOKO: Yes. It's normal for the mind to produce thoughts. Practice is to be aware of our thoughts without getting lost in them. And if we get lost, to notice that, too.

Zazen is actually not complicated. The real problem is, we don't want to do it. If my boyfriend begins to look at other women, how long am I going to be willing simply to experience that? We all have problems constantly, but our willingness just to be is very low on our list of priorities, until we have practiced long enough to have faith in just being, so that solutions can appear naturally. Another mark of a maturing practice is the development of such trust and faith.

STUDENT: What is the difference between being totally absorbed in hammering the nails and being aware that you're totally absorbed in hammering the nails?

JOKO: Being aware that you're absorbed in hammering the nails is still dualistic. You're thinking, "I am totally absorbed in hammering the nails." That is not true mindfulness. In true mindfulness, one is just doing it. Awareness that one is absorbed in an experience can be a useful step on the way, but it's not quite it, because one is still thinking about it. There's still a separation between awareness and the object of awareness. When we're just hammering the nails, we're not thinking about practice. In good practice, we're not thinking, "I have to practice." Good practice is simply doing what we're doing and noticing when we drift off. When we've been sitting for many years, we know almost instantaneously when we've started to drift.

Focusing on something called "Zen practice" is not necessary. If from morning to night we just took care of one thing after another, thoroughly and completely and without accompanying thoughts, such as "I'm a good person for doing this" or "Isn't it wonderful, that I can take care of everything?," then that would be sufficient.

STUDENT: My life seems to consist of layers upon layers of activity, all going on simultaneously. If I did only one thing at a time, then went on to the next, I wouldn't accomplish what I usually do in a day.

JOKO: I question that. Doing one thing at a time and giving oneself wholly to doing it is the most efficient way one can possibly live, because there's no blockage in the organism whatsoever. When we live and work in that way, we are extremely efficient without being rushed. Life is very smooth.

STUDENT: But when one of the things I have to do is think something through, and another is to answer a ringing phone, and another is to write a letter. . . .

JOKO: Still, each time we turn to another activity, if we are wholly present, just doing what we're doing, it gets done much more quickly and well. Usually, however, we bring into the activity various subliminal thoughts, such as "I have to get those other things done, too—or my life just doesn't measure up." Pure activity is very rare. There's nearly always a shadow, a film over it. We may not be aware of that; we may just be aware of some tension. There's no tension in pure activity, beyond the physical contraction required to do the activity itself.

Years ago in sesshin I often had the experience of just becoming cooking or weeding or whatever it was that I had to do, but there was still a subtle subject in there. And sure enough, as soon as the sesshin had faded a little bit, I was right back into the same old stuff. I had not become one with the object.

STUDENT: Back to the example of hammering the nails: if we're really just doing it, then we're not aware of ourselves at all, whereas if we remember that we're doing it, we're back into a dualism of subject and object and are not simply engaged in pure activity. Doesn't that mean, however, that when we're just hammering nails, we're not there at all? We no longer exist?

JOKO: When we're engaged in pure activity, we're a presence, an awareness. But that's all we are. And that doesn't feel like anything. People suppose that the so-called enlightened state is flooded with emotional and loving feelings. But true love or compassion is simply to be nonseparate from the object. Essentially it's a flow of activity in which we do not exist as a being separate from our activity.

There is always some value in practice that has dualistic characteristics. A certain amount of training and deconditioning goes on in any sitting practice. Until we have gone beyond that dualism, however, we cannot know any ultimate freedom. There is no ultimate freedom until there's just no one here.

We may think that we don't care about ultimate freedom in that sense. The truth is, however, that we do want it.

STUDENT: If one person is caught in an emotion of love and another person is caught in an emotion of hatred, is there a difference in how they should practice?

JOKO: No. Genuine love or compassion is an absence of both such personally conceived emotions. Only a person can love or hate in the usual sense. If there's no person, if we're just absorbed in living, such emotions will be absent.

In the concentrative practice I first described, since the feeling of anger is an object, what we do is just ignore it. We push the emotion to the side and empty the koan of content. The problem with that approach is that when we return to daily life, we don't know what to do about our emotions, because they have not been resolved; they are foreign territory to classic Zen practice. In an awareness practice, we simply experience the emotion-thought and its accompanying sensations. The results are very different.

STUDENT: In the shikantaza practice I was taught, the emotions are part of the practice: they come up and we sit with them.

JOKO: Yes, shikantaza practice can be understood in that way. We just need to be aware of the pitfalls.

STUDENT: In the longer, more difficult sesshins, sometimes I feel like Gordon Liddy, holding my hand over a candle in order to see how much pain I can endure. In the old style of samadhi practice, I think that the test of one's samadhi was one's ability to obliterate pain through bliss and concentration.

JOKO: Right. Then the object is blanked out.

STUDENT: In that style of practice, sesshin becomes a kind of endurance contest. Could you say something about how pain functions in this system so that it's not masochism?

JOKO: Moderate pain is a good teacher. Life itself presents pain as well as inconvenience. If we don't know how we deal with pain and inconvenience, we don't know much about ourselves. Extreme pain is not necessary, however. If the pain is excessive, it's okay to use a bench or chair, or even to lie down. Still, there is some value in just being willing to be the pain. Subject-object separation occurs because we're not willing to be the pain that we associate with the object. That's why we distance ourselves from it. If we don't understand ourselves in relation to pain, we run from it when it appears, and we lose the great treasure of awareness with its direct experience of life. So up to a point, it's useful to sit with pain, so that we can regain fuller awareness of our life as it is.

When I see students in daisan,* most of the time my knees are hurting. So they're hurting: that's just how it is. Particularly as we grow older, it's useful to be able simply to be with our experience and live our lives fully, anyway. Part of what we're here to learn is to be with discomfort and inconvenience. In moderate degrees, pain is a great teacher. Without some degree of discomfort, most of us would learn very little. Pain, discomfort, difficulty, even tragedy can be great teachers, especially as we get older.

STUDENT: In ordinary consciousness, is everything besides ourselves an object?

---

*Daisan: a formal interview between student and teacher during the course of meditative practice.

JOKO: If we think of the self as one object among others, even the self is an object. I can observe myself, I can hear my voice, I can poke my legs. From that point of view, I am an object also.

STUDENT: So objects include feelings and states of mind, as well as things in the world?

JOKO: Yes. Though we think of our self as a subject and everything else as an object, that's an error. When we separate things from one another, everything becomes an object. There's only one true subject—which is nothing at all. What is it?

STUDENT: Awareness.

JOKO: Yes, awareness, though the word is inadequate. Awareness isn't anything, and yet the whole universe exists through it.

Integration

There is a traditional story about a Zen teacher who was reciting sutras* and was accosted by a thief, demanding his money
or his life. The teacher told the thief where to find the money,
asking only that some be left to pay his taxes and that when
the thief was ready to leave he thank the teacher for the gift.
The thief complied. A few days later he was apprehended and
confessed to several crimes, including the offense against the
Zen teacher. But the teacher insisted that he had not been a victim of theft, because he had given the man his money and the
man had thanked him for it. After the man had finished serving his prison term, he returned to the teacher and became one
of his disciples.

Such stories sound romantic and wonderful. But suppose
somebody borrows money from us and doesn't return it. Or
someone steals our credit card and uses it. How would we respond? A problem with classic Zen stories like this is that they
have the feel of long ago and far away. With that distance from
our time, we may fail to get the point. The point is not that
somebody took some money or what the master did. The point
is that the master did not judge the thief. It doesn't follow that
the best thing is always to give the thief what he wants; sometimes that might not be the best action. I'm sure that the master
looked at the situation, saw immediately who the man was
(perhaps just a kid who picked up a sword and hoped he
could seize a little quick money), and intuitively knew what to
do. It's not so much what the master did as the way he did it.
The attitude of the master was crucial. Instead of making a

---

*Sutra: a traditional Buddhist text, often chanted aloud.

judgment, he simply dealt with the situation. Had the situation been different, his response might have been different.

We don't see that we are all teachers. Everything we do from morning to night is a teaching: the way we speak to someone at lunch, the way we transact our business at the bank, our reaction when the paper we submit is accepted or rejected—everything we do and everything we say reflects our practice. But we can't just want to be like Shichiri Kogen. That's a pitfall of training, to conclude, "Oh, I should be like that." Students do great harm by dragging such ideals into practice. They imagine that "I should be selfless, giving, and noble like the great Zen master." The master in each of these stories was effective because he was what he was. He didn't think twice about it. When we try to be something that we are not, we become the slave of a rigid, fixed mind, following a rule about how things have to be. The violence and the anger in us remain unnoticed, because we are caught in our pictures of how we should be. If we can use the stories rightly, they are wonderful. But we should not simply try to copy them in our lives. Intrinsically, we are perfect in being as we are. We *are* enlightened. But until we really understand this, we will do deluded things.

Zen centers and other places of spiritual practice often ignore what has to happen to a human being for true enlightenment to take place. The first thing that has to happen—with many steps, many byways and pitfalls—is the integration of ourselves as human beings, so that mind and body become one. For many people, this enterprise takes an entire lifetime. When mind and body are one, we are not constantly being pulled this way and that way, back and forth. As long as we are controlled by our self-centered emotions (and most of us have thousands of these illusions), we haven't accomplished this step. To take a person who has not yet integrated body and mind and push him or her through the narrow concentrated gate to enlightenment can indeed produce a powerful experience; but the person won't know what to do with it.

Momentarily seeing the oneness of the universe doesn't necessarily mean that our lives will be freer. For example, as long as we worry about what someone's done to us, like taking our money, we are not truly integrated. Whose money is it, anyway? And what makes a piece of land ours? Our sense of ownership arises because we're afraid and insecure—and so we want to own things. We want to own people. We want to own ideas. We want to own our opinions. We want to have a strategy for living. As long as we are doing all these things, the idea that we could naturally act like Master Kogen is quite farfetched.

The important thing is who we are at any given moment and how we handle what life brings to us. As body and mind become more integrated, the work becomes paradoxically far easier. Our job is to be integrated with the whole world. As the Buddha said, "The whole world are my children." Once we are relatively at peace with ourselves, integration with the rest of the world becomes easier. What takes the greatest time and work is the first part. And once that has been relatively accomplished, there are many areas of life that have the quality of an enlightened life. The first years are more difficult than the later years. The most difficult is the first sesshin, the most difficult months of sitting are in the first year, the second year is easier, and so it goes.

Later on another crisis may arise, perhaps after five or ten years of sitting, when we begin to understand that we are going to get nothing out of sitting—nothing whatsoever. The dream is gone—the dream of the personal glory we think we're going to get out of practice. The ego is fading; this can be a dry, difficult period. As I teach, I see people's personal agendas cracking up. That happens in the first part of the journey. It's really wonderful, though it is the hard part. Practice becomes unromantic: it doesn't sound like what we read about in books. Then real practice begins: moment by moment, just facing the moment. Our minds no longer are so obstreperous; they don't dominate us anymore. Genuine renunciation of our personal agendas begins, though even then it may be interrupted by all sorts of difficult episodes. The path is never direct and smooth. In fact, the rockier the better. The ego needs rocks to challenge it.

As practice progresses, we notice that the episodes, the rocks in our path, are not as difficult as they once would have been. We don't have quite the same agenda that we had before, not the same drive to be important or to be judgmental. If we sit with even forty percent awareness, little chips come off of our personal agendas. The longer we sit, the less eventful our sitting becomes. How long can we stand to look at our ego stuff? How long can we look at it without letting it go and just returning to being here? The process is a slow wearing away—not a matter of gaining virtue, but of gaining understanding.

In addition to labeling our thoughts, we need to stay with our body sensations. If we work at both with the utmost patience, we slowly open up to a new vision of life.

We want a life that is as rich and wide—as beneficial—as it possibly can be. We all have the possibility for such a life. Intelligence helps; the people who come to Zen centers are typically quite bright. But bright people also tend to get caught up in too much thinking and analyzing. No matter what the discipline—art, music, physics, philosophy—we can pervert it and use it to avoid practice. But if we don't do it, life gives us kick after kick after kick, until we learn what we need to learn. No one can do this practice for us; we have to do it by ourselves. The only test of whether we are doing it is our lives.

The Tomato Fighters

A moment ago I had a call from a friend on the East Coast who is dying. She said that she had perhaps three or four days left and that she was calling to say good-bye. After the call, I was reminded of the preciousness of this jewel we call life—and of how little we know or appreciate it. Even if we know it a bit, how little we take care of it!

Some, especially those in spiritual communities, may imagine that the jewel of life never has conflict, argument, or upset—just calmness, peacefulness. That's a great mistake, because if we don't understand how conflict is generated, we can wreck our lives and the lives of others. First, we need to see that we are all afraid. Our basic fear is of death, and this fear is the basis of all other fears. Our fear of our own annihilation leads to useless behaviors, including the effort to protect our self-image, or ego. Out of that need to protect comes anger. Out of anger comes conflict. And conflict destroys our relationships with others.

I don't mean to imply that a good life has no heated arguments, no disagreements; that's silly. When I was growing up I knew a couple of old men and their families very well. The families were friendly and often went off together for weekends. These two men competed on every front, but most especially during the tomato season. They would both enter their best tomatoes in the local fair. Their arguments about their tomatoes were classic: they raised their voices until the walls shook. And in fact, they both won "Best in Fair." It was delightful to watch them because they both knew the arguing was just fun. The test of a good conflict, a good exchange of opinions, is that when the conflict is over there is no residue of coolness or bitterness, no clinging to an idea that "I won, and you didn't." Arguments are fine, but only if they are fun. If we have a fight with someone close to us and afterward we supposedly forgive and forget, but in fact remain cool and distant, it's time to look more closely.

A verse from the *Tao Te Ching* states, "The best athlete / wants his opponent at his best. / The best general / enters the mind of his enemy. / The best businessman / serves the communal good. / The best leader / follows the will of the people. // All of them embody / the virtue of non-competition. / Not that they don't love to compete, / but they do it in the spirit of play. / In this they are like children / and in harmony with the Tao." If our arguments are in that spirit, that's fine. But how often is this the case?

Suzuki Roshi was once asked if anger could be like a pure wind that wipes everything clean. He said, "Yes, but I don't think you need to worry about that." He said that he himself had never had an anger that was like the pure wind. And our anger is surely not that pure, either, because of the fear that lies beneath the anger. Unless we contact and experience our fear, we will have harmful anger.

A good example is in our efforts to be honest. Honesty is the absolute basis of our practice. But what does that mean? Suppose we say to another, "I want to be honest with you. I want to share with you how I see our relationship." What we say could be helpful. But often our efforts to be honest don't come from real honesty, from a spirit of play, from including the other—even though we may pretend that. As long as we have any intention to be right, to show or teach the other person something, we should be wary. So long as our words have the slightest ego attachment, they are dishonest. True words come when we understand what it is to know we're angry, to know we're fearful, and to wait. The ancient words say, "Do you have the patience to *wait* until your mind settles and the water is clear? Can you remain unmoving until the right action arises by itself?" That's a wonderful way of putting the point: can we be quiet for a moment, until the right words arise by themselves—honest words, words that don't hurt others? Such words may be very frank. They may exactly communicate what we need to say. They may even be the same words we might have spoken out of our ego, but there will be a difference. To live in this way is not easy; none of us can do it all of the time. Our first reaction comes out of self-preservation and fear, and then anger jumps right in. Our feelings are hurt, we are frightened, and so we get angry.

If we have the patience to wait until the mud (our mind) settles and the water is clear, if we remain unmoving till the right action arises by itself, the right words will arise, without our thinking about them. We won't need to justify what we are saying with multiple reasons; we won't have to give reasons at all. The right words will say themselves if we have settled down. We can't do this without sincere practice. It may not be a formal practice; sometimes we just take a deep breath, wait for a second, feel our guts, and then speak. On the other hand, if we're having a major conflict with somebody, we may need more time. It might be better to say nothing for a month.

My old friends who argued about the tomatoes had no intent to harm. Despite the noise, there was practically no ego involvement. They had been playing this game for years. Often from students I hear tales about dealings with friends, what has gone wrong, and what they want to do to "right" it. "My friend did something mean. My friend was lacking. I'll let him know how I feel." About such situations, Jesus said, "Let him who is without sin throw the first stone." We are all lacking. I'm lacking; you're lacking; we're all lacking. But our ego tells us only that the *other* fellow is lacking. Much of what we call communicating with others during our conflicts boils down to telling them how they are lacking. Then they naturally want to tell us how we are lacking. And so it goes, back and forth, back and forth, back and forth. Nothing useful or true is communicated. The persons speaking are like two ships that pass in the night. People object to waiting until the mud clears, however; we're afraid we will be taken advantage of. But can we truly be taken advantage of?

STUDENT: We can't be taken advantage of, but we sure feel like it much of the time.

JOKO: Yes, we often feel that we are being taken advantage of. Suppose a person owes us money and doesn't pay it. Or someone breaks a promise to us. Or someone talks about us behind our back. And so on; we all do such things. Are such actions grounds for abandoning a friendship, a partner, a child, or a parent? Do we have the patience to wait till our mud settles and the water is clear? Can we remain unmoving till the right action arises by itself? Sometimes we are angry with ourselves. When this happens, we usually are using words that are false, springing out of our propensity to feel injured or hurt. Instead of directing the angry words at someone else, we have turned them on ourselves. But only out of the Tao—the emptiness, the quiet—can arise right words and right action. Right words and right action *are* the Tao.

As I teach, I'm less interested in the conflicts students have than in the character of their words and where the words come from. With people who have been practicing a while, the words may sound better but still come from the wrong place. "I know it's all me. I know it's got nothing to do with you. I don't want to be picky or fussy, *but* . . ." The judgment is still there, just disguised. They might as well say, "Damn it! Why don't you pick up your clothes?" Though it's nice for clothes to be picked up, that's not the way to make it happen. Can we remain unmoving, can we keep our mouths shut until the right action or the right word arises by itself? Most of the time, there's no harm in doing *nothing*. Most of what we do doesn't make much difference, anyway; we just think it does.

We are all angry people because we are all frightened. Luckily, we often have the opportunity of practicing with anger with people who are difficult for us. We may try to deal with such persons by cutting them out of our lives. Why do we do this?

STUDENT: To make our life easier.

STUDENT: Because we think they're the cause of our problem.

STUDENT: Because they don't do what we want them to.

STUDENT: Because they might show us something about ourselves that we don't want to see.

STUDENT: To avoid our own guilt.

STUDENT: We might want to punish them.

STUDENT: Perhaps the last time we were together was too confusing and painful, and we don't want to get near that spot.

JOKO: We need to be willing to rest in the confusion and unpleasantness, to let the mud settle until we can see more clearly. With such practice we can uncover the precious jewel of our life; then there will be an absence of squabbling. We may still have arguments, but like the tomato fighters—playfully. When we study anger fully, it disappears. As Dogen Zenji said, to study Buddhism is to study the self, and to study the self is to forget the self. When our anger resolves into emptiness, there's no problem; the right action arises by itself. In intensive retreats, this process is accelerated. The self-centered self becomes more transparent, clearer, so that we can settle right through it. As the mud settles and the water becomes clearer, we can see the jewel—almost as if we were in tropical waters and could look into the depths and see the colored fish and plants. Then we can speak true words, as opposed to self-centered words, which always create disharmony.

STUDENT: Joko, what do you say to somebody who is dying?

JOKO: Not much, or "I love you." Even when we are dying, we still want to be part of the human experience.

STUDENT: Sometimes when I have a conflict, if I just come out and say something in the best way that I can, even if it is not perfect, I learn a lot about myself that I don't want to know, and it's very valuable. And then I can be honest about that instead of waiting.

JOKO: Yes, I understand. When I say to wait, I'm not talking about a formula. I'm talking about an attitude of learning. Sometimes it is useful to say something before the mud settles; it depends on the attitude, the spirit of the words. Even if the spirit is somewhat off, if we're learning fast as we do it, that can be okay, too. If we do it badly, then we apologize. We should always be ready to apologize; we all have something to apologize about.

STUDENT: Often I really think I am being honest, and only in retrospect do I see that I was in the midst of self-deception.

JOKO: Yes. The test of a good conflict as opposed to one that is harmful is that there is no residue afterward. Everyone feels good afterward. It's clear. It's over. The air is pleasant. It's great, though rare.

STUDENT: It seems that there are some things that we just can't fix, however.

JOKO: I'm not talking about fixing things; that's trying to control the world, to run the universe.

STUDENT: Sometimes I allow people to abuse me. When I do that, it is important to speak up. If I speak up, sometimes I get good results.

JOKO: It's fine to speak up, if we can speak up with true words. And if we feel that we have been abused, we need to recognize that we may have allowed the abuse. When we see this, it may be unnecessary to say anything. Instead of trying to educate or save the other person (which is never our business), we can simply learn.

Do Not Judge

There's a passage in the *Dhammapada*, verse 50: "Let none find fault in others. Let none see omissions and commissions in others. But let one see one's own acts, done and undone." This is a key aspect of our practice. Though practice may make us more aware of our tendency to judge others, in ordinary life we still do it. Because we are human, we judge one another. Someone does something that seems to us rude or unkind or thoughtless, and we can't help noticing it. Many times a day, we see people doing things that seem lacking in some way.

It's not that everyone always acts appropriately. People often do just what we are objecting to. When they do what they do, however, it's not necessary for us to judge them. I'm not immune from this; I find myself judging others, also. We all do. So I recommend a practice to help us catch ourselves in the act of judging: whenever we say the name of another person, we should watch what we add to the name. What do we say or think about the person? What kind of label do we use? Do we put the person into some category? No person should be reduced to a label; yet because of our preferences and dislikes, we do it anyway.

I suspect that if you do this practice, you'll find that you can't go for five minutes without judgment. It's amazing. We want other people's behavior to be just what we want—and when it's not, we judge them. Our waking life is full of such judgments.

Few of us hurt other people physically. The main way we hurt others is with our mouths. As someone said, "There are two times to keep your mouth shut: when you're swimming—

and when you're angry." When we judge others to be wrong, we get to be right—which we like.

As the passage says, we should be concerned for our own behavior, instead. "But let one see one's own acts, done and undone." Instead of looking around constantly and judging everybody else, let us see our own behavior: what we have done and what we have not done. We don't need to judge ourselves, but simply notice how we act. If we start judging ourselves, we have set up an ideal, a certain way we think we must be. This also is not helpful. We need to see our actual thoughts, to be aware of what is actually true for us. If we do this, we will notice that whenever we judge, our body tightens up. Behind the judgment is a self-centered thought that produces tension in our body. Over time, that tension is harmful to us, and indirectly harmful to others. Not only is the tension harmful; the judgments we express about others (and ourselves) are harmful, too.

Whenever we say a person's name, it's useful to notice whether we have stated more than a fact. For example, the judgment "she's thoughtless" goes beyond the facts. The facts are, she did what she did—for example, she said she'd call me, and she didn't. That she was thoughtless is my own negative judgment, added onto that fact. We will find ourselves making such judgments over and over. Practice means to become aware when we do this. It's important not to slither unaware over great areas of our life, and much of our life involves talking.

STUDENT: Is it okay to say, "She said she'd call, and she didn't"?

JOKO: It depends upon how it's said. If we "state the facts" in an accusing way, we're clearly making a judgment, even if the words seem factual.

STUDENT: When we notice other people's mistakes, it helps us to know what not to do. In a way we should be grateful for their errors.

JOKO: Yes, it's useful to see others as our teachers. But if our learning involves seeing others as "wrong," we're still caught in judgment.

If we stay awake and are not wrapped up in our emotions, we tend to learn. Nearly always, however, what we do is to get upset in some way. Out of our upset, we judge others and judge ourselves. Either is harmful—and unfruitful.

STUDENT: I tend to keep my mouth shut about others. But I notice that when I get angry or upset, my judgments come out indirectly, in my attitude and in passive-aggressive behavior. I find that really hard to work with.

JOKO: The key phrase here is, "Let one see one's own acts, done and undone." That means simply to notice our attitude, our thoughts, and our behavior. *And*, to return to our basic bodily experience of the anger, to really feel it.

STUDENT: At work we sometimes get into complaining and gossiping about the boss. If I refuse to participate, it's as if I'm being aloof or arrogant and believe I'm better than they are.

JOKO: That is a difficult situation to work with. One of the marks of skillful practice is to be present without participating in harmful actions. For you that would mean to be in a group that is judging and being critical, yet to remain noncritical and not be seen as acting superior or different. It can be done. How might we manage to do it? What would be useful?

STUDENT: Humor.

JOKO: Yes, humor helps. What else?

STUDENT: Not judging the other people who are being critical.

JOKO: Yes. If everyone else is gossiping and we've decided that we're not going to do that, we're probably feeling superior, "holier than thou." We may be feeling anger at them, too. If our attitude is angry and superior, that judgment will come through. If we have honestly practiced with our anger, however, it may be minimal and not a problem. We can just be present in the group naturally.

STUDENT: I've noticed that when I'm in a group that is gossiping or being critical about others, if I just let them talk without myself joining in any judgment, they often come around eventually to see the other side. If I try to nip it in the bud at the beginning, however, the judging escalates. If I argue or try to point out the good qualities of the person they are criticizing, it all gets confused.

JOKO: Yes. As we become clearer with our own practice, we tend to find more skillful means to deal with whatever comes up.

STUDENT: Rather than talking about the person being criticized, it helps to come back to the person who is judging and show some sympathetic understanding of his or her feelings. For example, if someone says, "That guy is always late," we can say, "It must be difficult for you to have to wait. I can see that you're upset."

STUDENT: What about positive judgments? There's a school of thought about working with children that holds that it's not healthy for children to label them in any way, negatively *or* positively. When we say, "You're such a good boy!" or "You're smart!," we put them in a box.

JOKO: It's better not to judge the person at all. We can be approving of their actions, however. To a child, we might say, "That's a great drawing!" The more specific we can be, the better. Instead of "Great paper!" we can say, "The opening is particularly good" or "You give good examples to back up your points."

Children are less threatening to us than adults. We expect adults to know what they're doing, and so we're very ready to judge them and find fault. Likewise with ourselves: we think we should know what we're doing.

STUDENT: When I find myself judging others, what should I do?

JOKO: When we catch ourselves judging, we need to notice the thoughts that comprise the judgment, such as "thinking that she's stupid," and feel the tension in our body. Behind our judgments is always anger or fear. It's helpful to experience the anger or fear directly, rather than letting them drive our actions.

The problem is that we enjoy talking about people critically, and that constantly causes problems. If something happens that we feel fairly neutral about, we usually handle it quite well. But about most things we aren't particularly neutral. That's why our practice is so valuable.

STUDENT: I notice that if I judge people in my first contact with them, that judgment colors my whole relationship with them. I tend to hang on to my judgments and just forget about practicing with it.

JOKO: Yes. We form a fixed notion. The next time we meet them, our notion is already fixed, and we can observe even less about how they actually are.

STUDENT: Criticizing the person to someone else seems to make the judgment even stronger. If, for example, another person and I agree that someone is thoughtless, the judgment becomes really solid and difficult to shake.

JOKO: Yes. Much of what we call friendship amounts to shared judgments and critical attitudes about other people and events.

STUDENT: Aren't judgments always false? We see such a little bit of each person.

JOKO: I wouldn't say we're always mistaken. We're incomplete. For example: everyone is sometimes thoughtless; we just don't think things through, we just don't pay attention fully.

When we label others "thoughtless," however, we don't see the hundreds and thousands of other things they do. We tend to be interested only in what affects us directly. That's why when we remember our childhoods, we always remember the bad stuff. We're not as interested in the good things that people did to us. We tend to remember anything that felt threatening. If someone hurts us, we're not interested in the other things she does. So far as we're concerned, she's unacceptable.

If we complain about her to others and they agree with us, a solid network of judgment is set up. The negative attitude we have formed about her poisons the way she is received by others, including those who have no personal experience of her. Having heard the gossip, they dismiss her, too. Such cumulative judgment is the most harmful thing humans do to each other. We judge people and reject them without knowing them at all.

Have you ever had the experience of hearing people described whom you have never met? You feel that you know them before you've ever met them. And when you meet them, they're totally different from the description. It's amazing.

STUDENT: Sometimes it feels therapeutic to talk to a friendly ear about a difficult situation I have with someone else. Is that ever okay?

JOKO: Only if the exchange is completely confidential. And even then, it's better simply to describe the other person's behavior in factual terms, and then talk about your own feelings. We need to be very careful. If we can stick to "I notice myself thinking that she's thoughtless" or "I feel really upset and tight," that's okay. But when we slip into "She's really thoughtless, isn't she?" we've lost our practice.

STUDENT: I think it's important to remember your point that when we do speak ill of another person, then we are hurting ourselves. There's a contraction that occurs when we speak ill of someone or even think ill of someone.

JOKO: Yes. Our body and mind are contracted. We always pay for that, in many ways. Other people pay, too. I suggest that the minute somebody's name escapes our mouth, we watch what we've added on. Is what we've said a fact? Or is it a judgment? For example, if Lisa has left something where I might trip over it, we can say, "Lisa left something where I might trip over it. I'd better be careful" or we can say, "Lisa's a pain. She's so thoughtless!" That's not a fact, but my judgment.

STUDENT: My judgments seem very persistent. I go through periods where I have negative thoughts about a person, over and over. It seems as though I label it a million times and still miss another million times.

JOKO: Yes. We may have to do that many, many times over before it fades.

STUDENT: I'm puzzling over the difference between facts and judgments. Suppose that someone really does pick on me repeatedly. If I say, "She's always picking on me," is that a fact or a judgment?

JOKO: The difference is in how we say it and the feeling behind it. If we're simply observing, "Yes, it's true. She does pick on me," that's simply a fact. If we're complaining, that's a judgment. The tone of voice is one clue.

STUDENT: If we catch ourselves just as we're about to judge another person, and we don't say anything, it seems like we have to be willing to be nothing in that moment.

JOKO: That's true. When we judge, we reinforce our separate identity as a person who judges. When we keep our mouth shut, we have to give that identity up for a moment. That's why the technique I have suggested is really training in what Buddhism calls "no self."

STUDENT: I find that when I encounter persons whom I don't know, if I deliberately refrain from saying anything about them, I don't seem to be able to get a handle on opinions about them. That makes me realize how important talking is in forming judgments.

JOKO: Yes, though we can also form judgments without saying anything at all. Again, we need to notice the judgment we have formed. We need to remember that most of practice can be summed up in *kindness*. In any situation, what is kindness?

IV

CHANGE

Preparing the Ground

From time to time, one of my students has a little break-through, a small realization or kensho. Some Zen centers focus on such experiences and make much out of them. That's not true here. The experiences are interesting: if for a moment one comes into the absolute present, a shift takes place. The shift does not last; we always slip back into our usual ways of doing things. But for a while—perhaps for just a second, perhaps for an hour, perhaps for weeks—everything that was a problem is not a problem. Troublesome ailments and struggles of various kinds suddenly quiet down. Life has been turned upside down for a moment; we see how things really are. Having such an experience doesn't mean much by itself. But it may point the way for us to be in the absolute present more and more. Being in the present is the point of sitting and of practice in general: it helps us to be wiser about life, more compassionate, more oriented to what needs to be done. We become more effective in our work. Such outcomes are wonderful; yet we cannot strive for them or make them happen. All that we can do is to prepare the neces-sary conditions. We need to be sure that the soil is well pre-pared, rich and loose and fertile, so that if the seed falls, it will spring forth rapidly. The student's job is not to be hunting for outcomes, but to be preparing the way. As the Bible says, "Pre-pare ye the way of the Lord." That is our work.

In a sense, our path is no path. The object is not to get some-where. There is no great mystery, really; what we need to do is straightforward. I don't mean that it is easy; the "path" of practice is not a smooth road. It is littered with sharp rocks that can make us stumble or that can cut right through our shoes. Life itself is hazardous. Encountering the hazards is usually what brings people into Zen centers. The path of life seems to be mostly difficulties, things that give trouble. Yet the longer we practice, the more we begin to understand that those sharp rocks on the road are in fact like precious jewels; they help us to prepare the proper condition for our lives. The rocks are different for each person. One person might desperately need more time alone; another might desperately need more time with other people. The sharp rock might be working with a nasty person or living with somebody who is hard to get along with. The sharp rocks might be your children, your parents, anyone. Not feeling well could be your sharp rock. Losing your job could be it, or getting a new job and being worried about it. There are sharp rocks everywhere. What changes from years of practice is coming to know something you didn't know before: that there are no sharp rocks—the road is covered with diamonds. What are other sharp rocks that are really diamonds?

STUDENT: My husband's death.

STUDENT: Deadlines.

STUDENT: Illness.

JOKO: Yes, good. What is necessary for us to begin to realize that the sharp stones of our lives are really diamonds? What are some of the conditions that make it possible for us to practice?

If we are very new to practice, it may be impossible for us to see a huge trauma as a gift, to see a sharp rock as a diamond. It is usually best to begin to practice at a time when one's life is not too upset. For example, when one has a new baby, the first month is not a good time to begin practice—as I well remember. It is usually advisable to begin practice in a relatively calm period. It's better to be in fairly good health. Mildly poor health does not rule out practice, but severe illness makes it extremely difficult to begin. It helps to be in reasonably good physical condition, too. Practice is physically demanding.

The longer we practice, the less important are these prerequisites. But without them at the beginning, the rocks are just too big. We can't see any way to practice. When one has been up all night with a screaming baby and has had two hours' sleep, that's not a good time to begin to do zazen. If one's body is falling apart, if one is thoroughly miserable, that's not a good time to begin. But the longer we practice, the very difficulties that life presents more and more can be seen as jewels. Increasingly, problems do not rule out practice, but support it. Instead of finding that practice is too difficult, that we have too many problems, we see that the problems themselves are the jewels, and we devote ourselves to being with them in a way we never dreamt of before. In my interviews with students, I constantly hear about such shifts: "Three years ago, I couldn't possibly have handled this situation, but now . . ." That's the turning over, preparing the ground. That's what is necessary for the body and mind truly to transform. It's not that problems disappear or that life "improves," but that life slowly transforms—and the sharp rocks that we hated become welcome jewels. We may not delight to see them when they appear, but we appreciate the opportunity that they give, and so we embrace them rather than running away from them. This is the end of complaints about our life. Even that difficult person, the one who criticizes you, the one who doesn't respect your opinion, or whatever—everybody has somebody or something, some sharp rock. Such a rock is precious; it is an opportunity, a jewel to embrace.

No one sees the jewel all at once; no one sees it completely. Sometimes we may see it in one area but not in another. Sometimes we can see the jewel, and sometimes we absolutely cannot see it. We may absolutely refuse to see it; we may not want to have anything to do with it.

Yet we must constantly wrestle with this basic problem. Because we are human, much of the time we don't even want to know about it. Why? Because to wrestle with it means a life that is open to difficulty rather than hiding from it. We are usually trying to substitute something for the difficulty. When we are fed up with our children, for example, we'd like to turn them in and get new ones. Even when we stay stuck with them, we find subtle ways of "turning them in," instead of being with the reality of who they really are. We deal with other problems in the same way: we have subtle ways of turning almost anything in, of choosing not to deal with it.

Wrestling with the reality of our lives is part of the endless preparation of the ground. Sometimes we prepare a little piece of ground well. We may have little insights, moments that spring out. Still, there are acres of land that are not yet prepared—so we keep going, opening up more and more of our life. This is all that really matters. Human life should be like a vow, dedicated to uncovering the meaning of life. The meaning of life is in fact not complicated; yet it is veiled from us by the way we see our difficulties. It takes the most patient practice to begin to see through that, to discover that the sharp rocks are truly jewels.

None of this has anything to do with judgment, with being "good" or "bad" persons. We just do the best we can at any given moment; what we don't see, we don't see. That's the point of practice: to enlarge that little "peek hole" we get sometimes, so that it becomes bigger and bigger. No one sees it all the time. I certainly don't. And so we keep poking away.

In a way, practice is fun: to look at my own life and be honest about it is fun. It is difficult, humiliating, discouraging; yet in another sense, it's fun—because it's alive. To see myself and my life as they truly are is joy. After all the struggle and avoiding and denying and going the other way, it is deeply satisfying for a second to be there with life as it is. The satisfaction is the very core of ourselves. Who we are is beyond words—just that open power of life, manifesting constantly in all sorts of interesting things, even in our own misery and struggles. The hassle is both horrendous and wholesome. That's what it means to prepare the ground. We don't need to worry about the little moments or openings that pop up. If we have fertile, well-prepared soil, we can throw anything in there and it will grow.

As we patiently do this work, we come to a different sense of our lives. Recently, I had a call from a student who lives some distance away who told me, "I can't believe it. Most of the time my life is very enjoyable." I thought, yes, that's great, but . . . *life* is enjoyable. An enjoyable life includes heartache, disappointment, grief. That's part of the flow of life, to let such experiences be. They come and go, and the grief finally dissolves into something else. But if we are complaining and holding on and being rigid (which is what we like to do), then we have very little enjoyment. If we have been aware of the process of our lives, including moments that we hate, and are just aware of our hating—"I don't want to do it, but I'll do it anyway"— that very awareness is life itself. When we stay with that awareness, we don't have that reactive feeling about it; we're just doing it. Then for a second we begin to see, "Oh, this is terrible—and at the same time, it's really quite enjoyable." We just keep going, preparing the ground. That's enough.

Experiences and Experiencing

At each second, we are at a crossroad: between unawareness and awareness, between being absent and being present—or between experiences and experiencing. Practice is about moving from experiences to experiencing. What is meant by this?

We tend to overwork the word *experience,* and when we say, "Be with your experience," we are speaking carelessly. It may not be helpful to follow this advice. Ordinarily we see our lives as series of experiences. For example, I have an experience of one or another person, an experience of my lunch or my office. From this point of view, my life is nothing but having one experience after another. Entwined around each experience there may be a slight halo or a neurotic emotional veil. Often the veil takes the form of memories, fantasies, or hopes for the future—the associations we bring to experience, as a result of our past conditioning. When we do zazen, our experience may be dominated by our memories, which can be overwhelming.

Is there anything wrong with this? Humans *do* have memories, fantasies, hopes; that's natural. When we clothe our experience with these associations, however, experience becomes an object: a noun rather than a verb. So our lives become encounters with one object after another: persons, my lunch, my office. Memories and hopes are similar: life becomes a series of "this" and "that." We ordinarily see our lives as encounters with things "out there." Life becomes dualistic: subject and object, me and that.

There's no problem with this process—unless we believe it. For when we really believe that we're meeting objects all day long, we're enslaved. Why? Because any object "out there" will have a slight veil of emotional context. And we then react in terms of our emotional associations. In classical Zen teaching, we are enslaved by greed, anger, and ignorance. To see the world exclusively in this way is to be in chains. When our world consists of objects, we guide our lives by what we can expect from each object: "Does he like me?" "Is that to my advantage?" "Should I be afraid of her?" Our history and our memories take over, and we divide the world up into things to avoid and things to pursue.

The trouble with this way of living is that what benefits me now may hurt me later, and vice versa. The world is constantly changing, and so our associations lead us astray. There's nothing safe about a world of objects. We're constantly wary, even of those people whom we say we love and are close to. As long as another person is an object to us, we can be sure that there's no genuine love or compassion between us.

If having experiences is our ordinary world, what is the other world, the other fork in the road? What is the difference between experiences and experiencing? What is genuine hearing, touching, tasting, seeing, and so on?

When experiencing occurs, in that very moment, experiencing is not in space or time. It can't be; for when it's in space or time, we've made an object of it. As we touch and look and hear, we're creating the world of space and time, but the actual life we lead is not in space or time; it's just experiencing. The world of space and time arises when experiencing becomes reduced to a series of experiences. In the precise moment of hearing, for example, there is just hearing, hearing, hearing, hearing, which creates the sound of the airplane or whatever. Thup, thup, thup, thup . . . : there's space between each; and each one is absolute hearing, hearing, hearing. That's our life, as we create our world. We're creating with all our senses so quickly that we can't possibly keep track of it. The world of our experiences is being created out of nothing, second by second by second.

In the service we do, one of the dedications states, "Unceasing change turns the wheel of life." Experiencing, experiencing, experiencing; change, change, change. "Unceasing change turns the wheel of life, and so reality is shown in all its many forms. Peaceful dwelling as change itself liberates all suffering sentient beings and brings them to great joy." Peaceful dwelling as change itself means feeling the throbbing pain in my legs, hearing the sound of a car: just experiencing, experiencing. Just dwelling with experience itself. Even the pain is changing minutely, second by second by second. "Peaceful dwelling as change itself liberates all suffering sentient beings and brings them to great joy."

If this process were absolutely clear, we'd have no need to practice. The enlightened state is not *having* an experience; instead, it's an absence of all experience. The enlightened state is pure, unadulterated experiencing. And that is utterly different from "having an enlightenment experience." Enlightenment is the demolition of all experience built of thoughts, fantasies, memories, and hopes. Frankly, we're not interested in demolishing our lives as we have ordinarily known them. We demolish the false structures of our lives by labeling our thoughts, by saying for the five hundredth time, "Having a thought that such-and-such will happen." When we've said it five hundred times, we see it for what it is. It's just empty energy spinning out of our conditioning, with no reality whatsoever. There is no intrinsic truth in it; it's just changing, changing, changing.

It's easy for us to talk about this process, but there's nothing that we are less interested in doing than demolishing our fantasy structures. We have a secret fear that if we demolished them all, we'd be demolishing ourselves.

There's an old Sufi story about a man who dropped his keys on the dark side of the street at night, then crossed the street to the lamppost where it was bright to look for the keys. When a friend asked why he was looking under the lamp instead of where he dropped the keys, he replied, "I'm looking here because there is more light." That's what we do with our lives: the familiar framework is where we want to look. If we have a problem, we follow a familiar framework: thinking, stewing, analyzing, keeping the crazy business of our lives going because that's what we're used to doing. Never mind that it doesn't work. We just get more determined, and keep searching under the lamppost. We're not interested in that life which is out of space and time, constantly creating the world of space and time. We're not interested in that; in fact, it's frightening to us.

What pushes us to abandon this melodrama, to sit through the confusion? At bottom, it comes down to the unease we have with the way we are living our lives. Beyond a life of having experiences is a life of experiencing, a life of compassion and joy. For true compassion and joy are not things to be experienced. Our true master is just this: changing, changing, changing; experiencing, experiencing, experiencing. The master is not in space and time—yet none other than space and time. Our experiencing of life is also the creating of life itself. "Unceasing change turns the wheel of life and so reality is shown in all its many forms."

A poem by W. H. Auden captures much of our ordinary state:

> We would rather be ruined than changed,
> We would rather die in our dread
> Than climb the cross of the moment
> And let our illusions die.

We would rather be ruined than changed—even though change is who we are. We would rather die in our anxiety, our fear, our loneliness, than climb the cross of the moment and let our illusions die. And the cross is also the crossroads, the choice. We are here to make that choice.

The Icy Couch

In experiencing we lose our seemingly dual relationship to other people and things, which is, "I see you, I comment on you, I have thoughts about you or myself," or whatever. Dual relationship is not hard to talk about; but nondual relationship—experiencing—is harder to describe. I want to consider how we get away from living a life that's experiential, how we fall out of the Garden of Eden.

Every human being while growing up decides that he or she needs a strategy, because we cannot grow up without meeting opposition from what we might call the "not-self," that which is seemingly external to us. Often we meet apparent opposition from our parents, friends and relatives, and others. Sometimes the apparent opposition is severe; sometimes it's fairly mild. But no one grows up without developing a strategy to deal with it.

We may decide that our best option for pleasant survival is to be a conforming, "nice" person. If that doesn't seem to work, we may learn to attack others before they can get at us, or we may withdraw. So there are three major strategies for coping: conforming to please, attacking, or withdrawing. Everyone in some way employs one or another of those strategies.

In order to maintain our strategy, we have to think. So the growing child relies more and more on thinking to elaborate that strategy. Any situation or person encountered begins to be evaluated from the standpoint of the chosen strategy. Eventually we approach the whole world as if it were on trial, asking, "Will that individual or event hurt me or not?" Even though we may do it with a social, smiling face, we ask that question of everything we meet.

Eventually we perfect our strategy so that we no longer know it consciously; it's now in the body. For example, suppose we develop a strategy of withdrawing. When we meet anything or anybody, we tighten the body; the response is habitual. We may tighten our shoulders, our face, our stomach, or some other part of the body. The particular style is unique to each person. And we don't even know we're doing it because once the contraction is established, it is in every cell of our body. We don't have to know about it; it's just there. Although the response is unconscious, it makes our life unpleasant because it is a withdrawal from life and a separation from it. The contraction is painful.

Yet everybody has it. Even when we think we're relatively happy, we may be able to detect a mild tension throughout the body. It's nothing spectacular and may be very mild. When everything is going our way, we don't feel bad; yet the mild contraction never ceases. It's always there, with every person on earth.

Children learn how to elaborate their strategies, incorporating everything that happens to them into the framework of their personal systems. Our perceptions become selective, incorporating those events that fit our system and screening out events that don't fit. Because the system is supposed to keep us safe and secure, we're not interested in having it weakened by contradictory information. By the time we reach adulthood the system is ourselves. It's what we call the *ego*. We live our life from it, trying to find people, situations, jobs, that will confirm our strategy and avoiding those that threaten it.

But such maneuvers are never completely satisfactory, because as long as we live, we can never quite know what will happen next. Even if we get most of life under control we never know how to achieve this totally, and we know that we don't know. So there's always an element of fear. It has to be there. Not knowing what to do, the average person seeks everywhere for an answer. We have a problem, and we don't really know what it is. Life becomes for us the promise that is never kept because the answer eludes us. That's when we may start to practice. Only a few lucky people on the planet begin to see what needs to be done to recover the Garden of Eden, our genuine functioning self.

Perhaps we get a new partner who's just wonderful. (Particularly in relationships, delusion reigns supreme.) Then we marry or live with him or her, and . . . whoops! If we're practicing, this "whoops" can be immensely interesting and instructive. If we're not practicing, we may trade that partner in and look around for a new one. It seems as if the promise has not been kept. Or we start a new job or a new endeavor. At first it's fine, but then we begin to see some harsh realities, and the disillusion begins to set in. If we're living out of our strategy, nothing seems to work, because phenomenal life by definition is a promise that is never kept. If we fulfill a desire, we're happy for a brief moment, but the nature of fulfilling one desire is immediately to find another one, and another one, and another one. There's no way of being free from that pressure or stress. We can't settle. We find no peace.

As we sit, the endless spinning in our heads reveals to us our strategy. If we label our thoughts long enough, we're going to recognize our strategy. It's the strategy itself that generates the buzzing thoughts. Only one thing in our life is not caught by this strategy, and that's the physical, organic life of the body.

Of course, the body is taking punishment because it reflects our self-centeredness. The body has to obey the mind, so if the mind is saying that the world is a terrible place, the body says, "Oh, I'm so depressed!" The minute the images appear—thinking, fantasizing, hoping—the body has to respond. It has a chronic response, and at times that response exacerbates into depression or illness.

The main teacher I've had all my life has been a book. It may be the best book on Zen ever written. However, it's a translation from French, and the writing is unwieldy, with sentences that are whole paragraphs. After reading one of those sentences, you may ask yourself in puzzlement, "*What* did he say?" So it's a difficult book; still, it's the best explanation of the human problem that I've ever found. I studied it at one time for ten or fifteen years. I have a copy that looks like it's been through the washing machine. The book is *The Supreme Doctrine* by Hubert Benoit, a French psychiatrist who was in a severe accident that left him almost completely helpless for years. All he could do was just lie there. The human problem was his all-consuming interest, so he used those years of recovery to thoroughly delve into it.

Benoit's term for the emotional contraction arising from our efforts to protect ourselves is "spasm." He calls the ceaseless chatter of our internal dialogue "the imaginary film." The turning point for him comes when he realizes "that this spasm, which I have called abnormal is on the road that leads to satori [enlightenment]. . . . One can indeed say that what should be perceived, under the imaginary film, is a certain profound sensation of cramp, of a paralyzing grip, of immobilizing cold . . . and that it is on this hard couch, immobile and cold, that our attention should remain fixed; as though we tranquilly stretched out our body on a hard but friendly rock that was exactly molded to our form."

What Benoit is saying is that when we rest at peace with our pain, this repose *is* the "gateless gate." And it's the last place we want to be; it's not pleasant, and our whole strategic drive is for pleasantness. No, we want somebody to comfort us, save us, give us peace. Our ceaseless thinking, planning, and plotting are always about this. Only when we stay with what is beneath the imaginary film and rest there, do we begin to have a clue. The way I usually explain it is: instead of remaining with our thoughts, we label them until they settle down a little and then we do our best to stay with that which really is, the nonduality that is the sensation of our life at this very moment. That goes against everything we want, everything our culture teaches us. But it's the only real solution, the only gate to peace.

As we settle into our sensation of pain, we find it so appalling that we skitter off again. The minute we land in the sensation of discomfort, we spin back again into the imaginary film. We simply don't want to be in the reality of what we are. That's human, neither good nor bad, and it takes years of patient practice to begin to touch this reality more and more, becoming comfortable in resting there—until finally, as Benoit says, it's just a hard and friendly rock that is molded to us, and where we can finally rest and be at peace.

Sometimes we can rest for a short time, but because we are so habituated, we soon go back into the same old mental stuff. And so we go through the process again and again. Over time, it's that ceaseless process that brings us to peace. If it's complete, it can be called satori, or enlightenment.

The imaginary film generates the spasm, and the spasm generates the imaginary film. It's a ceaseless cycle, and it's only broken when we have become willing to rest in our pain. The ability to do this means we have become somewhat disillusioned, no longer hoping that our thoughts and feelings will be a solution to anything. As long as we hold out hope that the promise will be kept, we're not going to rest in the painful body sensations.

So there are two parts of practice. One is endless disappointment. Everything in our life that disappoints us is a kind friend. And we're all being disappointed in some way or other. If we're not disappointed, we never wear out our desire to think and reestablish ourself at the top of the heap with victory. Nobody wins in the end; nobody's going to survive. But that's still our drive, our system. It can only be worn out by years of sitting and by life; that's why our practice and our life have to be the same thing.

We have the illusion that other people are going to make us happy, that they're going to make our lives work. Until we wear out that illusion, there will be no real solution. Other people are for enjoyment, not for any other purpose. They are part of the wonder that life is; they're not here to do something for us. Until this illusion begins to wear out, we're not going to be content to stay with the spasm, the emotional contraction. We'll spin right off and go right back into our thoughts: "Yes, but if I do this, things will be better. . . ."

Life is a series of endless disappointments, and it's wonderful just because it doesn't give us what we want. To go down this path takes courage, and many people in this lifetime will not do it. We're all at different places on the path, which is fine. Only a very few who are enormously persistent and who take everything in life as an opportunity, and not as an insult, will finally understand. So if we spend all of our effort in trying to make our strategy work better, then we're just spinning our wheels. Our misery goes on till the day we die.

So there's nothing in life but opportunity, nothing. And that includes anything we can think of. Until we are disillusioned about the imaginary film that we spin endlessly (we hardly open our eyes in the morning before it begins), we won't stay with the cramp. We'll spin some more. I suppose that is what is meant by the wheel of karma.

Now, I'm not asking anyone to adopt this description as some sort of belief system. The only way we know the reality of such practice is by doing it. Eventually for a few people (sometimes intermittently but finally most of the time), there is what Christians call "the peace which passeth all understanding."

It has often helped me in difficult times to think of that cold, immobile couch and instead of fighting and struggling, just to be willing to rest on it. Over time we find the couch is the only place that is peaceful, the source of clear action.

As a dharma talk, this all sounds forbidding. Yet the people who endlessly practice are the ones who are enjoying life. This is the gateless gate to joy. People who understand and have the courage to do this are the ones who eventually know what joy is. I'm not talking about endless happiness (there's no such thing), but joy.

STUDENT: Do you often find that people choose one of the strategies, but as time goes by they may move to another one of these strategies? People who may have chosen to, say, withdraw and not participate may, as they become stronger, decide, "Well, maybe I'm up to conforming and pleasing a little bit." Do people sometimes move away from the wall and out into the crowd?

JOKO: I've often noticed that people who've been dependent and conforming begin to move to a false independence. That's natural, a stage before we can really just be ourselves. The more we practice with the cramp, the more the transformation accelerates. From the standpoint of the phenomenal world, we make progress, though in an absolute sense we're always fine, just as we are.

STUDENT: Resting with our discomfort, we find that it's not so scary and we can venture forth a little bit?

JOKO: Right. For example, we may learn that we can be depressed and still function. We just go ahead and do it. We don't have to feel good to function. The more we can go against our rigid system, the better.

STUDENT: When you talk about the cramp, it sounds like it's part of the rigid system.

JOKO: No, it is produced by the rigid system, but it's the only part of that system that is open to giving you a solution. For example, if we have angry thoughts, the body has to tighten up. We can't have an angry thought about somebody and not tighten up. And if we habitually have a strategy that is angry and attacking, the body will be contracted most of the time. But it's the only part of that system that gives us a gate to go through; because we can experience that cramp and leave it alone, it is free to open up. It might take five years, but it will happen.

STUDENT: I read the other day that whatever our chief feature is, it is good to exaggerate it. For me, however, that would mean to be very angry and to attack others.

JOKO: You may do it in private.

STUDENT: But if I really exaggerate anger and attack to make it more conscious, won't I hurt someone?

JOKO: No. Please remember that the only way to exaggerate is to exaggerate the *sensation* that the cramp is. We shouldn't exaggerate angry behavior. The system is totally unconscious, so as we consciously experience the cramp, it can dissolve itself.

STUDENT: I find from my experience that I'm in this terrible cramp, and then all of a sudden it will change. Something will open up, and I'll be in a space where I feel open and free, and then for no apparent reason I go back into my upset.

JOKO: Evidently you return into your habitual self-centered thinking.

STUDENT: Sometimes it seems like a muscle that was tight and is now relaxing.

JOKO: Yes, but the real cause is not a matter of muscles. Our basic desire to survive lies behind all of our troubles. If there was some way of managing muscles, then all body workers would produce enlightened subjects.

STUDENT: I find that the unpleasant sensation is not a static state. It's constantly in flux, changing all the time. So I'm in and out, all over the place, because it's pure energy, not static.

JOKO: The only thing that interferes with the flow is the fact that we believe our thoughts again. And that's almost habitual with us. We have to sit for many, many years before we don't believe our thoughts. We really do.

STUDENT: Until we wear out the project of trying to protect ourselves against life or fighting the way things are being presented to us at this moment, we will consistently return to the state of contraction, which is, "I don't like this!" It happens all the time.

STUDENT: Where is the cramp located?

JOKO: Wherever you feel it. It could be the face, the shoulders, anywhere. Frequently it's in the lower back.

STUDENT: I'm becoming more aware that some of my thoughts seem simply givens, pictures I have of myself that don't seem like thoughts, or that sound so good that I don't label them. Then there are thoughts that don't get labeled because they sound like good Zen practice.

JOKO: Yes; it's the thought we don't catch that will be running the show.

STUDENT: A lot of my conditioning seems unconscious or subconscious. So I may consciously feel very clear and light, and yet the conditioning is still there, and it does return me to the cramp or the hard bed, the spasm, even though I don't see anything happening in my conscious mind.

JOKO: Right. Remember that in a way there is no such thing as the unconscious, but what is revealed may be very subtle. A lot of what we're talking about isn't a major cramp like what is called a "charley horse."

STUDENT: You said that in good practice the companion to labeling thoughts is experiencing. Does that mean that the thought you're not catching might reveal itself if you are truly experiencing the cramp?

JOKO: Yes. The more we practice and make things conscious, the more the thought we're not conscious of will begin to float up to the surface. All of a sudden it hits us, "Oh, I never realized that before." It just floats up.

STUDENT: What's the repetitive spasm or bodily shaking that tends to come at times in this kind of practice?

JOKO: If we stay with the spasm, quite often the body will shake, or tears may come, because if we really put our attention on the body and give it freedom to be itself, it will begin to open up and the energy that was blocked will begin to surface. It may take the form of crying, shaking, or other involuntary movements.

STUDENT: Could you talk more about feelings?

JOKO: Feelings are simply thoughts plus bodily sensations.

STUDENT: And if a feeling comes up?

JOKO: Break it down. Either see what the thoughts are, or go into the body.

STUDENT: As we are experiencing, does the experiencing actually trigger memories or insights?

JOKO: Yes, sometimes. If we keep experiencing, the cramp sometimes will crack open. We'll see certain pictures from the past, but I wouldn't worry about them. Just let them come and go. Practice is not about analyzing ourselves, because there is no self. However, in a practice based on experiencing, our life will more and more spring from no-self as a life of direct and effective functioning and—yes!—clear and valuable thinking. Experiencing is the key.

Melting Ice Cubes

It's useful to understand the technical side of practice, the theoretical basis of sitting. But students often dislike technical explanations and want concrete analogies. Sometimes the best way to explain is through simple, even silly metaphors. So I'd like to talk about Zen practice as "the way of the ice cube."

Let's imagine for a moment that humans are large ice cubes, about two feet along each edge, with little heads and spindly feet. This is our life as humans most of the time, running about like ice cubes, bumping into one another sharply. Often we hit each other hard enough to shatter our edges. To protect ourselves we freeze as hard as we can and hope that when we collide with others, they will shatter before we do. We freeze because we're afraid. Our fear makes us rigid, fixed, and hard, and we create mayhem as we bump into others. Any obstacle or unexpected difficulty is likely to shatter us.

Ice cubes hurt. Ice cubes have a hard time. When we're hard and rigid, no matter how careful we are, we tend to slip and slide out of control. We have sharp edges that do damage, and we hurt not only others, but ourselves.

Because we're frozen, we have no water to drink, and so we're thirsty all of the time. At cocktail parties we soften up a bit and drink, but such drinking is not really satisfying because of our underlying fear, which keeps us frozen and parched. The softening is only temporary and superficial; underneath, we're still thirsty and yearning for satisfaction.

Some of the more intelligent ice cubes seek other ways out of their miserable lives. Noticing their sharp edges and their difficulties in meeting one another, they'll try to be nice and cooperative. That helps somewhat; still, an ice cube is an ice cube, and the basic sharpness remains.

A lucky few, however, may meet an ice cube that has actually melted and become a puddle. What happens if an ice cube meets a puddle? The warmer water in the puddle begins to melt the ice cube. Thirst is less and less of a problem. The ice cube begins to realize that it does not have to be hard, rigid, and cold; there is another way to be in the world. The ice cube learns how to create its own heat, by the simple process of observation. The fire of attention begins to melt its hardness. Observing how it bumps into others and causes hurt, seeing its own sharp edges, the ice cube begins to realize how cold and rigid it has been. A strange thing begins to happen. As ice cubes begin to notice their own activities, to observe their "ice cubeness," they become softer and mushier, and their understanding grows, simply by observing what they are.

The results are contagious. Suppose that two ice cubes are married. Each is protecting itself and trying to change the other. But neither can really change or "fix" the other, since they both are rigid and hard, with sharp edges. If one ice cube begins to melt, however, the other ice cube—if it gets close at all—has to begin to melt also. And it, too, begins to gain some wisdom and insight. Instead of seeing the other ice cube as the problem, it begins to be aware of its own ice cubeness. Both learn that the witness, the awareness of one's own activity, is like a fire. The fire cannot be stoked by effort; one cannot try to melt oneself. The melting is the work of the witness, which in one sense is nothing at all and in another sense is everything— "Not I, but my Father in me," as Christ said. The awareness, the witness within, is "the Father"—which is what we truly are. In order to allow the witness to do its work, however, we must not be caught up in stiffening and hardening ourselves, throwing our weight around, bumping into others and trying to change them. If we do these things, we must be aware so that the witness can do its work.

Some ice cubes begin to get the idea and do the necessary work. They may even get a little mushy. The first thing I notice about Zen students who are practicing is that their faces change. They're softer. They laugh differently. They get a little mushy. But the work is difficult, and some ice cubes, even as they begin to soften, get sick of the process. They say, "I just want to go back to being a comfortable ice cube. True, it's lonely and cold, but at least I didn't feel so much distress. I just don't want to be aware anymore." The truth is, however, that once one softens and becomes a bit mushy, one can't become hard again. You might say that that's one of "the laws of ice cubes" (with apologies to physics). An ice cube that has become mushy can never forget its mushiness. That's why I say to people, "Don't practice unless you're ready for the next stage." We can't go back. Once we start to practice, once we're a little mushy, we're a little mushy, and that's that. We may think we can return to life as it was before, and we may even try to do it, but we can't violate the process, the basic "law of ice cubes." Once we're a bit mushy, we're forever a bit mushy.

Some ice cubes, because they have only a sporadic practice, change only slightly over a lifetime, becoming just a little mushy. Those who truly understand the path and practice diligently, however, actually turn into a puddle. The funny thing about such puddles is that as other ice cubes walk through them, these ice cubes begin to melt and get a little mushy. Even if we only melt slightly, others around us soften, too. It's a fascinating process.

Many of my students are mushy. They often hate to go through the process. When we come down to it, however, the work of an ice cube is to melt. When we're still frozen solid, we think that our work is to go around slamming other ice cubes or being slammed by them. In such a life, no one ever really meets another. Like bumper cars, we hit and bounce off of others, and then pass on. It's a very lonely and cold life. In fact, what we really want is to melt. We want to be a puddle. Perhaps all that we can say about practice is that we're learning how to melt. At intervals, we say, "Let me alone. Stay away; just let me be an ice cube." Once we've started to melt at all, however, we can't forget. Eventually what we are as ice cubes is destroyed. But if the ice cube has become a puddle, is it truly destroyed? We could say that it's no longer an ice cube, but its essential self is realized.

The comparison of human life to an ice cube is of course silly. I see people battering one another, however, hoping that by battering others, something will be gained. It never is. Someone has to stop battering and just sit with being an ice cube. We need to just sit and watch, and feel what it's like to be what we are—really experience that. We can't do much about the other ice cubes. In fact, it's not our business to do so. The only thing we can do is more and more to summon that witness. When we turn to the witness, we begin to melt. If we melt, other ice cubes do, too, little by little. Once we've begun to melt, it's perfectly natural to resist the melting, to want to go back to being frozen, trying to control and manipulate all the other frozen creatures we meet. I never worry about that, because for anyone who's been practicing for a while, there's too much knowing. We can't become rigid again, because deep within us, we know something we didn't know before. We can't go back.

The next time we speak sharply or complain or try to fix others or analyze them, we're playing a futile ice cube game. Such efforts just don't work. What works is to cultivate the witness, which is always there, though we can't see it if we're busy banging other ice cubes. Even though we may not allow space in our lives for the witness, it's always there. It's who we are. Though we all often try to avoid it, we can't.

As we become softer, we find that to be a puddle attracts a lot of other ice cubes. Sometimes even the puddle would rather be an ice cube. The more like a puddle we become, the more work there is to be done. A puddle acts as a magnet for the ice cubes that want to melt. So as we begin to drip more, we attract more work to ourselves—and that's fine.

STUDENT: I like the analogy because when the puddle is clear it contains the whole in the reflection. Could you talk more about how the witness is born?

JOKO: The witness is always there. But as long as an ice cube can't see anything to do except to bump other ice cubes, or to avoid them, it's as though the witness can't function. There has to be a change in the ice cube to allow it to become aware of its own activity. As long as our total awareness is turned to what the other ice cubes are doing, the witness can't appear, even though it's always present. When we begin to see, "Oh, the problem isn't with the other ice cubes. I guess I have to look at myself," the witness automatically appears. We begin to realize that the problem is not "out there"; it's always here.

STUDENT: In the ice cube state, I can entertain the delusion that nothing can get in or out, so I'm protected. When the mushiness starts, however, then it dawns on me that everything interpenetrates—including pollution, war, hopelessness, and so forth. The insight into this interpenetration can be frightening and discouraging. Could you talk about the fear and the other emotional states that arise when one is between being an ice cube and a puddle?

JOKO: It's true, the intermediary stage of being mushy involves a lot of fear and resistance. In a way, being an ice cube works, or seems to work. It's just that the ice cube is lonely and thirsty. When we're mushy, we're more vulnerable to others. If we don't see what's happening, we experience more fear. So that mushy stage, which is the beginning of the melting, is always accompanied by resistance, by fear of having the world rush in on us. We want to stiffen ourselves up again, because we're beginning to have demands put upon us that we don't know how to handle. The demands may be unwelcome. Our resistance will attempt to solidify itself. Still, the resistance can't last.

People sometimes tell me, "I've been practicing six months, and everything in my life is worse." Before practice, they had the illusion of knowing who they were. Now, they are confused and that doesn't feel good—it may feel terrible. But it's absolutely necessary. Unless we realize this fact, we may become totally discouraged. Practice is sometimes most unpleasant. The idea that everything feels steadily better, onward and upward, is quite untrue.

STUDENT: When I first started sitting, it was like being dead from the neck down. I felt just like the ice cube you described: a head on top, feet on the bottom, and a walking, dead computer in between. Practice has released a lot of feeling in me; for example, I have done a great deal of crying, which feels like melting down into a puddle.

JOKO: Good. In most of my students, I observe melting going on. It's often not pleasant, but in a way it's wonderful, too. We sense that we're becoming more truly who we really are. There's always resistance, too. The two go hand in hand. People think resistance is something terrible. It's the very nature of practice to resist. It's not something extra.

STUDENT: Does being a mother tend to make one mushy? I would think that mothers have to open up to their children and that would tend to melt the ice cube.

JOKO: Being a mother can be excellent training. Still, I've known mothers who were pretty good ice cubes, including myself at one time.

The Castle and the Moat

As long as I've been teaching, I've met very few people who weren't in some degree immersed in what they regarded as a problem. It's as though our lives are buried under a deep, thick cloud, or as though we are in a dark room, wrestling with our nemesis. When we're caught up in this struggle, we shut out the world. Frankly, we don't have any time for it, because we're busy with our worries. Our only concern is to solve our problem. We don't see through the illusion, which is that the problem we are preoccupied with is not the *real* problem. I hear any number of variations: "I'm so lonely," "Life is empty and meaningless," "I have everything, but still . . . ," and many more. We don't see that our surface problem is merely the tip of the iceberg. In fact, what we think of as our problem is really a pseudoproblem.

It doesn't feel that way to us, of course. For example, if I'm married and my husband suddenly walks out on me, I certainly don't think that's a pseudoproblem. It will take a long time for me to see that what I am calling my problem isn't the real one. Yet the real problem is not the part we can easily see, sticking up in the air; it is the part of the iceberg under the water. For one person, the iceberg could be a pervasive belief that "I have to control everything"; for another, it may be "I have to do things perfectly." But in truth I can't control the world by being very helpful, I can't control it by being helpless, I can't control it with my charm or success or aggressiveness; I can't control it with my blandness or my sweetness or my drama of being the victim. Underneath the presenting problem is a more fundamental pattern that we must become acquainted with. That underlying problem is a chronic, pervasive attitude toward life, an ancient decision arising from our childish fears. If we fail to see it, and instead stay lost in trying to handle the pseudoproblem that presents itself, we remain blind to people and events.

Only when our blind approach to life begins to fail do we begin to have a faint inkling that our pseudoproblem is a gloomy castle in which we are imprisoned. The first step in any practice is to know that we're imprisoned. Most people have no inkling: "Oh, everything's fine with me." Only when we begin to recognize that we're imprisoned can we begin to find a door and leave the prison. We have awakened enough that we know that we're in a prison.

It's as if my problem is a dark, forbidding castle, surrounded by water. I find myself a little boat, and I begin to row away. As I row away, I look back at the castle. It's becoming smaller in my sight as I get some distance from it. The moat is enormous, but finally I cross it to the other shore. Now when I look back at the castle, it looks very small. Because it has receded, it no longer has the interest it once had for me. So I begin to pay more attention to where I am right now. I look at the water, the trees, and the birds. Perhaps there are people out boating on the water, enjoying the fresh air. One day as I'm enjoying the scene, I look over to where the castle was, and it's gone.

Practice is like the process of rowing across the moat. First, we're caught in our particular pseudoproblem. At some point, however, we realize that what seemed to be the problem is not the problem after all—that our problem is something much deeper. A light begins to dawn. We're able to find a door to the outside and get some distance or perspective on our struggles. The problem may still overshadow us, like an enormous gloomy castle, but at least we're outside it and looking up at it. As we begin to row away, the water may be choppy and rough, making our rowing difficult. A storm may even throw us back against the shore, so that we can't get away for a while. Still, we keep trying, and at some point we put some distance between ourselves and the gloomy castle. We begin to enjoy life outside that castle a little bit. Eventually we may enjoy life enough that the castle itself now seems to be just another piece of debris floating in the water, no more important than anything else.

What is your castle? What is your pseudoproblem? And what is the iceberg underneath, the deeper problem that runs your life? The castle and the iceberg are one and the same. What are they for you? The answer is different for each person.

If we begin to see that the current problem that upsets us is not the real issue in our lives, but merely a symptom of a deeper pattern, then we're beginning to know our castle. When we know it well enough, we're beginning to find our way out.

We might ask why we remain imprisoned in the castle. We remain imprisoned because we don't recognize the castle or how to win our freedom. The first step in practice is always to see and acknowledge our castle or prison. People are imprisoned in many different ways. For example, one castle can be the constant pursuit of an exciting and vibrant life, full of new things and enjoyment. People who live in this way are stimulating but hard to be around. So living in a castle doesn't necessarily mean a life of worry, anxiety, and depression. The more subtle prisons don't look like this at all. The more successful we are in the outer world, the harder it may be to see the castle that imprisons us. Success is fine in itself; yet if we don't know ourselves, it can be a prison. I've known people who were world famous in their fields, and who were nevertheless imprisoned in their own castle. Such persons come into practice only when something begins to break down in their life—though outward success often makes the disintegration harder to recognize and acknowledge. When real cracks appear in the castle wall, we may begin to investigate our lives. The first years of practice are coming to know the castle where we are imprisoned and beginning to find the rowboat. The journey across the moat may be tortuous, especially at the beginning. We may encounter storms and high seas as we separate ourselves from our dream of how we are and how we think our life should be.

Only one thing accomplishes this journey for us: awareness of what's going on. The ability to maintain awareness when pseudoproblems come up gradually grows through practice, though not effort. When events occur that we don't like, we create pseudoproblems and get caught in them: "You insulted me! Of course, I'm angry!" "I'm so lonely. Nobody really cares about me." "I've had a hard life. I've been abused." Our journey isn't finished (and perhaps in a human lifetime it is never completely finished) until we see there is no castle and no problem. The expanse of water we cross in our boat is always just as it is. How could there be a problem? My "problem" is that I don't like it. I don't like it, I don't want it that way, life doesn't suit me. So out of my opinions, reactions, and judgments I build a castle in which I imprison myself.

Practice helps me to understand this process. Instead of losing myself in an upset, I notice my thoughts and the contraction in my body. I begin to see that the incident that upset me is not the real problem; instead, my upset arises out of my particular way of looking at life. I pick this apart and begin to demolish my dream. Bit by bit, I gain some perspective. My rowboat moves away from the castle I have built, and I am no longer so caught.

The longer we practice, the more quickly we move through this process each time it arises. The work is slow and discouraging at first, but as our understanding and skill increase, it moves faster, and we come to see that there is no problem. We may develop ill health, we may lose what little money we have; yet there is no problem.

But we don't see life that way. The minute something is thrown up that we don't like, from our point of view we have a problem. So Zen practice isn't about adjusting to the problem. It is seeing that there isn't any. It is a very different road than most of us are used to. Most of us simply try to fix up the castle, instead of seeing through it and finding the moat to separate us from it—which is what practice comes down to.

The truth is, most of us don't want to leave the castle. We may not realize it, but we love our problems. We want to stay imprisoned in our constructions, to spin and twist and be the victim, to feel sorry for ourselves. Eventually we may come to see that such a life does not work very well. That's when we may begin looking for the moat. Even then, we continue to fool ourselves, seeking solutions that leave the castle intact and keep us imprisoned. For example, if a relationship seems to be the problem, we may jump into another relationship rather than discovering the underlying issue, which is our fundamental decision about life, the castle we have constructed.

"I've got a broken leg." "I'm upset with my girlfriend." "My parents don't understand me." "My son is into drugs." And so on. What is it right now that separates us from life and prevents us from seeing things as just being as they are? Only when life is appreciated in all its moments can we say that we know something about the religious life.

Understanding is the key. Still, it takes lots of practice to begin to understand what I am describing, and it takes courage to venture out across the moat and move away from the castle. So long as we stay in the castle, we can feel important. It takes endless training and skill to cross that moat quickly and efficiently. We're not very willing to leave the castle. If we're terribly depressed, depression is nevertheless what we know; heaven forbid that we should abandon our depression. It's frightening to get out in our little boat and leave behind all the things we have called our life. Imprisoned in the castle, we're caught in a constricted, small space. Our life is dark and gloomy, whether we realize it or not. Luckily, freedom (our true self) never ceases to call us.

STUDENT: It seems to me that there is no way to get into that boat and begin crossing the moat until the magic of practice has been taking place for months, or maybe a year.

JOKO: Some people come into practice when their lives are falling apart and their personal dream is failing. Such people are often ready to begin demolishing the castle. For others, the process happens more slowly. The process of sitting brings our personal castle under attack; before long, we begin to see cracks in it, even if before it seemed solid. We become aware—perhaps with shock—of that first rift.

STUDENT: If a problem *feels* like a problem, isn't it a real problem? What makes it a false problem?

JOKO: Suppose someone I love has been assigned to work in Europe for two years, but my responsibilities keep me here. That looks like a problem to me. My life has been entwined with this person, and I'm very unhappy with the separation. From my personal point of view, that's a real problem; yet from the point of view of life itself, my lover is simply in Europe, and I'm simply here. Period. The only "problem" is my opinion about it.

STUDENT: Are you saying not to do something about it, to just passively accept whatever happens?

JOKO: No, not at all; that's not the point. If I have an option to move to Europe to be with my lover, and if that's okay for all concerned, fine. But often we find ourselves in situations that we can't do anything about. We can't always remake the world to fit our preferences. Practice helps us to deal with things as they are, and not add anything onto that.

STUDENT: How do we discover what our castle is? What is the strategy?

JOKO: The key is to notice what makes us upset. The castle is constructed from personally centered emotion. What are some examples of being upset?

STUDENT: Anger; somebody says something I don't like.

STUDENT: Depression.

JOKO: Depression is usually a sign that life is not going the way we want.

STUDENT: Jealousy. I don't like the way he's looking at her.

STUDENT: Resentment, because I did everything and they didn't appreciate me.

JOKO: That's a common one in parents: "I did everything for you, and what thanks do I get? I gave you the best years of my life!"

Every castle involves a personal agenda. The castle may be built on what seems a noble intention, yet conceal self-centered thoughts. For example, working for the homeless may be the way we prove to ourselves and others that we are good people, that we are caring. (The question is not whether we should help the homeless, but why we do it.)

STUDENT: Can something that brings us happiness be part of the castle? For example, if we listen to beautiful music as a way of coping with upset?

JOKO: Yes, if the music is used as an escape, it's part of the castle.

STUDENT: To the persons who live in them, castles always look as if they're based in reality, right?

JOKO: Yes, but they're not. Our deep decision that this is the way life is creates the castle. Whenever that decision is questioned in any way, our castle will shake.

STUDENT: The decision we have made stems from some experience we've had in the past, right?

JOKO: Yes, though we may not remember that experience.

STUDENT: Can we have more than one castle? Or does each person live in one general castle?

JOKO: Most people live in just one castle, but with a lot of rooms. For most people, the castle arises from one basic decision about life, though that decision can show up in many different ways. We have to discover the various ways we play out our decision; we have to know our castle well.

STUDENT: Knowing our castle means becoming aware of tension in our body?

JOKO: Yes—and seeing and labeling our thoughts. As we do this, we slowly unlock the door to the castle and find our way to the boat that takes us across the moat. It's a gradual process: there's no sharp dividing line. And we don't leave our castle once and for all. Sometimes it will seem very distant—and then something comes up that we haven't seen through—and we're right back in the castle. Nobody fully knows every room in the castle.

STUDENT: The analogy of the castle and the moat is helpful, but I know that the minute I stop sitting and go back to the rest of my life, I'll lose my clarity.

JOKO: The point of sitting and the point of a talk like this is to clarify the problems we meet when we return to the rest of our lives and help us to deal with them. With good practice, that ability does increase over time. It's true that we can easily get sucked back into our old patterns. In itself, a talk like this can do nothing; the only thing that counts is what people do with it. Can we look frankly at our areas of upset and watch ourselves being upset? Can we get some perspective? That's the point of the moat: to look back to the castle and see it more clearly. Though it sounds easy, it's monumentally difficult, especially in the beginning. The difficulty is not a bad thing; that's just the way it is.

STUDENT: Would you say that the castle is one's whole personality? Or just one's particular opinions and personal agenda?

JOKO: *Personality* suggests a rigid or permanent inner structure. Our personality is the strategy we have devised to cope with life. In this sense, the castle *is* our personality. As we sit over time, dominant features of our personality fade. In those who have been sitting well for a long time, personality tends to disappear and leave openness. In a sense, the more we sit, the less personality we have.

STUDENT: I've known you for many years, and you seem to have more personality now than you've ever had.

JOKO: Over time, good practice does make us more responsive to what's going on. Instead of an unvarying response, however, we respond more freely in a way that fits the situation. Practice enhances our ability to respond appropriately. Personality no longer gets in the way.

V

AWARENESS

The Paradox of Awareness

When we're sitting, it's important to maintain absolute still-ness as much as possible: to be aware of the tongue in its space, the eyeballs, the fidgeting of the fingers. When they do move, it's important to be aware of the movement. When we want to think, our eyeballs will move. We have very subtle ways of escaping from ourselves. Absolute stillness is for us a restrictive and unpleasant directive. It is for me. When I have been sitting for a number of periods, I want to do something, adjust something, take care of something. We should not be stiff or tight, but simply maintain stillness as much as we can. To be simply what we are is the last thing we want to do.

We all have great desires: for comfort, for success, for love, for enlightenment, for buddhahood. As the desires come up, we strain, trying to shift life into something other than what it is. So the last thing we want to do is to be still. In absolute still-ness, we become aware of our unwillingness to be what we are, this very second. And that's extremely annoying; we sim-ply don't want to do it. Master Rinzai said, "Do not spend even one thought in chasing after buddhahood." That means to be ourselves as we are, in each moment, moment by mo-ment. It's all we ever need to do, but the human desire is to chase something. What are some of the things we chase after as we sit?

STUDENT: Comfort.

STUDENT: Trying to stop thinking.

JOKO: We're trying to stop thinking instead of being aware of our thinking.

STUDENT: Having some sort of intense body experience, an altered state of consciousness.

STUDENT: Peace.

STUDENT: To be more awake, less sleepy. Or to get rid of anger: "As soon as I get rid of this anger, I'll be closer to buddhahood."

JOKO: Or we may remember some stretch of time when things felt good, and we're trying to regain that feeling. If we don't have one thought of chasing after buddhahood, what would we be doing?

STUDENT: Not clinging.

JOKO: Not clinging, and being willing to be . . .

STUDENT: Who we are and where we are.

JOKO: Yes—who we are and where we are, right here and right now. When we sit, we're willing to do that for about three seconds; then almost immediately the desire to move, to fidget, to think, to do something is there.

In simplest terms, there are two kinds of practices. One is to try to steadily improve ourselves. We raise our energy. We eat better. We purify ourselves in some way. We force ourselves to have a clear mind. People think that enlightenment is the result of such efforts, but it's not. Of course, it's good to eat rightly, to exercise, to do what will make us healthier. And this effort to improve our lives, to follow a path that will lead us somewhere, can produce people who seem to be very saintly, very calm, very impressive.

From the point of view of the second kind of practice, however, this notion of making ourselves into something different and better is nonsense. Why? Because being just as we are, we're fine. Since how we are doesn't feel fine, however, we are confused, upset, angry. The statement that we're fine just as we are doesn't make any sense to us.

We can make the point in another way. If we're aware of our thoughts, they tend to disappear. We can't be aware of thinking without thinking beginning to shut down, to fade away. A thought is simply a little blip of energy, but we add to the thought our conditioned beliefs, and we try to hold on to them. When we look at our thoughts with impersonal awareness, they disappear. When we look at a person, however, does she disappear? No, she remains. And that's the difference between reality and the illusory view of reality that we have when we live in our thoughts: when truly looked at, one remains, and one vanishes. The personal version of life just dissolves. What we want is simply to be a life that's real. That's different from a life that is saintly.

All of us are drawn by the first kind of practice: we want to become other than we are. We think that when we sit sesshin, we're making ourselves over into something that is improved. Even when we know better, the desire is deep in us to want something other than just what's here. We don't have to get rid of our thoughts; we just need to keep looking at them, looking at them, looking at them. If we do, they fade into nothing. Anything that fades into nothing isn't very real. But reality doesn't disappear just by being looked at.

STUDENT: Don't we need goals of some kind in order to have a process at all, to accomplish anything?

JOKO: What do you mean by a process?

STUDENT: A process is doing something.

JOKO: Is awareness a doing? There is a difference between doing something—for example, "I'm going to become a nice person"—and simple awareness of what I'm doing. Suppose that I'm gossiping. The gossiping is doing something, but the awareness of it is not a doing, not a making something happen. The basis of doing is a thought that things should be different than they are.

Instead of saying to myself, "I have to become a nicer person" and trying to do that, I should simply be aware of what I'm doing—for example, noticing that every time I meet a certain person I cut her off. When I've seen myself doing that a hundred times, something happens. The pattern drops away, and I'm a nicer person, though I'm not acting on the sentence "I should be a nicer person." Awareness has no sentences, no thoughts in that sense; it's simply awareness. This is what sitting is: not getting caught in our minds, not getting caught in the effort to get somewhere, to become a buddha.

STUDENT: It seems like a paradox. At one level, our minds are actively doing something, and at another level, we're being aware of what our minds are doing. What's the point of awareness?

JOKO: In ordinary thinking, the mind always has an objective, something it's going to get. If we're caught in that wanting, then our awareness of reality is gone. We've substituted a personal dream for awareness. Awareness doesn't move, doesn't bury itself in dreams; it just stays as it is.

At first, the distinction between ordinary thinking and awareness seems subtle and elusive. As we practice, however, the distinction gradually becomes clearer: we begin to notice more and more how our thoughts are occupied with trying to get somewhere and how we become caught in them so that we fail to notice what's really present in our lives.

STUDENT: It seems as if we're either noticing what's happening or getting stuck in the content of our thoughts.

JOKO: Right. There's nothing wrong with a thought *per se*; it's just an energy blip. But when we are caught in the content, the words of that thought, then we've made it into our personal domain, and we want to hold onto it.

STUDENT: Holding onto the thought involves a belief. Last night, as I was traveling somewhere, my mind was full of thoughts and feelings. I believed I was practicing: I knew I was angry, I knew I was tense, I knew I was rushing, and my clue was that I was getting madder and madder and more upset. Suddenly I said to myself, "What is practice right now?" And a thousand flashlights shone on what was happening in my mind. From a completely impersonal perspective, there was still the same stuff—anger, rushing, physical tension—but it had nothing to do with me. It was almost like watching a roach on the kitchen floor.

JOKO: And as we begin watching the thoughts and feelings, they begin to dissolve. They can't maintain themselves without our belief in them.

STUDENT: When we get so caught up in our thoughts, our world narrows. We haven't got a perspective on the whole. When we bring our awareness to our thoughts, the narrowness widens, and the restrictive thoughts begin to fall away.

JOKO: Yes. If our lives are not changing as we practice, then there's something wrong with what we're doing.

STUDENT: When we get caught in our thoughts, we generate anxiety, don't we?

JOKO: Yes. Anxiety is always a gap between the way things are and the way we think they ought to be. Anxiety is something that stretches between the real and unreal. Our human desire is to avoid what's real and instead to be with our ideas about the world: "I'm terrible." "You're terrible." "You're wonderful." The idea is separated from reality, and anxiety is the gap between the idea and the reality that things are just as they are. When we cease to believe in the object that we've created—which is off to one side of reality, so to speak—things snap back to the center. That's what being centered means. The anxiety then fades out.

STUDENT: I seem to get very uptight about trying to hold onto awareness.

JOKO: If you're trying to hold onto awareness, that's a thought. We use a word like *awareness*, and then people make it into something special. If we're not thinking (try it for just ten seconds: just stop thinking), our bodies relax, and we can hear and notice everything that's going on. In the minute we stop thinking, we're aware. Awareness is not something we have to try to be; it's an absence of something. What is it an absence of?

STUDENT: Aren't we just changing what we're aware of? Didn't we decide that we're always aware? My premise is that life is always awareness; we're always aware of something. When we sit (in a way it's a paradox), we have an objective in sitting: we are refocusing our awareness, perhaps sharpening it on something.

JOKO: No, that makes awareness into doing something. Awareness is like rising heat on a summer's day: the clouds in the sky just disappear. When we are aware, the unreal just disappears; we don't have to do anything.

STUDENT: Is there more awareness after sesshin than before?

JOKO: No; the difference is that we're not blocking it. Awareness is what we are. But we block it with self-centered thinking: with dreaming, with fantasizing, with whatever it is we want to do. Trying to be aware is just ordinary thinking, not awareness. All we have to do is to be aware of our self-centered thoughts. Finally they drift away, and we're just here. Although one could say that we're doing something, awareness is not a thing or a person. Awareness is our life when we're not doing something else.

STUDENT: Simple awareness lacks everything else. Awareness lacks space, time, everything.

JOKO: Right, awareness has no space, time, or identity—and yet it's who we are. The minute we talk about it, it's gone. In terms of practice, we don't have to try to be aware. What we have to do is to watch our thoughts. We should not try to be aware; we're always aware unless we're caught in our self-centered thinking. That's the point of labeling our thoughts.

STUDENT: So sometimes we're aware and we just don't notice it.

JOKO: Right.

STUDENT: Perhaps the difference between ordinary thoughts that we believe and awareness is that a believed thought is not held in awareness; it's not recognized as just being a thought.

JOKO: Right. It's not seen as just the energy fragment it is. We take it for real, and we believe in it; then it begins to run the show, instead of awareness running the show, which is what should be.

STUDENT: I usually notice awareness more sharply when I haven't been aware. For example: I suddenly realize that I'm at work and I don't know how I got there—and I wake up.

JOKO: Except for a buddha, everybody drifts in and out of awareness. But the longer we practice, the greater the percentage of our lives that is lived in awareness. I doubt that anyone ever lives totally in awareness.

STUDENT: You say "the longer we practice," but really do you mean the consistency with which we bring the attention to the present?

JOKO: Yes. It's possible to sit for twenty years and still have no idea what sitting is about. But if we're sitting and practicing with our whole lives, then definitely the amount of awareness increases. I used to spend half of my life daydreaming. It was "pleasant."

STUDENT: For years, my sitting practice consisted of first tuning out the environment, then tuning out my body, and then reciting Mu over and over again. I was totally aware of nothing.

JOKO: Yes, that's a form of concentrated practice that for some produces quick and dramatic effects that are pleasing. It doesn't do much for one's life. Mu does not have to be practiced in that way, however.

STUDENT: When I focus on awareness, I seem to notice more pain in my body. But if I just space out, I have no problem with pain; I just don't feel it. Then I wake up and become aware—

and there's the pain, again. Why does the pain go away when I space out?

JOKO: Well, our dreams are powerful narcotics. That's why we like them so much. Our dreams and fantasies are addictive, just like addictive substances.

STUDENT: Isn't there separation from reality involved if we feel pain?

JOKO: Not if we totally feel it.

STUDENT: If I really become the pain, the pain just fades away. But as soon as I have a thought about it, I suffer. When I notice the pain and have the thought that it's painful, the suffering remains. But if I simply notice it as a strong sensation, the suffering disappears.

JOKO: When we can see the pain as just a steady sensation with many little variations, it becomes interesting and even beautiful. But if we approach it with the thought that we're going to make it go away, that's just another way of seeking after buddhahood.

STUDENT: When I begin to sit, I usually become aware of being very tense, with a tight pain in my body. I feel it as just outside of my awareness. For years, people would say to me, "You're so tense." I'd say, "I'm not tense." Now I realize that my tension was just unexperienced, but there. I used my thoughts to block awareness of it. The tension and pain were there, just unexperienced.

JOKO: Are the tension and pain real? Something is there, but what is it? One night recently I was walking along the ocean with the moonlight shining on the water. I could see a shimmer of light on the ocean, but was the moonlight really there? Did the ocean really have anything on it? What is that color? Is it real or not? Neither is quite correct. From my perspective, the moonlight was on the water. But if I had been closer to the surface, I wouldn't see any moonlight on the water. I would just see whatever I would see at that point. There is no such thing as moonlight literally on the water. As for clouds in the sky: if we are in a cloud, we call it fog. We likewise give a kind of false reality to our thoughts. It's true that we always live within a certain perspective. Practice is about learning to live in that relative reality, enjoying it, but seeing it for what it is. Like the moonlight on the water, it's there—from a certain relative perspective—and it's not real, it's not the absolute. Even the water itself has only relative reality. When there is no light on the water, we see the water as black. I've had dinner at a restaurant by the ocean and watched the water turn from blue to dark blue to darker purple, and finally it can't be seen at all. What is real? In absolute terms, none of it is real. In terms of our practice, however, we must begin with our experience, with this meticulous work with awareness. We need to return to the reality of our lives. We have pains and aches, we have troubles, we like people or we don't like them: this is the stuff of our lives. This is where our work with awareness begins.

Coming to Our Senses

We all desire wholeness. We want to be whole persons; we want a sense of completeness; we want to be at rest in our lives. We try to figure out this problem, to think our way to wholeness. The effort never works; we need a different approach.

Suppose we're hiking in the mountains, and we sit down by a stream. What would it mean to be "whole" in this moment?

STUDENT: Being whole would mean feeling the air on my skin and hearing the sounds.

JOKO: Yes. . . .

STUDENT: Thinking about myself.

JOKO: When we think about ourselves, we separate ourselves from our experience, and we're no longer whole.

STUDENT: Feeling myself sitting on the ground, making contact with the leaves and soil. Observing myself thinking about myself.

JOKO: Yes, that's awareness.

STUDENT: Seeing the stream, smelling the natural smells of the earth, feeling the sun on my back.

JOKO: Yes, these are also part of the experience.

STUDENT: Feeling what is not present. For example, when I'm in a peaceful place I may feel the absence of pain. That's a good feeling: that there is no pain.

JOKO: That's a kind of thinking that takes us away from awareness or wholeness. There's nothing wrong with it, but it's still extra. It's as if, in the middle of appreciating a beautiful sunset, we say, "Oh, this is a beautiful sunset!" We have slightly removed ourselves.

While we're sitting by the stream, we probably won't be having sensations of taste. But suppose we're eating Thanksgiving dinner: it's surprising how few people actually taste the food they eat.

STUDENT: Sitting by a brook, sometimes it seems that I can almost feel the brook in my body.

JOKO: You may be talking not about a sensation, but about a very subtle thought, the kind that makes people write books about being with nature.

If we're just sitting by the stream and sensing all there is to sense, it's no big deal: we're just sitting there. Suppose, however, that we begin to think about our troubles in life. We become absorbed in our thoughts, poring over how we feel about our problems and what we can do about them—and suddenly we're oblivious to everything we were sensing a moment ago. We no longer see the water, smell the woods, feel our body. The sensations are gone. We have sacrificed our life in this moment in order to think about things that are not present, not real, here and now.

The next time you are eating Thanksgiving dinner—or any meal, for that matter—ask yourself whether you are truly tasting your food. For most of us, the experience of eating a meal is at best partial.

Without awareness of our sensations, we are not fully alive. Life is unsatisfactory for most people because they are absent from their experience much of the time. If we have been sitting for several years, we do it somewhat less. I don't know anyone who is fully present all of the time, however.

We're like the fish that is swimming about, looking for the great ocean of life, yet oblivious to its surroundings. Like the fish, we wonder about the meaning of life, not awake to the water all around us and the ocean that we are. The fish finally met a teacher who understood. The fish asked, "What is the great ocean?" And the teacher simply laughed. Why?

STUDENT: Because the fish was already in the ocean and just didn't realize it.

JOKO: Yes. The ocean *was* its life. Separate a fish from water, and there is no life for the fish. Likewise, if we separate ourselves from our life, which is what we see, hear, touch, smell, and so on, we have lost touch with what we are.

Our life is always just this life. Our personal commentary on life—all the opinions we have about it—is the cause of our difficulties. We couldn't be upset if we weren't leaving out our life. If we weren't leaving out the hearing, seeing, smelling, tasting, the kinesthetic sense of just feeling our body, we couldn't be upset. Why is that?

STUDENT: Because we're in the present.

JOKO: Yes. We *can't* be upset unless our mind takes us out of the present, into unreal thoughts. Whenever we're upset, we're literally out of it: we've left something out. We're like a fish out of water. When we're present, fully aware, we can't have a thought such as "Oh, this is such a difficult life. It's so meaningless!" If we do this, we've left something out. Just like that!

A good student recognizes when he or she has drifted away and returns to immediate experience. Sometimes we just shake our head and reestablish the basis of our life, the foundation in experience. Out of that foundation will come perfectly adequate thinking, action, creativity. It's all born in this space of experiencing, just letting the senses be open.

When I was sixteen or seventeen years old, I liked to play Bach chorales on the piano. One that I particularly loved was called "In Thine Arms I Rest Me." The translation goes on, "Foes who would molest me cannot find me here." Though it is from the Christian tradition, which is often dualistic, this chorale is about being present and aware. There is a place of rest in our lives, a place where we must be if we are to function well. This place of resting—the arms of God, if you will—is simply here and now: seeing, hearing, touching, smelling, tasting our life as it is. We can even add thinking to the list, if we understand thinking as simply functional thinking rather than ego thinking based on fear and attachment. Just thinking in the functional sense includes abstract thinking, creative thinking, or planning what we have to do today. Too often, however, we add nonfunctional, ego-based thinking, which gets us in trouble and takes us from the arms of God.

A life that works rests on these six legs: the five senses plus functional thought. When our lives rest on these six supports, no problem or upset can reach us.

It's one thing to hear a dharma talk on these truths, however, and another to live by them. The minute something upsets us, we fly into our heads and try to figure it out. We try to regain our safety by thinking. We ask how we can change ourselves or something outside ourselves—and we're lost. To reestablish our lives on a secure foundation, we have to return to these six legs of reality, over and over and over again. That's all the practice we need. If I have the faintest thought of irritability about anybody, the first thing I do is not to begin figuring out in my mind how to fix the situation, but simply to ask myself, "Can I really hear the cars in the alley?" When we fully establish one sense, such as hearing, we establish them all, since all are functioning in the present moment. Once we reestablish awareness, we see what to do about the situation. Action that arises out of awakened experience is nearly always satisfactory. It works.

You may say, "That may be true with simple problems, but I doubt that it will work with the big, complex problems I face." In fact, however, the process works, no matter how "big" the problem is. We may not get the solution we were looking for, and the resolution may not be immediate, but we will see what step to take next. Over time, we learn to trust the process, to have faith that things will work out as best they can under the circumstances. The person we counted on who didn't come through, the job we failed to get, the physical ailment that worries us: instead of going round and round in our thoughts, worrying about the problem, if we reestablish the foundation of our lives in immediate experience, we will see how to act appropriately.

I'm not suggesting that we should act blindly, out of mere impulse. We need to be informed, to know the obvious things about the problem; we need to use our natural intelligence, our functional thinking. For example, suppose I have a twinge in my tooth. If I begin to think of how I hate dental work, the drilling and the needles and the discomfort, I'll go round and round in my head and create a huge problem for myself. If I return to the foundation of my life in my direct experience, on the other hand, I'll say to myself, "Well, it's just a twinge, right now. I'll keep an eye on it and go about my business. If the twinge persists or gets worse, I'll call the dentist and make an appointment." With that approach everything falls into place.

STUDENT: The danger for me in returning to my ordinary sensations is that I may block out my anxiety or worry entirely, as if it didn't exist.

JOKO: The anxiety is no more than certain thoughts and an accompanying tension or contraction in the body. Returning to our senses means to notice the thoughts for what they are, and to be aware of the tension in the body. Awareness of the tension is, after all, just another physical sensation, along with seeing, smelling, and the like.

It sounds crazy to say that when we have a problem we should listen to the traffic. But if we truly listen, our other senses come to life also. We feel the contraction in our body, too. When we do that, something shifts, and how to respond becomes clearer.

STUDENT: Aren't the senses on a kind of "time-share" basis? If we totally listen to a sound, don't we block out smell, taste, and so on? Really listening to the traffic may mean that I'm ignoring the rest of my body.

JOKO: That kind of exclusive attention to one mode of sensation is the result of subtle thinking, perhaps an anxious thought that "I have to do this" or "I'm in danger." If we're fully open, we engage all of our senses simultaneously.

STUDENT: Returning to the senses doesn't always happen quickly with me. If I'm worried about a problem, I may think about it for a week, despite my efforts to pay attention to the traffic or whatever.

JOKO: Yes, depending upon how long and how well we have practiced, the process does take time. The ability to move quickly is the mark of a practice that has gone on for many years. Some people can hold on to their misery for a long time. They really enjoy it. Someone was telling me recently how much she enjoys her self-righteousness. Who wants to listen to the traffic when we can enjoy our self-righteousness? We don't want to abandon our patterns, our thoughts of who we are, even when we recognize intellectually that they get us into trouble. So we cling to them and return to them, even after reminding ourselves to come back to our senses. We're not ready to trust the process fully, to have faith in our direct experience.

STUDENT: I have another question about the "time-share" issue. You included functional thinking as one of the six legs of real experience. Suppose I'm working at a computer or fixing a watch; isn't it natural to block out other sensations in order to give full attention to what I'm doing?

JOKO: Yes, there can be a mechanical narrowing of attention for a specific task. That's different from the psychological narrowing that comes from self-centered thinking, which generates a subtle rigidity.

STUDENT: So if one of my tasks while I'm sitting by the stream is to plan the day's menu, that's okay?

JOKO: Yes, assuming that planning the menu is an appropriate task for that moment, instead of arising out of anxious thoughts about oneself. We just do what needs to be done, when it needs to be done. Once we've handled the task, we turn to whatever else is going on. It's okay to narrow attention as needed to undertake a task. That's different from shutting out our life because we are thinking about ourselves, which is an unnecessary psychological impediment.

The distinction concerns false emotion versus true emotion. If a remark made to us days ago is still upsetting us, that's false emotion. A true emotion is immediate to the situation: maybe someone hits me, or I see somebody in trouble. For a second I'm upset and I do something—and it's over. The emotions are a response to a real event; when the event is no longer going on, then the emotions settle back. That's a natural response to life. There's nothing wrong with true emotion. Most people run their lives out of false emotion, however. They carry memories from the past or worries about the future and create upset for themselves. The upset is unrelated to what's happening in the moment. We're stewing about what happened last week, and we can't sleep.

STUDENT: Even though the memory is generating false emotion, there is a present sensation in the body. The emotion is stuck in me; I can feel it.

JOKO: Yes. So we notice the accompanying thoughts and feel the tension in the body. When we do that enough times, the blockage eases. Something shifts.

STUDENT: If my day is particularly busy, a lot of anxiety can build up, and it feels more comfortable to be daydreaming. Is that wrong?

JOKO: If you do it, you do it. The problem is that by daydreaming, we cut ourselves off from life. When we're cut off from life, we overlook things, and we get into trouble. It's as though we're floating down a turbulent stream. Here and there are rocks and tree stumps projecting out of the water. Looking at them may make us anxious. But if we ignore them and instead just gaze at the beautiful clouds in the sky, sooner or later we're in the drink. Paying attention to the white water and rocks may feel scary, but it's a very good idea, nonetheless.

STUDENT: Gazing up at the sky gives me the illusion that I can control things. Returning to the senses, I often have a fear of loss of control. It feels reassuring to stay in the old conditioning and try to figure everything out in my head.

JOKO: Yes. All practice brings up fear. So we alternate between experiencing the fear and retreating into thinking. Most people's lives consist of a rapid alternation, in and out of direct experience. No wonder life feels jangly.

STUDENT: Returning to direct experience feels like a grounding of one's life.

JOKO: Yes. The minute we feel the sensory input of life, we are grounded. If we are still upset, it means that we are not fully feeling it; there is still some thinking.

STUDENT: When I was learning to play tennis, my teacher kept saying, "You can't hit the ball properly unless you've got your two feet on the ground. If you have one leg up in the air, you are out of balance."

JOKO: If we don't maintain our groundedness, we tend not to see what's going on around us, and we'll hit the tree stump or the rock, or whatever. An awakened life is not some airy-fairy thing. It's very down-to-earth.

STUDENT: When I lived on a mountaintop in Maui, it was very easy to lie down on the earth and reconnect with my sensations, but when I'm in the middle of a noisy classroom with all of the children screaming, I don't want to experience it all, including the noise and the tension in my stomach.

JOKO: Right. Yet the point remains: to negotiate our lives effectively, we need to stay in touch as much as possible.

STUDENT: In the past, instead of simply opening up to my experience, I have tended to exaggerate the process by wallowing in my sensations, chasing after them and going round and round in them.

JOKO: There's thinking behind that effort: "I have to get into my drama."

STUDENT: Now, I'm beginning to learn another way. I ask myself, "Where's the tension in my body?" Without forcing it, I just stay with the sensations. Eventually I feel a soft spreading out and sinking feeling inside, and I'm more aware of my connection to everything.

JOKO: Good. As that happens, we have a much clearer space in which to act. We simply know what to do, without calculating or guessing. The degree of clarity we find is a function of how long and how well we have practiced. It's important, however, not to create another ideal in our minds ("I have to make that happen!") and strive to achieve it. Where we are is where we need to be.

As the chorale said, there is a foundation for our lives, a place in which our life rests. That place is nothing but this present moment, as we see, hear, experience what is. If we do not return to that place, we live our lives out of our heads. We blame others; we complain; we feel sorry for ourselves. All of these symptoms show that we're stuck in our thoughts. We're out of touch with the open space that is always right here. Only after years of practice are we able to live in an open, aware space most of the time.

STUDENT: I tend to seek out quiet, calming places where it's easier for me to open up to the present and to avoid places, such as the noisy classroom, where I get tense and distracted.

JOKO: Yes, that's a natural impulse, and there's nothing wrong with it. Still, it's a kind of avoidance. As our practice becomes stronger, we are able to maintain openness and steadiness in situations where we formerly would have lost it. The important thing is to learn to be open to whatever life brings, wherever we are. If we are alert enough, we notice our impulse to avoid, and we can return to awareness of the present, without flinching. These endless little jogs of attention are practice itself. When we're trying to avoid or escape something, we're back in thought rather than direct experience.

STUDENT: Sometimes when I try to concentrate on my experience—say, my feeling of anger, or the tension in my jaw—it seems to expand to fill the whole room. All of my other sensations disappear.

JOKO: There's some veiled thought behind such experiences and not just open sensation. If we fully experience one sense, we experience all the rest as well. If we name our anger and concentrate on it to the exclusion of everything else, we haven't really encountered our life.

STUDENT: What about simply observing one's sensations?

JOKO: There's value in that. But it's transitional; there's still an element of thinking, of subject-object duality. If we truly hear the traffic, we are absorbed in it. There's no me, and there's no traffic. There's no observer and no object of sensation. We return to what we are, which is simply life itself.

Attention Means Attention

There's an old Zen story: a student said to Master Ichu, "Please write for me something of great wisdom." Master Ichu picked up his brush and wrote one word: "Attention." The student said, "Is that all?" The master wrote, "Attention. Attention." The student became irritable. "That doesn't seem profound or subtle to me." In response, Master Ichu wrote simply, "Attention. Attention. Attention." In frustration, the student demanded, "What does this word *attention* mean?" Master Ichu replied, "Attention means attention."

For *attention*, we could substitute the word *awareness*. Attention or awareness is the secret of life, and the heart of practice. Like the student in the story, we find such a teaching disappointing; it seems dry and uninteresting. We want something exciting in our practice! Simple attention is boring; we ask, is that all there is to practice?

When students come in to see me, I hear complaint after complaint: about the schedule of the retreat, about the food, about the service, about me, on and on. But the issues that people bring to me are no more relevant or important than a "trivial" event, such as stubbing a toe. How do we place our cushions? How do we brush our teeth? How do we sweep the floor, or slice a carrot? We think we're here to deal with "more important" issues, such as our problems with our partner, our jobs, our health, and the like. We don't want to bother with the "little" things, like how we hold our chopsticks or where we place our spoon. Yet these acts are the stuff of our life, moment to moment. It's not a question of importance; it's a question of paying attention, being aware. Why? Because every moment in life is absolute in itself. That's all there is. There is nothing other than this present moment; there is no past, there is no future; there is nothing but this. So when we don't pay attention to each little *this,* we miss the whole thing. And the contents of *this* can be anything. *This* can be straightening our sitting mats, chopping an onion, visiting someone we don't want to visit. It doesn't matter what the contents of the moment are; each moment is absolute. That's all there is and all there ever will be. If we could totally pay attention, we would never be upset. If we're upset, it's axiomatic that we're not paying attention. If we miss not just one moment but one moment after another, we're in trouble.

Suppose I'm condemned to have my head chopped off in a guillotine. Now I'm being marched up the steps onto the platform. Can I maintain attention to the moment? Can I be aware of each step, step-by-step? Can I place my head in the guillotine carefully so that I serve the executioner well? If I am able to live and die in this way, no problem arises.

Our problems arise when we subordinate this moment to something else, to our self-centered thoughts: not just this moment, but what *I want.* We bring to the moment our personal priorities, all day long. And so our troubles arise.

Another old story concerns a group of thieves who broke into the study of a Zen master and told him that they were going to slice off his head. He said, "Please wait until morning; I have some work to complete." So he spent the night completing his work, drinking tea, and enjoying himself. He wrote a simple poem, comparing the severing of his head to a spring breeze, and gave it to the thieves as a present when they returned. The master understood practice well.

We have trouble comprehending this story because we are so attached to keeping our heads on our shoulders. We don't particularly want our heads severed. We're determined that life go as *we* want it to go. When it doesn't, we're angry, confused, depressed, or otherwise upset. To have such feelings is not bad in itself, but who wants a life dominated by such feelings?

When attention to the present moment falters and we drift into some version of "I have to have it *my* way," a gap is created in our awareness of reality as it is, right now. Into that gap pours all the mischief of our life. We create gap after gap after gap, all day long. The point of practice is to close these gaps, to reduce the amount of time that we spend being absent, caught in our self-centered dream.

We make a mistake, however, if we think that the solution is that *I* pay attention. Not "*I* sweep the floor," "*I* slice the onions," "*I* drive the car." Though such practice is okay in the preliminary stages, it preserves self-centered thought in naming oneself as an "I" to which experience is present. A better understanding is simple awareness: just experiencing, experiencing, experiencing. In mere awareness there is no gap, no space for self-centered thoughts to arise.

At some Zen centers, students are asked to engage in exaggerated slow-motion actions, such as slowly putting things down and slowly picking them up. Such self-conscious attention is different from simple awareness, just doing it. The recipe for living is simply to do what we're doing. Don't be self-conscious about it; just do it. When self-centered thoughts come up, then we've missed the boat; we've got a gap. That gap is the birthplace of the troubles and upsets that plague us.

Many forms of practice, commonly called concentrative meditation, seek to narrow awareness in some way. Examples include reciting a mantra, focusing on a visualization, working on Mu (if done in a concentrated way), even following the breath if that involves shutting out the other senses. In narrowing the attention, such practices quickly create certain pleasant states. We may feel that we have escaped from our troubles because we feel calmer. As we settle into this narrow focus, we may eventually go into a trance, like a drugged and peaceful state in which everything escapes us. Though at times useful, any practice that narrows our awareness is limited. If we don't take into account everything in our world, both mental and physical, we miss something. A narrow practice does not transfer well to the rest of our life; when we take it into the world, we don't know how to act and may still get quite upset. A concentrative practice, if we're very persistent (as I used to be), may momentarily force us through our resistance, to a glimpse of the absolute. Such a forced opening isn't truly genuine; it misses something. Though we get a glimpse of the other side of the phenomenal world, into nothingness or pure emptiness, there's still *me* realizing that. The experience remains dualistic and limited in its usefulness.

In contrast, ours is an awareness practice that takes in everything. The "absolute" is simply everything in our world, emptied of personal emotional content. We begin to empty ourselves of such self-centered thoughts by learning more and more to be aware in all our moments. Whereas a concentrative practice might focus on the breath, but block out the sound of cars or the talking in our minds (leaving us at a loss when we allow any and all experience back into consciousness), awareness practice is open to any present experience—all this upsetting universe—and it helps us slowly to extricate ourselves from our emotional reactions and attachments.

Every time we have a complaint about our lives, we're in a gap. In awareness practice, we notice our thoughts and the contraction in our body, taking it all in and returning to the present moment. That's the hardest kind of practice. We'd rather escape this scene entirely or else stay immersed in our little upsets. After all, our upsets keep us the center of things, or so we think. The pull of our self-centered thoughts is like walking through molasses: our feet come out of the molasses with difficulty and then rapidly get stuck again. We *can* slowly liberate ourselves, but if we think it's easy, we are kidding ourselves.

Whenever we're upset, we're in the gap; our self-centered emotions, what *we* want out of life, are dominant. Yet our emotions of the moment are no more important than is replacing the chair at the table or putting the cushion where it should be.

Most emotions do not arise out of the immediate moment, such as when we witness a child hit by a car, but are generated by our self-centered demands that life be the way *we* want it to be. Though it's not bad to have such emotions, we learn through practice that they have no importance in themselves. Straightening the pencils on our desk is just as important as feeling bereft or lonely, for example. If we can experience being lonely and see our thoughts about being lonely, then we can move out of the gap. Practice is that movement, over and over and over again. If we remember something that happened six months ago and with the memory come upset feelings, our feelings should be looked at with interest, nothing more. Though that sounds cold, it's necessary in order to be a genuinely warm and compassionate person. If we find ourselves thinking that our feelings are more important than what is happening at the moment, we need to notice this thought. Sweeping the walk is reality; our feelings are something we've made up, like a web we have spun in which we catch ourselves. It's an amazing process that we put ourselves through; in a way, we are all crazy.

When I see my thoughts and note my bodily sensations, recognize my resistance to practicing with them, and then return to finishing the letter I'm writing, then I've moved out of the gap into awareness. If we are truly persistent, day after day, we gradually find our way out of the gooey mess of our personal lives. The key is attention, attention, attention.

Writing a check is just as important as the anguished thought that we won't see a loved one. When we don't work with the gap created by inattention, everyone pays the price.

Practice is necessary for me, too. Suppose I hope that my daughter will visit me at Christmas, and she calls to say she's not coming. Practice helps me to continue to love her, rather than becoming upset that she's not doing what *I* want. With practice, I can love her more fully. Without practice, I would simply be a lonely and cantankerous old lady. In a sense, love is simply attention, simply awareness. When I maintain awareness, I can teach well, which is a form of love; I can place fewer expectations on others and serve them better; when I see my daughter again, I don't have to bring old resentments into the meeting and am able to see her with fresh eyes. So the priority is right here and now. In fact, there's only one priority, and that's attention to the present moment, whatever its content. Attention means attention.

False Generalizations

Nasrudin, the Sufi sage and fool, was once in his flower garden, sprinkling bread crumbs over everything. When a neighbor asked him why, he said, "To keep the tigers away." The neighbor said, "But there aren't any tigers within a thousand miles of here." And Nasrudin said, "Effective, isn't it?"

We laugh because we're sure that the two things—bread crumbs and tigers—have nothing to do with each other. Yet as with Nasrudin, our practice and our lives are often based upon false generalizations that have little to do with reality. If our lives are based upon generalized concepts, we may be like Nasrudin, spreading bread crumbs to keep away tigers. We say, for example, "I love people," or "I love my husband." The truth is that no one loves everyone all the time, and no one loves a spouse all the time. Such generalities obscure the specific, concrete reality of our lives, what is happening for us at this moment.

One may, of course, love one's husband most of the time. Still, the flat generalization leaves out the shifting, changing reality of an actual relationship. Likewise with "I love my work," or "Life is hard on me." When we begin practice, we usually believe and express many generalized opinions. We may think, for instance, "I'm a kind person," or "I'm a terrible person." But in fact, life is never general. Life is always specific: it's what's happening this very moment. Sitting helps us to cut through the fog of generalizations about our lives. As we practice, we tend to drop our generalized concepts in favor of more specific observations. For example, instead of "I can't stand my husband," we notice "I can't stand my husband when he doesn't pick up after himself," or "I can't stand myself when I do such and such." Instead of generalized concepts, we see more clearly what's going on. We're not covering events with a broad brush.

Our experience of another person or situation isn't just one thing. It can include a thousand minor thoughts and reactions. A parent may say, "I love my daughter"; yet this generalization ignores moments, such as "Why is she so immature?" or "She's being stupid." As we sit, observing and labeling our thoughts, we become more acquainted with the incessant outpouring of our opinions about anything and everything. Instead of just plastering the whole world with generalizations, we become aware of our specific concepts and judgments. As we become more acquainted with our thinking, we discover that we're shifting, moment by moment, as our thinking shifts.

Let's listen to a young woman. She's been going out with a young man for a little while. She feels that it's going well. If asked, she would say that she really cares about him. Now he has just called her. Let's listen not only to what she says to him, but also to what she's thinking to herself:

"Oh, it's so nice to hear from you. You sound great." ("He could have called me a little sooner.")

"Oh, you took so-and-so out to lunch. Yes, she's a charming person. I know you enjoyed her company." ("I could kill him!")

"You think I don't have much to say? That I'm not a very verbal person? Well, I appreciate your opinion." ("You hardly know me! How dare you make generalizations about me!")

"You did well on your test? I'm glad. Good for you!" ("He's always talking about himself. Does he have any interest in *my* life?")

"You'd like to go out to dinner tomorrow night? I'd love to go. It would be wonderful to see you again!" ("At last, he asked me! I wish he wouldn't wait until the last minute!")

This is a perfectly common interchange between two people, the sort of pretense that passes for communication. These people probably do care for each other. Still, she had one concept after another, about him and about herself. The exchange was a sea of conceptual material; their conversation was like two ships passing in the night—no contact took place.

In Zen practice, we tend to toss around many fancy concepts: "Everything is perfect in being as it is." "We're all doing the best that we can." "Things are all one." "I'm one with him." We can call this Zen bullshit, though other religions have their own versions. It's not that the statements are false. The world *is* one. I *am* you. Everything *is* perfect in being as it is. Every human being on the planet *is* doing the best he or she can at this moment. True enough. But if we stop there, we have turned our practice into an exercise of concepts, and we've lost awareness of what's going on with us right this second.

Good practice always entails moving through our concepts. Concepts are sometimes useful in daily life; we have to use them. But we need to recognize that a concept is just a concept and not reality and that this recognition or knowledge slowly develops as we practice. Gradually, we stop "buying into" our concepts. We no longer make such general judgments: "He's a terrible person," or "I'm a terrible person." We notice our thoughts: "I wish he wouldn't take her out to lunch." Then we have to experience the pain that accompanies the thought. When we can stay with the pain as a pure physical sensation, at some point it will dissolve, and then we move into the truth, which is that everything is perfect in being as it is. Everyone *is* doing the best that he or she can. But we have to move from experience, which is often painful, into truth and not plaster thoughts over our experience. Intellectual people are particularly prone to this error: they think that the rational world of concepts is the real world. The rational world of concepts is not the real world, but simply a description of it, a finger pointing at the moon.

Take the experience of having been hurt. When we've been criticized or treated unfairly, it's important to note the thoughts we have and move into the cellular level of being hurt, so that our awareness becomes simply raw sensation: our trembling jaw, the contraction in our chest, whatever we may be feeling in the cells of our body. This pure experiencing is zazen. As we stay with it, our desire to think comes up again and again: judgments, opinions, blame, retorts. So we label our thoughts and again return into our cellular experience, which is almost indescribable, perhaps just a light shimmering of energy, perhaps something stronger. In that space there is no "me" or "you." When we are this nondual experiencing we can see our situation more clearly. We can see that "she is doing the best she can." We can see that *we* are doing the best we can. If we say such sentences without the bodily component of experiencing, however, we will not know what true practice is. A calm, cool, rational perspective must be grounded in that pure cellular level. We need to know our thoughts. But that doesn't mean that we must think they're real, or that we must act on them. After observing our self-centered thoughts, moment by moment, the emotions tend to even out. This serenity can never be found by plastering some philosophical concept on top of what is actually happening.

Only when we move through the experiential level does life have meaning. This is what Jews and Christians mean by being with God. Experiencing is out of time: it is not the past, not the future, not even the present in the usual sense. We can't say what it is; we can only be it. In traditional Buddhist terms, such a life is being buddha nature itself. Compassion grows from such roots.

We all have our favorite concepts. "I'm sensitive. I'm easily hurt." "I'm a pushy kind of person." "I'm an intellectual." Our concepts may be useful on an everyday level, but we need to see their actual nature. Unexperienced concepts are a source of confusion, anxiety, depression; they tend to produce behavior that is not good for ourselves or for others.

To do the work of practice, we need endless patience, which also means recognizing when we have no patience. So we need to be patient with our lack of patience: to recognize when we don't want to practice is also part of practice. Our avoidance and resistance are part of the conceptual framework that we're not yet ready to look at. It's okay not to be ready. As we become ready, bit by bit, a space opens up, and we'll be ready to experience a little more, and then a little more. Resistance and practice go hand in hand. We all resist our practice, because we all resist our lives. And if we believe in concepts instead of experiencing the moment, we're like Nasrudin: we're sprinkling bread crumbs on the flower beds to keep the tigers away.

STUDENT: Concepts are sometimes necessary. What's the difference between a concept that serves me and a concept that confuses me? For example, "Look both ways before you cross the street" is a useful generalization.

JOKO: That's a good example, a sensible use of the human mind. Much of the thought going on in our minds is not related to reality, however.

STUDENT: If the generalization or concept comes from a self-centered emotion, then it may not be useful.

JOKO: In the young woman's phone conversations, the judgments came from hidden emotions and opinions; they were ego-centered. Her judgments about him were expressions of her own need and had nothing to do with him. False generalizations—harmful concepts—always have a personal emotional shade. On the other hand, observations about how to get work done efficiently or how to solve a math problem have little or no emotional context. That's useful thinking.

STUDENT: The experiential, cellular level seems so covered up to me.

JOKO: Remember that the experiential level is not some strange, exotic thing. It may be a tingling of the skin or a contraction in the chest or a tight face—the experiential level is quite basic and never far away. It's what we are right now. The experiential level is nothing special, and the longer we sit, the more basic we know it to be. In the early years of practice, however, there's more to experience, because of the emotional turmoil we're in, which generates a lot of sensation.

We never completely avoid the cellular level. Even if we're with our breath for only a split second between thoughts, we're at the cellular level to some degree. The more we label our thoughts and keep coming back to whatever's going on in our experience, the better. Moving into a more experiential life will sometimes go very slowly and sometimes very quickly, depending on the intensity of practice. When we realize that we need to practice twenty-four hours a day, it's impossible to avoid the experiential level.

STUDENT: A concept that at one time is very emotional for me may not bother me at all at another time. For example, I may be worried about getting a job. Before the interview, I'll be really worried about it, and I'll generalize about the state of my career. After the interview is over, when I think the same thought, I can't imagine how it could have bothered me.

JOKO: All thoughts occur in a specific context. That's the whole point: to see the specific context, not just the general thought. Our reaction to a person or thought will be different today than next week, depending on each situation. If you had a million dollars in the bank, you probably wouldn't care whether you got that job or not. You'd sail in calmly and just enjoy the interview. All reality is specific, immediate. We can meet the same people and have one thought about them today, yet next week (depending on the changing personal situation) they'll look different to us.

STUDENT: If I'm always paying attention to sensations in my body, how can I pay attention to things around me or tasks that I have to do? For example, how can I play cards or drive a car and still pay attention to my bodily sensations?

JOKO: We can focus on one activity while still taking in a wide range of sensation. For example, as I talk to you now, I'm also well aware of everything that's going on with me. That doesn't mean I'm not paying full attention to you. "Paying attention to you" is part of the total sensory input that is my life right now. If we have full sensory awareness of our life it has to include everything. When a student and I are talking in daisan, my attention is totally on the student, but I always am aware of my life. I'm acting out of that total context and not just out of my head.

STUDENT: Concentration on what I'm doing right now is not exclusive. When I'm doing data analysis on my work, my mind is fully on my data analysis, but I can have full awareness of my body. It's not that I dwell on my body; I don't have time to do that. My bodily sensations are not the major focus of what I'm doing. But it's important at every moment to have awareness of physical sensations and also my reactions to everything that's going on. So I can be in the middle of statistical analysis and yet at the same time be aware of other things. Sometimes, of course, I get so engrossed in a particular activity that I become oblivious to everything else. But for the most part, my awareness is not that focused and exclusive.

JOKO: The essence of Zen practice is to be totally what you're doing. But we're not that way very much. When we're not, then our focus needs to shift back to our body. When we do this, it becomes easier to enter totally into what we're doing. We can be totally concentrating on one activity or aware of several. The point is to experience whatever is happening. A great chess master, for instance, has an enormous accumulation of learning and intellectual background; yet in the middle of the game, his awareness is totally on the present moment, and the right move just emerges. The technical learning is there, but it is subordinate to his intense awareness, which is the real master.

STUDENT: In practicing music, it's important to stay aware of all the levels of one's experience. When I am practicing something new on the piano, if I ignore my body I'm likely to develop tendinitis, for example. This often happens with new students. If I'm just noticing my emotional thoughts, I get careless about the notes I'm playing.

JOKO: Even a minimal awareness of how much time we spend buying into our self-centered thoughts is useful. Of course, in a few minutes, we'll all be doing it again.

Listening to the Body

Practice is not about adjusting this phenomenal self that we think we are to our life. In a way, we are phenomenal selves, but in another, we are not. One could say that we are both—or neither. Until we comprehend this point, our practice will founder.

Labeling our thoughts is a preliminary practice. On the phenomenal level much of our psychological self is revealed by labeling. We begin to observe where we get hung up in our likes and dislikes, in all of our habitual thoughts about our self and our life. This preliminary work is important and necessary—but not *it*. Labeling is a first step, but until we know what it means to stay with our experience, we won't taste the fruits of practice. If we don't taste the fruits of practice, we won't see what practice is and we'll complain: "I don't understand practice; I can't see what it's all about." The fact is, I can't tell you what it's all about; what I'm trying to explain really cannot be talked about. Fundamentally, practice is different from improving a skill such as tennis or golf; much of such learning can be described in words. But we can't explain our zazen practice in words.

Practice may founder on this dilemma, sometimes for a few months, sometimes for years. If it founders badly enough, students may leave practice—and continue to suffer—without yet grasping what their life is. So although practice cannot truly be explained in words, we may be helped by some minimal understanding—even if it is an intellectual, confused understanding—and avoid some of our futile wanderings. Even better than this confused understanding is simple willingness to persist in practice, even when we see no point in it.

Through labeling we come to see that we don't want to desert our own personal psychological drama—what we think of ourselves and others, how we feel about what's happening. We really want to spend our time with our personal drama until months of labeling have revealed its barren nature. When this labeling stage is well under way, we need to do a practice that has no apparent rewards in it: the experiencing of our bodily sensations, our hearing, seeing, feeling, smelling, tasting. Because such practice seems to us dull and pointless, we are often reluctant to persist in it. As a result, our practice may be weak, intermittent, and (often for a long time) ineffective. We feel that we have more important things to do. How can we spend our time in dull, dreary activities, such as sitting here feeling, seeing, smelling, tasting?

It's true that not much of importance seems to be happening as we sit. We feel sensations in the legs and in the knees, tightness in the face, itches; why on earth would we really want to do *this?* Students often complain to me, "It's *boring!* I don't want to do this." Still, if we persist, at some point there is a shift, and for a second there isn't myself *and* the world, but just—there are no words for it, because it is nondual. It is open, spacious, creative, compassionate, and, from the usual point of view, boring.

Every second we spend in that nondual experiencing transforms our life. We can't see that transformation because there is no drama in it. Drama is always in our self-centered mental creations. There is no drama in good sitting. We don't like this lack of excitement—until we begin really to taste it. Until we taste it, we will confuse practice with some sort of psychological endeavor. While strong practice includes psychological elements, that's not what it is.

When I tell students to experience the body, people tell me, "Oh yes, I'm feeling my body. I label my thoughts, and then I feel my body. But it doesn't solve anything." "Yes, I feel the tightness in my chest, and I just center in on it and hope it will disappear." Such comments reveal a personal agenda, a kind of ambition. At bottom, the thought is, "I'm going to do this

practice so that I—my little self—can get something out of it."
In fact, as long as our little self is talking like this, we are not
truly experiencing. Our practice is contaminated by such agendas, and we all sometimes have them.

We can get closer to an accurate understanding of experiencing by the word *listen.* Not "I'm going to *do* this experiencing,"
but "I'm simply going to *listen* to my bodily sensations." If I
truly listen to that ache in my left side, there's an element of
curiosity, of what *is* this? (If I'm not curious, I am always
caught up in my thoughts.) Like a good scientist who is simply
observant, without preconceived notions, we just watch or observe. We listen.

If our mind is stirred up with personal concerns, we can't
listen—or rather, we don't *want* to listen; we want to think.
That's why labeling, watching the mind and its activities, is
often necessary for quite a while before the second nonstate of
experiencing or being can even start. This nonstate is what
makes our practice religious. Experiencing is the realm of no
time, no space, true nature. Just is-ness, thus-ness, God.

At first our desire to think about ourselves is powerful and
seductive; it seems to hold out infinite promise to us. This desire is so powerful that depending on the individual, it can
take a year, five years, ten years, or more before the desire
weakens and we can truly just *sit.* Such sitting is surrender, because there's no self in it. It is surrender to what is, a religious
practice. Such practice is not undertaken primarily to benefit
ourselves.

Good practice is simply sitting here—it is absolutely un-
eventful. From the usual point of view, it's boring. Over time,
however, we learn in our bodies that what we used to call
"boring" is pure joy, and this joy is the source, the feeding
ground, for our life and actions. Sometimes it is called *samadhi;*
it is the very nonstate in which we should live our entire life:
teaching a class, seeing a client, taking care of a baby, playing
an instrument. When we live in such nondual samadhi, we
have no problems because there is nothing separate from us.

As our mind loses some of its obsession with self-centered thinking, our ability to stay in nonduality increases. If we're patient and persistent, we will eventually learn a great deal about nonduality. But until we truly taste that nonduality, our practice has not yet matured. We may promote our psychological integration by the early stages of practice, but until experiencing becomes the foundation of our existence, we still don't know what sitting is.

It's very subtle. That's why practice is difficult: I can't give you a precise map and describe where you're heading. A number of students leave practice after five years or so. That's a shame, because their lives are still mysteries to them. Until the value of experiencing is clear and obvious, it's hard to stay with what we have to stay with. Only a certain number of people will actually do it.

But please: don't give up. When we can "listen" to the body for longer and longer periods, our life will transform in the direction of peace, freedom, compassion. No book can teach us this, only our own practice. And yes, it can be done. Many have done it.

VI

FREEDOM

The Six Stages of Practice

The path of practice is clear and simple. When we don't understand it, however, it can seem confusing and pointless. It's a bit like learning to play the piano. Early in my piano training a teacher told me that to become a better pianist, I should practice the sequence of C, E, G over and over again, five thousand times. I wasn't given any reason; I was just told to do it.

Since I was a good girl when I was young, I probably did this without understanding why it was necessary. But we're not all good girls and boys. So I want to present the "why" of practice, by going through the steps of the path we have to take—why all the tedious, repetitive work is necessary. All of my talks are about aspects of this path; this is an overview, to put things into that perspective in an orderly way.

Most persons who have not engaged in any sort of a practice (many people are practicing in their own way, whether or not they are students of Zen) are in what I call the prepath. That was certainly true of me before I began to practice. To be in the prepath means to be wholly caught up in our emotional reactions to life, in the view that life is happening *to* us. We feel out of control, stuck in what seems a bewildering mess. This may often be true for those who practice as well. Most of us revert at times into this painful confusion. The Ox-herding Pictures* illustrate this point; we may work through the later stages and then under stress still jump back to an earlier stage. Sometimes we jump way back to the prepath, where we're totally caught

---

*The Ox-herding Pictures: a traditional series of drawings depicting the progress of practice from delusion to enlightenment, cast in the form of a man progressively taming a wild ox.

in our reactions. This reversion is neither good nor bad, just something that we do.

To be caught wholly in the prepath, however, is to have no inkling that there is any other way to see life. We step onto the path of practice when we begin to recognize our emotional reactions—for example, that we are getting angry and beginning to create chaos. We begin to discover how much fear we have or how often we have mean or jealous thoughts.

The first stage of practice is this process of becoming aware of our feelings and internal reactions. Labeling our thoughts helps us to do this. It's important to be consistent, however; otherwise, we will miss much of what goes on in our thoughts and feelings. We need to observe it *all*. The first six months or year of practice can be quite painful because we begin to see ourselves more clearly and recognize what we're really doing. We label thoughts, such as "I wish he'd just disappear!" and "I can't stand the way she fixes her pillows!" In an intensive retreat, such thoughts are likely to multiply as we become tired and irritable. In the first six months to a year, opening up to ourselves can be a major shock. Though this is the first stage of practice, elements of it continue into ten or fifteen years of practice, as we continue to see more and more of ourselves.

In the second stage, which typically begins from two to five years into practice, we are beginning to break down the emotional states into their physical and mental components. As we continue to label and as we begin to know what it means to experience ourselves, our bodies, and what we call the external world, the emotional states slowly begin to break down. They never entirely disappear. At any point we can—and often do—dive right back to the previous stage. Still, we're beginning the next stage. The demarcation between stages is never precise, of course; each flows into the next. It's a matter of emphasis.

Stage one is beginning to recognize what's going on and the harm it does. In stage two, we're motivated to break down the emotional reactions. In stage three, we begin to encounter some moments of pure experiencing without self-centered thought:

just pure experience itself. In some Zen centers, such states are sometimes called enlightenment experiences.

In stage four, we slowly move more consistently into a non-dual state of living where the basis is experiential, instead of being dominated by false thinking. It's important to remember that there are years and years of practice involved in all of these stages.

In stage five, eighty to ninety percent of one's life is lived from an experiential base. Life is quite different than it used to be. We can say that such a life is one of no-self, because the little self—the emotional stuff that we've been seeing through and breaking down—is largely gone. Prepath living, being caught in everything and stuck in one's emotional reactions, is now impossible. Even if one wanted to revert from stage five to a prepath state, one couldn't do it. In stage five, compassion and appreciation for life and for other people are much stronger. At stage five, it's possible to be a teacher, helping others along the path. Those who have reached stage five are probably already teachers in one way or another. Sentences such as "I am nothing" (and "Therefore I am everything") are no longer meaningless phrases from some book, but things one knows intuitively. Such knowledge is nothing special or strange.

Theoretically, there is a sixth stage, that of buddhahood, where purely experiential living is one hundred percent. I don't know about that, and I doubt that anybody fully achieves this stage.

By far the most difficult jump to make is from stage one to stage two. We must first become aware of our emotional reactions and our body tension, how we carry on about everything in our lives, even if we conceal our reactions. We have to move into clear awareness through labeling our thoughts and beginning to feel the tension in the body. We resist doing this work because it begins to tear apart who we think we are. At this stage it helps to be aware of our basic temperament, our strategy for coping with pressure in our lives. Therapy can also be useful at this stage, if it's intelligent therapy. Good therapy helps us to increase our awareness. Unfortunately, truly good therapists are somewhat rare; much of therapy is not intelligent and even encourages blaming others.

On this battleground of struggle from stage one to stage two, we begin to realize that we have a choice. What is that choice? One is to refuse to practice: "I'm not going to label these thoughts; it's boring. I'm going to just sit here and dream about something pleasant." The choice is to stay stuck and continue to suffer (which unfortunately means that we will make others suffer also)—or to find the courage to change. Where do we get the courage? The courage increases as our practice continues and we begin to be aware of our own suffering and (if we're really persistent) the suffering we're causing other people. We begin to see that if we refuse to do battle here, we do harm to life. We have to make a choice between living a dramatic but self-centered life and a life that is based upon practice. To move with any degree of solidity from stage one to stage two means that our drama slowly has to come to an end. From the standpoint of the little self, that's a tremendous sacrifice.

When we struggle between stages one and two, we make emotional judgments: "He really makes me angry!" "I feel rejected." "I feel hurt." "I feel annoyed and resentful." "I feel vengeful." Such sentences come shooting out of our emotions. It's all very juicy and even seductive: we get a first-rate drama going about our victimization in life, what's happened to us, how bad it all is. Despite our misery, we really love being the center of it all: "I feel depressed." "I feel bored." "I feel irritable." "I feel excited." This is our personal drama. We all have our versions of a personal drama, and it takes years of practice before we're willing seriously to consider moving away from them. People move at different speeds because of differences in background, in strength, and in determination. Still, if we're persistent, we will begin to shift from stage one to stage two.

As we move increasingly into the second stage, there begin to be more and more periods when we find ourselves saying "Oh, it's okay. I don't know why I thought that was such a problem." We find that we see everything with increasing compassion.

That process is never complete or final; at any point we can dive back into stage one. Still, on the whole, our appreciation increases, and we find that we can enjoy people whom formerly we couldn't stand. In a good practice there is an almost inexorable movement, but we must be willing to spend as long as it takes at each step. The process cannot be rushed.

So long as we insist upon the emotional judgments I mentioned above (and there are endless variations), we can be sure we haven't moved firmly into stage two. If we still believe that another person makes us angry, for example, we need to recognize exactly where our work is. Our ego is very powerful and insistent.

As we move next into stage three, we're slowly moving out of a dualistic state of judging—having thoughts, emotions, and opinions about ourselves and others, and about everything else in the world as well—toward a more nondual and satisfying life. Husbands and wives fight less with one another; we begin to let our kids alone a bit more; problems that we're facing ease as we more readily sense what is the appropriate thing to do. Something is really changing. How long does all this take? Five years? Ten years? It depends on the person.

The continuum of practice could be divided in different ways. We could simplify the analysis with an analogy: first there is the soil, which is whatever we are at this moment in time. The soil may be clay or sand, or rich with loam and compost. It may attract practically no worms or many worms, depending on its richness. The soil is neither good nor bad; it's what we are given to work with. We have practically no control over what our parents gave us in the way of heredity and conditioning. We can't be anything else than what we are, right at this moment. We have things to learn, of course; but at any given point, we are who we are. To think we should be anything else is ridiculous. We simply practice with what we are. That's the soil.

Working with the soil—cultivation—covers what I have called stages two through four. We work with what the ground is—the seeds, the compost, the worms—weeding, pruning, using natural methods to produce a good crop.

From the soil and its cultivation comes the harvest, which begins to be strongly evident in stage four and increases thereafter. The harvest is joy and peace. People complain to me, "There's no joy in my practice yet," as if I should give it to them. Who gives us that joy? We give it to ourselves, through our unrelenting practice. It's not something we can expect or demand. It shows up when it shows up. A life of joy doesn't mean that we're always happy, happy, happy. It means simply that life is rich and interesting. We may even hate certain aspects of living, but it's more and more satisfying to live on the whole. We no longer fight life.

To summarize: The first stage is becoming aware of what we are emotionally, including our desire to control. The second stage is breaking down the emotions into their physical and mental components. When this process becomes a bit more advanced, in the third stage we begin to have some moments of pure experiencing. The first stage is now quite remote. In the fourth stage, we move more fully from the effort of practice into experiential living. In the fifth stage, the experiential life is now strongly established. One's life is eighty to ninety percent experiential. Prepath living—being caught in our emotions and taking them out on others, thinking that others are to blame for our troubles—is impossible in this stage. From stage two on, compassion and appreciation begin to grow.

STUDENT: Your description of the stages of practice is helpful. It's like a map: it doesn't tell us how to get there, but it lets us know where we are along the way.

JOKO: How one "gets there" depends on the individual. We're all different, and ego patterns differ from person to person. Still, it's helpful to have a picture of the overall pattern.

What I have described is similar to the ten Ox-herding Pictures of classical Zen, but it's couched in more psychological terms because psychological approaches are more familiar to us in this day and age. Fundamentally, however, practice is practice; it takes everything we've got. We simply have to do it. C, E, G. C, E, G. C, E, G.

Curiosity and Obsession

One of my students told me recently that, for him, the whole motivation for sitting was curiosity. He expected me to disagree with him and to disapprove of his practice. The truth is, I thoroughly agree. Much of our lives we are caught in our thoughts, obsessed with this or that and not truly in the present. But sometimes we become puzzled about ourselves and our obsessions: "Why am I so anxious, or depressed, or harried?" Out of our puzzlement comes curiosity and a willingness just to observe ourselves and our thoughts, to see how we make ourselves so upset. The repeating loop of thought recedes, and we become aware of the present moment. So curiosity is in a sense the heart of practice.

If we are truly curious, we investigate without any preconceptions. We suspend our beliefs and just observe, just notice. We want to investigate ourselves, how we live our life. If we do this with intelligence, we experience life more directly and begin to see what it is. For example, we're sitting here. Suppose that instead of being preoccupied with something or other, we turn our attention to our immediate experience. We notice what we hear. We feel our sore knees and our other bodily sensations. Eventually we lose our focus and our thoughts bubble off into one loop or another. When we realize that we've drifted away, we come back and pay attention again. That's normal sitting—the usual pattern. What we're really doing is investigating ourselves, our thoughts, our experience: we hear things, we feel things, we smell things. Our sensations trigger thoughts, and our minds are off on another loop. So we notice the loop. Our investigative focus changes slightly, and we begin to look at: "What is all this thinking?" "What is it that I do?" "What am I thinking about?" "How does it happen that I am constantly thinking about this instead of that?"

If we notice our thinking rather than running with it, eventually our thinking calms down and we investigate the next moment. That awareness could be, "I've been sitting here for hours, and my whole body is beginning to hurt." So we investigate this. What hurts? What does it really feel like? Eventually we become aware not just of our physical sensations, but of our thoughts about them as well. We notice the fact that we don't want to be sitting here at all. We observe our rebellious thoughts: "When are they going to ring the bell so I can move?" Our noticing is a kind of curiosity, an investigation of what is. We are simply paying attention to that which is involved in our life or our sitting.

This process can occur not just in sitting, but elsewhere. Suppose I'm at the dentist's office to have a cavity filled. I notice my thoughts about the dentist's work: "I really don't like to have that needle put in my gum!" I notice the slight tension as the dentist walks into the room. As we exchange pleasantries— "Hi, how are you?"—I notice my body contracting. Then the needle arrives. I just feel it and stay with it. My dentist helps by directing, "Just keep breathing. Take a long breath. . . ." It's like training for natural childbirth: when we follow the breath, we don't think about the pain. We simply *are* the pain.

Or perhaps we're at work. We've got our morning's work outlined. Then the boss comes in and says, "We've got a deadline. Drop what you're doing. I've got to get this done. I need it in an hour." If we have a sitting practice, we immediately notice our bodily reactions, even as we begin the task. We notice that our body begins to tighten, and we have resentful thoughts. "If he had to do this himself, he wouldn't expect it done in one hour." We notice our thoughts and then drop them, and return to the task at hand. We settle down into it.

We can investigate all of our life in this way. "What am I feeling? What happens to me as life does what it does?" The boss's abrupt demands are just something that life does for me. Likewise, needing to have a tooth filled is what life does for me. I have my feelings and my thoughts about each incident. As I stay with the feelings and thoughts, I settle back into just being here, just being with things going on as they go on, just doing the next thing. At noon, the boss comes in and says, "You don't have that done yet?" He doesn't say, "What's wrong with you?," but we get the point. We feel our body tighten again. We notice our resentful thoughts about him. We take a short lunch instead of the long lunch hour we had planned. Then we rush back and go to work again.

When we're lucky enough to be doing work we really like to do, we notice that also. We notice that the body relaxes more. We notice that we get into the task more easily. We get absorbed, time goes by rapidly, and our thoughts are fewer because we enjoy the focus. What we like is not more important than what we don't like, however. The longer we practice, the more the moment-to-moment flow takes over regardless of our likes and dislikes. We are aware of the situation as it flows through us and past us. We're just doing what we're doing; we're aware of the flow of experience. Nothing special. More and more the flow takes over and makes for a rather good life.

It's not that everything becomes pleasant. We can't anticipate what life will bring. When we get up in the morning, we don't know that at two o'clock in the afternoon we're going to break a leg. We never know what's coming up; that's part of the fun of being alive.

Practice is nothing but that attitude of curiosity: "What's going on here, now? What am I thinking? What am I feeling? What is life presenting to me? What am I doing with this? What is an intelligent thing to do with this? What's an intelligent thing to do with a boss who's already harried, unreasonable? What do I do when filling my cavity turns out to be excruciating?" Practice is about such investigation. The more we come to terms with our own personal thoughts and reactions, the more we can just be with whatever needs to be done. That's essentially what Zen practice is about: functioning from moment to moment.

There's a fly in this ointment, however. The fly is that we're not often curious about life and open to it. Instead of examining that fussy boss with interest, we get caught up in thoughts and reactions to the situation. We get stuck in obsessive mental detours, loops of thought. If we have never practiced, we may be stuck in these loops ninety-five percent of the time. If we've been practicing well for a number of years, we might be in such loops only five or ten percent of the time.

With the fussy boss, our loop might be, "Who does he think he is? He thinks I'm going to get that done in an hour? That's ridiculous!" Resistance comes up. "I'll show him!" We may even sabotage the job that needs to be done. If we don't sabotage the job, we may sabotage ourselves by being stuck in our thoughts and our anger. At the end of the day, we'll go home exhausted and tell our partner how unreasonable our boss was today. "Nobody could work for him. He's wrecking my life." In our heated reactions, the investigative, curious mode wasn't there. Instead of an observant curiosity, we are caught in a loop of obsession. We don't just observe our thoughts about the boss; instead, we believe that there's some validity in spinning off into our angry thoughts for hours on end, instead of seeing them for what they are, sensing the bodily contractions that grow out of them, and as much as we can, returning to doing something about the work problem.

Sitting is exactly that: we're investigating our life. But when we get lost in our self-centered trains of thought, we're not investigating anymore. We're thinking about how bad it all is, or we're blaming somebody, or we're blaming ourself. Each person has his or her own style, which is how we justify our existence. We like to let our loops grow and grow. We really enjoy them—until we begin to realize that they wreck our lives.

People lose themselves in many different kinds of loops. For some, the loop is, "I can't do anything until I figure it all out." So we refuse to act until we have everything analyzed. Another will respond to the fussy boss by saying, "I'll do the work, but I'll do it my own way. And I won't do it unless I can do it perfectly." An obsessive perfectionism can be our loop. The loop can be philosophical, about having to get a complete picture of how everything fits together. This loop is about trying to make our life safe: we think that if we understand completely, we'll have more security. Another loop is becoming obsessively busy and working all the time. A related style is doing too many things at once. Our loops are our own style, and we find out what they are when we label our thoughts. That's why labeling thoughts is so important. We have to know where and how we like to loop; we have to know our own particular style of looping.

As we sit, we learn how we like to fool ourselves. When we're fooling ourselves, caught in our loop, we're not curious but mechanical, just following a basic unconscious decision we have made earlier: "I've gotta be like this, and I've gotta do it like this." We can't hear any input, and we can't see what's really going on. There's no true curiosity about how we're functioning and about other possible ways to act. The loop of self-centered, obsessive thinking blocks all that. Our basic openness and curiosity about life are gone with the wind.

Sitting is not based on hope; it's based on not knowing, a simple openness and curiosity: "I don't know, but I can investigate." We all have our own particular style of failing to do this. We like to think in loops; we like our loops better than we like life. The loop is who we think we are: "I'm this kind of person." We like those reinforcing thoughts and activities, even though they're barren of life.

The longer we sit and become really acquainted with ourselves, the more willing we are just to see our loops and to let them be, just to let them go. We begin to spend more time in the essential part of sitting, which is just being open and curious, just letting life alone. From the standpoint of a beginner, to sit in this way is the most boring thing in the world. When we sit, nothing's happening except that we hear a car goes by, our left arm has a slight twitch, and we feel the air. From the standpoint of anyone attached to their own personal loop, the question naturally comes up, "What do you want to do *this* for? Of what importance is *this*?" Yet such practice is of total importance, because in that space, life takes over. Life—the natural intelligence or functioning of things—knows what to do.

STUDENT: When I feel depressed, I like to get into a creative visualization of feeling good.

JOKO: That's a loop. We think that the way we are isn't interesting—that there's something wrong with feeling the way we do. So we substitute something "better" that we invent. If we can instead simply investigate feeling down or depressed and be interested in it, we'll discover certain bodily sensations and certain thoughts that feed into that state. When we do that, the depression tends to disappear, and we feel no need for a visualization or fantasy of another state.

STUDENT: Can't investigation itself be an obsessive loop? Poring over one's insides like a detective with a magnifying glass: "I did this, and then I did that, which caused me to do that . . . "

JOKO: It's one thing simply to observe our inner process as a fact, and another to get caught in why we do it, what's wrong with it. If we're trying to track it down like a detective uncovering a crime, that's still a loop.

STUDENT: Is there a danger in noticing the loop and following it wherever it goes? Could that process go on forever?

JOKO: No. If we're truly just noticing our obsessions and aren't caught in them, they tend to fade and die. We usually pursue our loops because we really want to get back into our self-centered thinking. The minute we simply observe our thinking, that self-centered attachment is severed, and the loop loses its fuel. We don't have to worry about endless noticing of thoughts. When we begin to sit, our obsessive thoughts or loops have a lot of energy, but that momentum dissipates as we sit for longer periods. More and more, our thoughts die down, and we are simply with our bodily sensations, with life as it is.

I don't want anyone simply to take my word for it. I want you to investigate for yourselves. That's what practice is: a process of discovery for ourselves about how we function and think.

STUDENT: Some activities seem to require pursuing and following a train of thought. For example, writing as a profession, or philosophical inquiry. These seem to depend upon the ability to sustain a "loop" or line of ideas for as long as possible.

JOKO: That's fine. It's quite different, however, from obsessive, self-centered thought. The creative function of a writer or philosopher can happen only if one is *not* caught in one's anxious personal thoughts. Noticing how our own mind works, seeing our obsessive loops for what they are, can free us to use our minds more imaginatively, without being stuck.

STUDENT: Is there a kind of thinking about oneself that's not self-centered?

JOKO: Yes. We often have to think about ourselves. For example, if I develop a cavity in my tooth, I need to arrange for a trip to the dentist. That's thinking about myself, but not necessarily in an obsessive or self-centered way.

STUDENT: Sometimes, thinking about practice is a loop. I may develop a fantasy of how wonderful my life will be if I'm always aware of my thoughts and feelings.

JOKO: Yes. Then we're not simply investigating our thoughts, but adding hope or expectation. It's no longer a curious, open investigation. As Master Rinzai said, "Place no head above your own." That's an extra head. With steady, careful sitting, we begin to separate out such loops and recognize them for what they are.

STUDENT: When I am engaged in a mental task, I often get caught in a strong self-critical loop. For example, when I'm writing, it's easy for me to interrupt the creative flow of my thoughts with critical judgments about what I'm doing. Then the whole process short-circuits, and I get stuck.

JOKO: Yes. How could you practice with that?

STUDENT: Just notice my self-critical thoughts and keep going.

JOKO: Right.

STUDENT: I realize that the possibility of having my self-centered thoughts actually die down is terrifying. My fear is, maybe I wouldn't exist at all without that fundamental attachment to self.

JOKO: Yes. Just notice that. The more we notice that we don't want that shift to happen, paradoxically, the more we become free to allow it. It can't be forced. There's nothing to force. We're just being aware, with openness and curiosity.

STUDENT: Some people say that too much meditation is depressing and needs to be balanced with other, happier activities, such as celebrations. What do you think about that?

JOKO: In itself, there is nothing in life that's good or bad. What is, is simply what is. Depression is no more than certain bodily sensations plus accompanying thoughts, both of which can be investigated. When we feel depressed, we need simply to observe our sensations and label our thoughts. If we set aside or push away the depression and try to replace it with, say, going to a party, we haven't investigated and understood the depression. Going to a party may cover up the depression for a while, but it will be back. Covering our feelings and thoughts is just another kind of loop.

STUDENT: One of my loops is worrying about work and financial things: "Am I going to have enough money for necessities? Can I support my family? Is my job secure?" I tend to get stuck in these anxious, worrying thoughts.

JOKO: Right. As we investigate such obsessive thoughts, we don't abandon them or banish them. But they slowly lose their power over us as we see what they are and feel the basic fear that's underneath them. They just fade slowly.

STUDENT: I realize that I think of activities as depressing or joyful in themselves and tend to forget that what we call depression and joy are just thoughts and feelings we have in re-action to things. Often, what we regard as "joyful" is just a momentary escape from what's going on inside us. So we're afraid to stop and let ourselves really feel.

JOKO: That's right. Genuine joy is being this moment, just as it is. Experiencing the moment can be feeling the contraction we call depression, or it can be feeling the contraction we call having good news. So genuine joy underlies both what we call depression and what we call elation. There's a kind of impersonal quality, or God's-eye view of things, that develops in someone who sits for a long time. I'm not talking about being cold and unfeeling or callous. I'm not a cold person, though I have developed this impersonal quality in my life.

STUDENT: I've known you for many years, and I have a sense of what you mean. In my opinion, as you have become more "impersonal," you have become warmer, more approachable.

JOKO: At one time, I was too scared to allow people to get close. Now, I look at what used to be very upsetting, and say, "Oh, that's going on. Interesting." It's simply a matter of investigation or curiosity: "What's happening now?" This is our life. For example, my car got smashed the other day. She wasn't looking, and I wasn't looking—and so we had an accident. I didn't have any reaction to that whatsoever. I'm not saying that's good or bad, but it certainly is easier on the adrenals. If somebody had gotten hurt, I might have had a stronger reaction, though I'm sure it would have been different than many years ago. It's all just life, a gift for us to experience.

Transformation

In southern California we bandy around words describing personal growth, such as *change* and *transformation*. I doubt that you hear that kind of talk often in Kansas. Much of such talk is silly, reflecting little real understanding. "Personal growth" is often merely cosmetic change, like adding a chair to the living room. In true transformation, on the other hand, there is an implication that something genuinely new has come into being. It's as though what was there before has disappeared, and something different has taken its place. When I hear the word *transformation*, I think of those line drawings that look like a vase and then suddenly switch into a face. That's transformation.

Zen practice is sometimes called the way of transformation. Many who enter Zen practice, however, are merely seeking incremental change: "I want to be happier." "I want to be less anxious." We hope that Zen practice will bring us these feelings. But if we are transformed, our life shifts to an entirely new basis. It's as if anything can happen—a rosebush transformed into a lily, or a person with a rough, abrasive nature and bad temper transformed into a gentle person. Cosmetic surgery won't do it. True transformation implies that even the aim of the "I" that wants to be happy is transformed. For example, suppose I see myself as a person who is basically depressed or fearful or whatever. Transformation isn't merely that I deal with what I call my depression; it means that the "I," the whole individual, the whole syndrome that I call "I," is transformed. This is a very different view of practice than is held by most Zen students. We don't like to approach practice in this way because it means that if we want to be genuinely joyful, we have to be willing to be anything. We have to be open to the transformation that life wants us to go through. I have to be prepared for the possibility that I will become a bag lady, for example. Now, I don't really want to be a bag lady. We fantasize that when we practice, we're going to be comfortable with ourselves and life is going to be very smooth. We think we're going to be wonderful new versions of who we are now. Yet true transformation means that maybe the next step *is* to be a bag lady.

That certainly isn't what brings people to Zen practice. We're here to get our present model repainted a little bit. If the car of our life is a deep gray, we want to turn it into lavender or pink. But transformation means that the car may disappear altogether. Maybe instead of a car it will be a turtle. We don't even want to hear of such possibilities. We hope that the teacher will tell us something that will fix our present model. A lot of therapies merely provide techniques for improving the model. They tinker here and there, and we may even feel a lot better. Still, that is not transformation. Transformation arises from a willingness that develops very slowly over time to be what life asks of us.

Most of us (myself included at times) are like children: we want something or somebody to give us what a small child wants from its parents. We want to be given peace, attention, comfort, understanding. If our life doesn't give us this, we think, "A few years of Zen practice will do this for me." No, they won't. That's not what practice is about. Practice is about opening ourselves so that this little "I" that wants and wants and wants and wants and wants—that wants the whole world to be its parents, really—grows up. Growing up doesn't interest us very much.

A lot of my students try to turn me into a substitute parent. That is not my role. Students in difficulty often come running to me; as much as possible, I set them to dealing with the problem themselves. Once students have some idea of how they might deal with the problem, the best thing to do is to let them struggle. Then there is some possibility of transformation.

Transformation is allowing ourselves to participate in our life right this second. That's scary business. There is no guarantee of comfort, of peace, of money, of anything. We have to be what we are. Most of us, however, have other ideas. It's as though we are a tree that produces leaves and fruit of a certain kind. We want to produce this because it's comfortable. Transformation, however, is to produce what life chooses to produce through us. We can't know what this is going to be. It might mean any kind of a transformation—in the work we do, in the way we live, in our health (it might even get worse, not better).

Still, transformation is joy. Transformation means that however life is—whether difficult, easy, comforting, or noncomforting—it is joy. By joy I don't mean happiness. Joy has more to do with curiosity. Think of babies about nine months to a year, crawling about, encountering all kinds of marvels: one can see the curiosity and wonder on their faces. They're not crawling in order to absorb information, they're not trying to be better babies who can crawl more efficiently; in fact, they're not crawling for any reason. They are simply crawling for sheer enjoyment and curiosity. We need to regain the capacity to feel curiosity about everything in our life, even the disasters. For instance, suppose that a long-time partner walks out on us unexpectedly. Such a dire event can plunge us into a melodrama of reaction. Can you imagine being able to view that with curiosity instead? What would it mean to view such a disaster with curiosity?

STUDENT: We would be in a state of wonder.

JOKO: That's right. We would be interested in the whole thing, including our emotional reactions: our screaming, our mood swings, our physical sensations—just curiosity, second after second after second. That may sound cold, but it's not; it means that for the first time we're open to the situation and can learn from it and handle it. That curiosity is also part of joy, a state of wonder. We don't care about curiosity and wonder, however. We'd rather fix things so we'll feel good. But the curiosity I'm speaking of can be there, whether we feel good or bad.

Years ago I was associated with a top-notch scientist. I asked him what it meant to be a scientist. He said, "If there is a plate on a table near you, and you know there is something under the plate—but you don't know what it is—being a scientist means that you can't rest night or day until you've seen what's under the plate. You *have* to know." Practice should cultivate this kind of attitude. Through our efforts at self-protection, we've lost most of our curiosity about life. When we're depressed, we just want to make the depression stop. Likewise when we're worried, lonely, or confused. Instead, we need to approach our state of mind with curiosity and open wonder. That open, curious listening to life is joy—no matter what the mood of our life is.

This is the way of transformation. We become less wrapped up in our self-protected view of life—wanting what we want—less attached to pictures or fantasies of how our life must turn out. Practice, the way of transformation, is a slow shift over time into a new way of being in the world. This way will be therapeutic, to be sure, but that is not its purpose. A person who is totally curious is neither happy nor unhappy. A crawling baby who discovers a measuring cup we have put on the floor is neither happy nor unhappy. Instead of being "happy," the baby is absorbed. It's not ambitious; it's not a good or bad baby; it's simply absorbed in the wonder of what it is seeing.

Unfortunately, babies turn into adults. It's not that the best practice is to be like a baby. Ideally, we keep the openness and wonder of a baby, yet have the mature mind and abilities of an adult. Instead of seeing with curiosity and wonder, however, we approach life with a self-centered agenda, wanting everything to suit us and make us feel good. The people we like are the people who give us good sensations. The friends we really want to be around are the ones who make us feel good. People who consistently make us feel bad go onto another list. A person who is just open and curious, however, doesn't do this, at least not to the same degree.

As Carlos Castaneda writes, our practice needs to be *impeccable*. This means being as aware as we can be in every moment, so that our "personality," which is made up of our self-protective strategies, begins to break down and we can respond more and more simply to the moment. Impeccable practice means, for example, working with one or two projects in practice and just pounding away with no letup. Suppose we have a habit of believing thoughts such as, "I'm no good." Impeccable practice means we hardly ever let that thought slip by. Even though we will miss one now and then, impeccable practice means to keep that practice pressure on ourselves. It's not that we're trying to be better, or that we're bad when we fail. Still, we need to be meticulous. Impeccable practice means we never stop. The way of transformation doesn't mean, "Oh, I've practiced enough today; I think I'll go off and have a good time." There's nothing wrong with having a good time, but impeccable practice is to be aware of that, too. Otherwise, we're just kidding ourselves.

Though it is meticulous, a mature practice has no struggle. In the first few years, however, there's no way to avoid the struggle. Gradually, over the years, the struggle becomes less. Practice is also not something to set aside when things are rough. Instead of "Things are so tough right now, I'll practice next week," we need to practice right now, with the struggle itself; otherwise, practice is just one more toy we're playing with and a waste of time.

The way of transformation requires an impeccable warrior—which is not the same as being a perfect warrior. Instead, we constantly do our best, working with specific care. Instead of resolving, "I'm going to be aware," we need to resolve, "I'm going to be aware specifically when I do that." Instead of trying to work with everything at once, we work on one or two items at a time, maybe for two or three months, and just keep pounding away. If we let even one thought go by, such as "Oh, I'm really a hopeless person," without being aware of it until afterward, then we want to sit up a little straighter and try again. We need to apply ourselves steadily, to build up muscle for the long, hard journey. In the end, we realize that it's *not* a long, hard journey, but we won't see this until we see it.

When I'm away from the Zen Center of San Diego, people sometimes set up a two-day sitting and do it. That's good. Not everyone can participate; some people have young children, for example. Still, to undertake a sitting like that—to sit for two days, struggling to maintain awareness—is what we're talking about. In a serious practice there is no way to skip over this kind of struggle. There has to be a struggle for a long time. There is no way out of it. Struggling develops strength. It means growing up. When we complain, when we're bitter about what somebody did to us, bitter about what life has done to us, then we're being children. There's some big breast we're trying to hold onto. Zen practice is about growing up. We shouldn't enter a practice like this until we really want to do it. We must really want a life that's transformed.

The Natural Man

No matter how many years we've been practicing, we tend to misunderstand the nature of practice. In one way or another, we suppose that practice is about correcting an error. We imagine that if we do this or master that, we will finally overcome the error in ourselves. Our lives will "get fixed," and we'll somehow do better.

Many forms of therapy begin with the assumption that there's something wrong in the person seeking therapy, and therapy is about repairing that wrong. We carry this attitude—so widespread in our culture—into our own spiritual practice.

We assume there's something wrong with our lives because we don't feel content with ourselves. From our personal standpoint, something *is* wrong. What needs to be understood about this dilemma?

Consider a hurricane. From the standpoint of the hurricane itself, there's no problem in destroying thousands of trees, pulling down power lines, killing people, devastating beaches, and so on. That's just what hurricanes do. From our point of view, however—particularly if we have a house that has been battered by a hurricane—there's something very wrong. If we could, we'd be fixing hurricanes. We haven't figured out how to do it yet.

Unfortunately, when we try to fix things, we often create a whole new set of problems. The automobile is a fine invention that eases our lives in many ways; yet as we all know, it has brought us a whole host of major problems. Left to itself, nature makes all kinds of messes. But they seem to heal, and the natural process restores itself. When we get the idea that we need to solve all of the problems of life, however, we don't do so well. The reason for our failure is that our viewpoint is limited to our ego needs, to "what I want." If what was happening in our lives were okay with us, nothing would disturb us.

Should we just become passive and allow everything to be as it is, without doing anything at all? No. But we get ourselves into trouble by the emotional context we supply, the attitude that there's something wrong that needs fixing.

In particular, we want our personal selves to be different than they are. For example, we want to make ourselves "enlightened." We picture being an enlightened self as somehow glorified, different, and separated from the rest of poor ordinary mortals. Enlightenment seems to us to be a great achievement, the ultimate ego attainment. That eagerness to become enlightened pervades many spiritual centers as an undercurrent of excitement about spiritual practice. It's ridiculous, really.

Still, when we feel miserable, we like to imagine that we can find something that will fix us up, so that our relationships will be always wonderful. We imagine ourselves always feeling good, doing work that doesn't have any painful twists and turns.

Let's take a look at what we might call "a natural man." (We might just as well talk about "a natural woman," but in this example, let's talk about a male.) In the Bible a natural man would be Adam before he was expelled from the Garden of Eden—that is, before he became conscious of himself as a separate self. What was that natural man like? What would it be like to be a natural man?

STUDENT: A natural man would be full of wonder.

JOKO: That's true, though he wouldn't be aware that he was full of wonder.

STUDENT: There would be no sense of separation between himself and the world around him.

JOKO: That's also true. Again, he would have no awareness of his lack of separation.

STUDENT: He would just be.

JOKO: Yes. He would just be. How would he behave? For example, would he be saintly, or would he occasionally go out hunting?

STUDENT: He'd do whatever he needed to get by.

JOKO: He'd do what was needed to survive. If necessary, he would hunt, rather like the Native Americans who made offerings to the animals that they had to kill.

STUDENT: Would he have wars with his fellow tribespeople?

JOKO: Possibly, though I doubt that there would be bloodshed. Perhaps some disagreement here and there.

STUDENT: I think of a natural man as being like my cat: eating, sleeping, doing whatever comes up from moment to moment without any awareness or thought about it.

JOKO: That's about right. Dogs are a poor example, because we make them over into what we want them to be. But cats are more independent, more like a natural man.

The natural state is what practice is about. To be a natural person doesn't mean that one turns into some kind of a saint. Without a sense of separation from the world, however, there is always an innate goodness and appropriateness of action. For example, our two hands don't behave inappropriately toward each other, because they are part of the same body.

A natural man enjoys food. He enjoys loving. He gets upset now and then, but probably not for long. He may be fearful when his survival is threatened.

In contrast, our lives are very unnatural. We feel ourselves to be separated from the world, and that removes us from the Garden of Eden. In separating ourselves from the world, we have also separated the world into good and bad, satisfactory and not satisfactory, pleasant and painful. Having separated things in this way, we're always trying to steer to one side and avoid the other, so that we encounter only the parts of life that suit us.

Nature is like the hurricane. Whatever happens, happens. We don't want that in our life, however. We want a hurricane that takes other houses, but not ours. We constantly seek a safe little haven in the middle of the hurricane of life. There is no such place. Life is really about simply living and enjoying whatever comes up. Because we have ego-centered minds, however, we think that life is about protecting ourselves. And that keeps us entrapped. An ego-mind is self-centered. It spends its time thinking about how it's going to survive and be safe, comfortable, entertained, pleased, nonthreatened at every juncture. When we live in this way, we've missed the boat. We've lost our center. The further we go from the center, the more anxious and eccentric—that is, away from the center—our lives become.

From our earliest moments in life, we are developing an ego-mind. To be living from ego-mind is simply looking at life in a certain way. There's nothing intrinsically wrong with this; it's just that we see life only from our own viewpoint. Our essential nature remains undisturbed at all times. We can't see it, however, because we're now always looking from a limited, one-sided viewpoint.

We're far away from "just living," as a natural man or woman would live. We're thinking about living all of the time. We probably spend eighty or ninety percent of our time doing this. And we wonder why nothing feels right and isn't right. From our point of view, we're very uncomfortable.

Left to his own devices, the natural man is essentially good. He hunts when he has to. He does what he needs to do. Because he doesn't feel separate, however, he does very little harm. We have only to look at ourselves, to see how far we are from this kind of life.

Our essential task in practice is *not* to try to achieve something. Our true nature—buddha nature—is always there. It's always undisturbed. It's present. We recognize that we are just fine once we get in touch with it. We're not in touch with it, however, because we're off to the side, one-sided. And this creates problems in our lives.

It is often said that the essence of any religious practice is renunciation of the self. That's true enough, if we understand the words rightly. What do we have to renounce, however?

STUDENT: Attachment.

JOKO: Yes. Attachment is rooted in what?

STUDENT: Self-centered thought?

JOKO: Self-centered thought. Suppose someone says to me, "You're stupid, Joko." She's simply giving me her opinion. I fire back with my opinion: "I'm not stupid. You're the one who doesn't know what you're doing." And so we go back and forth. We fall into these games because of our self-centered, egotistical minds. From such a standpoint, there's always something wrong with the world. In fact, however, life itself is fine, quite undisturbed. What causes disturbance are our opinions.

Practice is not about finding something. We don't have to find enlightenment. We don't have to find our buddha nature. It's who we are. What we need to do is to remove our blindness, so we can once more see it. What are some practical ways to remove our blindness?

STUDENT: Label our thoughts.

JOKO: Yes, we can label thoughts so we see them as merely thoughts, something we cook up. We need to see that they have no essential reality.

STUDENT: I think one has to accept the fact of blindness. I can't label something until I'm willing to look at it.

JOKO: That's true. We are usually not willing to do the work of looking until we're suffering. That's bound to happen in an ego-centered life: suffering, in myself and in people around me.

Our little mind produces complaints. It produces bitterness and a feeling of victimization. It produces ill health. It's not the only cause of ill health; still, a body that is constantly tight has a double battle to fight. Little mind produces smugness and arrogance. It also prevents us from being in touch with our body sensations and with life itself. When we are in touch, on the other hand, our lives are more like that of the natural man. What does that mean?

STUDENT: It means a sense of appropriate action.

JOKO: Yes. What else?

STUDENT: Greater openness. Natural intelligence takes in information through the senses and functions as part of everything else.

JOKO: Yes. We tend to see clearly. We tend to know how to balance things out and what to do in a particular situation. We tend to remain calm, because we're not upset by every little thing. We tend to be more playful. We tend to be spontaneous. We tend to be more cooperative. We tend to see others more fully, instead of viewing them as things to be manipulated.

These results do not come easily. The work that we do on the cushion at times is very dreary. We get tired of labeling our thoughts and going back to our body sensations. This work is not pointless, but it takes years. We're stubborn, and we don't want to do any of the necessary work. When we don't, however, life is hard on us and on everybody else around us. Even so, we often fail to do the work that is needed.

Renunciation of self sounds exotic; we imagine Christ on the cross or some other remarkable action. But renunciation of self is mostly quite simple and basic. Renunciation of self happens each time we see our thoughts spinning and we label them and give up our little self—that's what the thoughts are—and return to what's happening. We return to taking in the body sensations, the sound of the cars, the smell of lunch. That is what renunciation of self means. When we sit for a week in retreat, we should do this ten thousand times: labeling our thoughts, seeing the fantasy, and returning to an awareness of what is, which is renunciation of little self for the sake of big self. The result: just life itself coming in.

There's nothing fancy about this. We do this perhaps ten times a sitting period; if we're really alert, perhaps twenty or thirty times. If we get lost in our thoughts for fifteen minutes, we cut out some of our work.

Nobody rushes up and gives us a gold star for doing this kind of work. Nobody. In order to do it, we have to understand what's involved. Everything—our whole life—is involved. Everything we really want is involved in this dull work that we do, over and over and over.

Then there are times when we simply aren't willing to do the work for a while. "No matter what Joko says, I'm going off into this daydream." So we run our little fantasy, and then we return to the work. Our mind comes out of its self-centered fantasy and goes back to feeling our knees, feeling the tightness in our body, just letting it be. In that second, we have renounced ourselves. That's the enlightened state: just being here.

We always return to our little self. But as we sit, gradually the intervals where we just stay with life as it is get a little longer, and the interruptions of our self-centeredness are a little shorter. The interruptions don't last as long, and we don't take them as seriously. Increasingly, they're like clouds that drift through the sky: we note them, but we are less controlled by them. Over time, this process makes a marked difference in our lives. We feel better. We function better. After an intensive retreat, for example, most people find that what was a problem before is now trivial, even funny. The "problem" hasn't changed, but the mind is different. The point of my talks—and of sesshin itself—lies in this return to daily life. When we get back to the more complex demands of our ordinary lives, however, we often forget to continue to practice. Instead of letting our little mind go haywire, we have to continue to watch and observe. If we don't, then the clarity we have gained begins to fade. That doesn't have to happen; we don't have to fight with someone the day after sesshin.

The longer we practice and the more the habits of practice become just who we are, the longer the benefits of sesshin last. Eventually we reach a point where there's no difference between sesshin and daily life.

It's important to remember that we're not fixing anything. We're not trying to be different from who we are. In fact, practice is simply returning to that which we always are. We're not doing anything special. We're not trying to be enlightened. We just keep returning, renouncing the little self, over and over.

As we do this work, we begin to feel life in a different way, and this is the only thing that can really teach us anything. Words like these come and go; if we don't do the work, the words don't mean anything. Reading a book or listening to a talk isn't enough by itself. It's the work that we do that gives us a taste of a different way of feeling about our life. As that taste gets stronger, we discover that we can't go home again, even if we want to. As we transform ourselves into more of who we truly are, the effects become established, and our lives change.

Are there any questions?

STUDENT: You describe practice as returning in each moment to sounds or body sensations, but what if I'm practicing with a strong emotion, such as grief or anger?

JOKO: What is an emotion? An emotion is simply a combination of body sensations and thoughts. The thoughts are self-centered thoughts. "How dare he go out with somebody else! He said he loved me." Such thoughts grip us like a fire. "How dare he do that!" Our thoughts spin and whirl. "He shouldn't do that!" On and on they go. Now as we think these thoughts, the body is tightening. Suppose, however, that we begin to label the thoughts. It may take days, but at some point our thoughts begin to collapse and we're just left with this tight, suffering body. If we just stay with the tight, suffering body, without thoughts, what happens? The tightness increases and then collapses—and the emotion is over.

The fact is, there's nothing real about a self-centered emotion. We all think our emotions are important; yet there's nothing less important than a self-centered emotion. The emotion is simply tension and thoughts that we've cooked up. The thoughts are essentially unreal; they're not related to reality. For example, I may think that the hurricane is unfair—that it shouldn't hit me. Such thoughts are futile, unrelated to reality. They're not important. My body sensations are simply what they are, neither good nor bad. When we understand self-centered emotion, we see that it is unnecessary.

STUDENT: When I'm labeling thoughts, and a thought gets up and starts walking into my head and halfway through I say, "Whoops, it's a thought," should I immediately go back to my body sensations, or is it a good idea first to observe the thought fully before I set it aside?

JOKO: If that thought has any great push in your life, it'll be back. You needn't worry about not finishing with it.

STUDENT: What is a true emotion?

JOKO: A true emotion is in response to reality. Suppose my friend falls over with a heart attack. I'd certainly have an emotion as I jumped to do something. On the other hand, when I'm angry about something that happened five minutes ago, that's not a real emotion. If someone has insulted me five minutes ago, I don't want to know that my emotion about that insult is unreal. Instead, I want to dwell on "He shouldn't do that. He's terrible!" When I take my little emotions seriously, then I reinforce my idea of myself so I can keep playing this game.

STUDENT: Can anger be a true emotion?

JOKO: It can be, but it's rare. If I see someone beating up another person and I jump in and do something to stop the harm, there is probably some anger in me. But that's more like a little storm than what we ordinarily call anger. Almost always, when we think we're expressing true anger, we're fooling ourselves.

STUDENT: Is there a true emotion of empathy?

JOKO: True empathy or compassion is not itself an emotion. It can contain emotions, such as love. But compassion as such is simply openness to what is. Since it is absolutely open, it will be receptive and able to see what is best to do and will do it. Compassion may be the end result of practice. Nobody is always compassionate, but if our practice is real, we'll become more compassionate. We become more aware of others as persons, not simply as things to be controlled or manipulated or fixed, but as centers of real awareness. That capacity grows with practice. If it doesn't, then we're not understanding practice, or we're simply not doing it.

I don't have to investigate what somebody is doing on the cushion if I see their behavior in the rest of their lives. It's obvious when a practice is growing. The feeling of victimization, of "poor me," goes down. The person has much more awareness of the needs of other people and increasing willingness to meet the needs—something very different from being a "do-gooder."

STUDENT: So compassion doesn't necessarily feel like something?

JOKO: No. If we're truly listening with compassion to another person, we may not feel much of anything; we simply listen and act appropriately. We confuse compassion with love. Compassion can contain love, which may be an emotion, but compassion is not itself an emotion. In true compassion there is no separation, which means there are no self-centered thoughts between me and whomever I'm with. No separation is compassion.

STUDENT: The dictionary definition of *empathy* is to feel what another is feeling. That doesn't necessarily mean reacting to what they're feeling, or sympathizing. Compassion means being with their experience, but not being in it.

JOKO: One who is truly compassionate never gives it a thought. It's simply absolutely natural. It's not a result of trying to be compassionate. Trying to be compassionate is like trying to be spontaneous. We either are, or we aren't. If we're not, we can be sure that we're caught in a self-centered dream of some sort. When we're caught in our thoughts, we won't be compassionate. So all of practice is to investigate the self-centered dream which we like so well. If we're not caught in that, we'll be compassionate.

STUDENT: Are love and compassion the same thing?

JOKO: Sometimes love has an emotional connotation for short periods. Truly loving somebody doesn't mean we feel emotional about them, however. We can love our children and wish they'd wipe their feet off before coming into the house. Being irritated that they don't wipe their feet is an emotion, but the underlying love is not. The love for one's children remains steady.

In the case of romantic love, there's nearly always an element of need, a thought that we're going to get something out of it. "I'm so excited to be with you." "I get such a good feeling when I'm around you." "You make me so happy." "I feel whole when I'm with you." "You meet all my needs." When something happens to destroy our fantasy, the words change: "I really hate him! I don't know what I ever saw in him."

In fact, nobody makes us happy or sad; we do that to ourselves. Romantic love is full of illusions; genuine love, or compassion, has no illusions. It is simply who we are.

VII

WONDER

The Fall

There was once a man who climbed to the top of a ten-story building and jumped off. As he passed the fifth floor on his way down, he was heard to say, "So far, so good!"

We laugh at the man because we see what's coming up for him in a moment. How can he say he's doing well, so far? What's the difference between the second when he is at the fifth floor and the second just before he hits the pavement? The second before hitting the pavement is what most of us would call a crisis. If we think that we have only a few minutes or days before we die, most of us would say, "This is a crisis." On the other hand, if our days are proceeding normally (the usual job, the usual people, the usual tasks), life may not seem wonderful, but at least we're used to it. At such times we don't feel we're in a crisis, and we may not feel impelled to practice with diligence. Let's look at this supposed difference between crisis and noncrisis.

Sesshin is an artificial crisis. When we commit ourselves to a retreat, we have to stay and struggle with a difficult situation. By the end of the retreat, most of us have gone through the crisis—at least enough so that we see our life somewhat differently. It's sad that we don't understand that each moment of our lives—drinking a cup of coffee, walking down the street to pick up a paper—is *it*. Why don't we grasp that truth? We don't get it because our little minds think that this second that we're living has hundreds of thousands of seconds that preceded it and hundreds of thousands of seconds still to come, so we turn away from truly living our life. Instead, we do what human beings spend all their time doing, which is a complete waste of time: we try mentally to scheme so that we will never have to suffer through a crisis. We spend all of our energies trying to be liked, successful, nice, agreeable, assertive (or non-assertive), depending upon what we think will do it for us. We have schemes. Most of our energies go into these schemes, as we try to handle our life so that we never hit the bottom. That's why it's so wonderful to get close to that bottom. That's why people who are seriously ill, or who have a devastating circumstance in their lives, often wake up. Wake up to what? What do we wake up to?

STUDENT: To the present?

JOKO: Yes. And what else?

STUDENT: To impermanence.

JOKO: Impermanence. All right, that's true.

STUDENT: To our bodily sensations.

JOKO: Yes, and more than that, we wake up to what?

STUDENT: The wonder of it all.

JOKO: The wonder of this second. When this second is not me, or anything else, but just, Oh!—and that doesn't mean some giant emotion, but just—then all of our worries are nonexistent. But usually we have such a realization only when we are pressed hard enough that our mind is pulled into the present moment; then we can forget all our schemes of fixing ourselves, somebody else, or circumstances. Most people spend fifty to ninety percent of their waking hours trying to avoid the bottom. Yet we can't avoid it. We're all on our way down, every one of us. We can't avoid the bottom, but we spend most of our life trying to do that.

Waking up means realizing that our situation is hopeless— and wonderful. There is nothing for us to do except simply to live this second. When we're in crisis, or in sesshin, we may not wake up fully, but we wake up enough so that the way we see our life shifts. We realize that our usual maneuvers—worrying about the past, projecting an imaginary future—don't make sense; they waste precious seconds.

From one point of view, we're always in crisis: we're always falling toward the bottom. From another point of view, there is no crisis. If we're going to die in one second, is there any crisis? No, there's just that second. One second we're alive; one second we're dead. There's no crisis; there's just what is. But the human urge to do the impossible keeps us mucked up. We spend our lives trying to avoid the unavoidable. Our energies, our emotions, our projects go into making money, being successful, having everybody like us, because we secretly believe that such things will protect us. One of our most powerful illusions is that being in love can give us real protection. In reality, there is no protection, no answer. Our lives are absolutely hopeless. That's why they're wonderful. And it's not a big deal.

Who wants to be successful? Who wants to be liked? All of us. There's nothing wrong with such wants—unless we believe the illusion. Even wanting to make a million dollars can be great fun—as good a game as any—if we see it simply as a fun game, and we don't hurt people as we play it. But we don't see it as a game, and so we hurt others as we pursue our lethal path.

Enlightenment is simply knowing the truth, not in the head but with one's whole being, knowing that "this is it." It's wonderful. Got a toothache? That's also it—wonderful. When we think about the toothache, of course we don't think it's wonderful. But it *is* wonderful simply to be what life is in this second, toothache and all.

Unfortunately, our human minds do us in. For the most part, animals are less manipulative with their lives. Sometimes they may try to play tricks; I once had a dog who didn't like to come home when he was called, so he'd stand behind the hedge on the opposite side of the street. That worked well in the summer: he'd stand hidden behind the hedge, just as quiet as could be. But when the leaves fell off in the fall, he'd still run there to hide, standing quietly—and completely visible! Still, dogs and other animals do not get as confused as we do about the purpose of their lives; unlike us, they just live.

Some of us are in the middle of "disasters"; others are not. Of course, we don't stay forever in the middle of a major disaster, but when we're in the middle of one we practice hard, showing up at the zendo more often, doing whatever we can to cope. Then when life settles down, we cease practicing with such intensity. One mark of maturing practice is to see that life is always totally a crisis and totally not a crisis: they're the same thing. In a mature practice, we practice just as hard whether there's a crisis or not. Crisis or no crisis, we just do it.

Nothing is really solved until we understand that there is *no solution*. We're falling, and there's no answer to that. We can't control it. We're spending our life trying to stop the falling; yet it never stops. There is no solution, no wonderful person who can make it stop. No success, no dream, no anything can make it stop. Our body is just going down.

The fall is a great blessing. If someone announced a pill that would cure death and allow us to live forever, that would be a true disaster. Picture yourself in six thousand years still thinking the same old thoughts! With a cure for death, the whole meaning of being on this planet would change. And where would we put the new babies being born?

All of us are aware of aging: gray hair, wrinkles, twinges. From the time we are conceived, we're dying. When I notice such signs, I don't rejoice. I don't like them any more than you do. Still, there's a big difference between disliking change and trying frantically to stop it.

Sooner or later we realize that the truth of life is the second we are living, no matter whether that second is at the ninth floor or the first. In a sense, our life has no duration whatsoever: we're always living the same second. There's nothing but that second, the timeless present moment. Whether we live the second at the fifth floor or right over the pavement, it's all the same second. With that realization, each second is a source of joy. Without that realization, each second is misery. (In fact, we often secretly want to be miserable; we *like* being at the center of a melodrama.)

Most of the time we don't think there's any crisis. ("So far, so good!") Or we think the crisis is the fact that we don't feel happy. That's not a crisis; that's an illusion. So we spend most of our life attempting to fix this nonexistent entity that we think we are. In fact, we are this second. What else could we be? And this second has no time or space. I can't be the second that was five minutes ago; how can I be that? I'm here. I'm now. I can't be the second that's going to arrive in ten minutes either. The only thing I can be is wiggling around on my cushion, feeling the pain in my left knee, experiencing whatever is happening now. That's who I am. I can't be anything else. I can imagine that in ten minutes I won't have a pain in my left knee, but that's sheer fantasy.

I can remember a time when I was young and pretty. That's sheer fantasy also. Most of our difficulties, our hopes, and our worries are simply fantasies. Nothing has ever existed except this moment. That's all there is. That's all we are. Yet most human beings spend fifty to ninety percent or more of their time in their imagination, living in fantasy. We think about what has happened to us, what might have happened, how we feel about it, how we should be different, how others should be different, how it's all a shame, and on and on; it's all fantasy, all imagination. Memory *is* imagination. Every memory that we stick to devastates our life.

Practical thinking—when we're not clinging to some fantasy but just getting something done—is another matter. If my knee hurts, perhaps I should investigate treatment for it. The thoughts that destroy us are the ones in which we're trying to stop the fall and not hit bottom. "I'm going to fix him." "I'm going to fix myself." Or "I'm going to understand myself. When I finally understand myself, I'll be at peace and then life will be all right." No, it won't be all right. It will be whatever it is, just this second. Just the wonder.

As we sit, can we sense the wonder? Can we feel the wonder in the fact that we're here, that as human beings we can appreciate this life? In this respect we are more fortunate than animals. I doubt that a cat or a beetle has this capacity to appreciate, though I may be wrong. And I can lose the appreciation, the wonder, if I wander from this moment. If someone yells at me, "Joko, you're a mess!" and I get lost in my reactions (my thoughts about protecting myself or retaliating), then I've lost the wonder. But if I stay with this moment, there's just being yelled at. It's nothing. But we all get stuck in our reactions.

As human beings, we have a wonderful capacity to see what life is. I don't know if any other animal has that ability. If we waste it and don't truly practice, everyone with whom we come in contact feels the effects. That means our partners, our children, our parents, our friends. Practice isn't something that we do just for ourselves. If it were, in a way it wouldn't make any difference. As our life shifts into reality, everyone we meet shifts too. If anything can affect this suffering universe, this is it.

The Sound of a Dove—
and a Critical Voice

I got a phone call recently from someone on the East Coast who told me, "In sitting this morning, it was quiet and suddenly there was just the sound of a dove. There wasn't any dove, there wasn't any me, there was just *this*." Then she waited for my comment. I replied, "That's wonderful! But suppose that instead of hearing the dove, you hear a critical voice finding fault with you. What's the difference between the sound of the dove and the sound of a critical voice?" Imagine we are sitting in the stillness of early morning and suddenly through an open window there is just "chirp, chirp, chirp." Such a moment can be enchanting. (Often we think that this is what Zen is.) But suppose our boss rushes in and screams, "I should have had your report yesterday. Where *is* it?" What is the same about the two sounds?

STUDENT: They're both just hearing.

JOKO: Yes, they're just *hearing*. Whatever happens to us all day long is simply input from one of the senses: just hearing, just seeing, just smelling, just touching, just tasting. We have said what is the same about the two sounds. So what is the difference? Or is there a difference?

STUDENT: We like one, and we don't like the other.

JOKO: Why is that true? After all, they're both just sounds. Why don't we like the critical voice as much as we like the sound of a dove?

STUDENT: We don't just hear the voice; we attach an opinion to what we hear.

JOKO: Right. We have an opinion about that criticism—strong thoughts and reactions, in fact.

In an earlier talk, I told the story of a man who jumped off a ten-story building, and as he fell past the fifth floor, he yelled, "So far, so good!" He was hoping that he would stay up forever. That's how we live our lives: hoping to avoid the critical voice, hoping to defy gravity and stay up forever.

Some do seem to defy gravity. A person who has given me pleasure over the years is Greg Louganis, probably the greatest diver who has ever lived. A superb diver like Louganis has the strength to achieve remarkable height at takeoff, allowing more room for movement on his way down to the water. Height gives him operating space. Another remarkable athlete who seems to defy gravity is the basketball player Michael Jordan, who sometimes seems like he is suspended in the air. Amazing. And we marvel at Baryshnikov, the great dancer. They all get remarkable height, but they all at some point come down. As common sense tells us, gravity always prevails.

But we do not live according to common sense. We don't like the critical voice; we don't like to come down. We don't like it at all. Yet like it or not, life consists of much unpleasant input. Seldom does life give us just what we want. So we spend all of our time trying to do what no human being can do. We try somehow to stay up there, so that we will never come down and crash. We try to avoid that which cannot be avoided.

There is no way to live a human life and avoid all unpleasant input. There is criticism, pain, being hurt, being sick, being disappointed. Our little mind says, "You can't depend on life. You'd better take out some insurance." We do our best to avoid any contact with painful reality.

As we sit in zazen, our mind is incessantly fantasizing, trying to "stay up there." We can't do it. Yet as human beings, we persist in trying to do that which cannot be done: avoiding all pain. "I will plan. I will find the best way. I'll find out what to do so I can survive and be safe." We try to transform reality with our thinking so that it can't get near us, not ever.

228

There's a story I've told before about sitting in a zendo next to a young woman who kept wiggling. She was fiddling with her ankle all the time. She would stretch it out, she would put it down, she would twist it behind her. She was constantly moving her ankle. The monitor leaned over and whispered to her, "You must be still. You must stop moving your ankle." She said, "But it *hurts*." He replied, "Well, there are many ankles in this room that hurt." And she said, "But it's *my* ankle!" If we have gone through certain kinds of pain, we have some sympathy for another person going through similar pain. But when another feels pain, it's simply not the same as when *we* feel it. When others say, "I feel for you," the truth is that they don't, not in the way that we do for ourselves. We have one primary objective: we want to keep pain away from ourselves so that we don't even know about it. We want to stay up in our clouds of thought about our enterprises and schemes for self-improvement.

There's nothing wrong with self-improvement as such; for example, we may decide to cut out junk food or get more exercise or more sleep. All fine. What's wrong is that we add on to such efforts the hope that self-improvement is going to insulate us from unpleasantness—the critical voice, the disappointment, the illness, the aging. By the time Michael Jordan is seventy years old, he's not likely to be floating around basketball rims as he does now. Likewise with relationships and marriage: what expectations do we load onto them?

STUDENT: We expect that they will guarantee happiness.

JOKO: Right. It's useful to work at making a good marriage. But we add on to that the hope that our partner will help us to defy gravity, and stop our fall.

As long as we think there is a difference between the sound of a dove and a critical voice, we will struggle. If we don't want that critical voice in our life and if we haven't handled our reaction to it, we are going to struggle. What is the struggle about? We all do it.

STUDENT: The struggle arises because of the difference between what's really happening and what is in our mind.

JOKO: Right. In its own subtle way, our mind is always adding, "This situation is something I do or don't like." We have an opinion.

In just hearing, there is no opinion. When the sound hits our eardrums, there is no opinion; there is just hearing. The struggle in practice is precisely at this point. All day long, sensory information comes in. But from the human point of view, only some of it is acceptable.

Does that mean that if you gently brush my hand or if you stick a sharp needle in it, I have to like them equally? No, I will have a preference. We all know that we prefer pleasant sensations. (I particularly hate to have a technician stick a needle in the end of my finger to draw blood.) There's nothing wrong with preferences as such; it's the emotion we add to them that gets us in trouble. Because of our emotions, we transform preferences into demands. Practice helps us to reverse this process, to dissolve demands back into simple preferences, without emotional freight. For example, if we have a picnic planned, a preference is, "I'd rather it didn't rain today." It has become a demand, however, if we get upset when it rains. "I got all this food and I did all this work—and now what am I going to do? Life is really unfair!"

Sitting helps us to gain an increasingly objective view of the mental creations by which we attempt to protect ourselves so we can "stay up there." We learn simply to watch the mental creations and to return to open experiencing of sensory input. Sitting is a simple endeavor.

If we are honest when we sit, however, what we find out is that we don't *want* to listen to our body. We want to *think*. We want to think about all those ideas that give us hope that our life is going to "stay up there." We don't want to give up that hope.

So the first step is to be honest. That means to see our thoughts as much as we can and to listen to the body. Until our hope is fading, we will not spend a lot of time listening to the body. Certainly we don't *want* to listen. Over years of sitting, however, that unwillingness slowly changes. Sitting is not about being blissful or happy. It's about finally seeing that there is no real difference between listening to a dove and listening to somebody criticizing us; the "difference" is only in our mind. This struggle is what practice is about. It's not about sitting in bliss for a period each morning; it's about facing our life directly, so that we see what we are really doing. Usually what we are doing is trying to manipulate our life or the lives of others. So we simply *observe* that we are trying to manipulate people or events so that "I"—this illusion built of self-centered thoughts—cannot be hurt.

Honesty: recognizing my opinions about my sitting, myself, the person sitting next to me. Honesty: "I'm really pretty irritable, pretty nasty." Such honesty enables us more and more to listen to the body—for two seconds, twenty seconds, or longer. The less hope we have that we can fix things by thinking, the longer we will be able to stay with listening to what is real. And finally we may begin to realize that there is no solution. Only egos must have solutions, but there are no solutions. At some point, we may even see that if there is no solution; there is no problem.

Talks like these are not words to ponder; we get something from them and then throw them away and return to simple, direct practice. Will we eventually be wonderful and perfect? No. We are not going to get anywhere. There is nowhere to get. We have already arrived at that place where there is no difference between the sound of a dove—and a critical voice. Our task is to recognize that we have arrived.

Joy

I'm often accused of emphasizing the difficulties in practice. The accusation is true. Believe me, the difficulties are there. If we don't recognize them and why they arise, we tend to fool ourselves. Still, the ultimate reality—not only in our sitting, but also in our lives—is joy. By joy I don't mean happiness; they're not the same. Happiness has an opposite; joy does not. As long as we seek happiness, we're going to have unhappiness, because we always swing from one pole to the other.

From time to time, we do experience joy. It can arise accidentally or in the course of our sitting or elsewhere in our lives. For a while after sesshin, we may experience joy. Over years of practice, our experience of joy deepens—if, that is, we understand practice and are willing to do it. Most people are not.

Joy isn't something we have to find. Joy is who we are if we're not preoccupied with something else. When we try to find joy, we are simply adding a thought—and an unhelpful one, at that—onto the basic fact of what we are. We don't need to go looking for joy. But we do need to do something. The question is, what? Our lives don't feel joyful, and we keep trying to find a remedy.

Our lives are basically about perception. By perception I mean whatever the senses bring in. We see, we hear, we touch, we smell, and so on. That's what life really is. Most of the time, however, we substitute another activity for perception; we cover it over with something else, which I'll call evaluation. By evaluation, I don't mean an objective, dispassionate analysis—as for example when we look over a messy room and consider or evaluate how to clean it up. The evaluation I have in mind is ego centered: "Is this next episode in my life going to bring me something I like, or not? Is it going to hurt, or isn't it? Is it pleasant or unpleasant? Does it make me important or unimportant? Does it give me something material?" It's our nature to evaluate in this way. To the extent that we give ourselves over to evaluation of this kind, joy will be missing from our lives.

It's amazing how quickly we can switch into evaluation. Perhaps we're functioning pretty well—and then suddenly somebody criticizes what we're doing. In a fraction of a second, we jump into our thoughts. We're quite willing to get into that interesting space of judging others or ourselves. There's a lot of drama in all of this, and we like it, more than we realize. Unless the drama becomes lengthy and punishing, we enter willingly into it, because as human beings we have a basic orientation toward drama. From an ordinary point of view, to be in a world of pure perception is pretty dull.

Suppose we've been away on vacation for a week, and we come back. Perhaps we've enjoyed ourselves, or we think we have. When we return to work, the "In" box is loaded with things to do, and scattered all over the desk are little messages, "While You Were Out." When people call us at work, it usually means that they want something. Perhaps the job we left for someone else to take care of has been neglected. Immediately, we're evaluating the situation. "Who fouled up?" "Who slacked off?" "Why is she calling? I bet it's the same old problem." "It's their responsibility anyway. Why are they calling me?" Likewise, at the end of sesshin we may experience the flow of a joyful life; then we wonder where it goes. Though it doesn't go anywhere, something has happened: a cloud covers the clarity.

Until we know that joy is exactly what's happening, minus our opinion of it, we're going to have only a small amount of joy. When we stay with perception rather than getting lost in evaluation, however, joy can be the person who didn't do the job while we were gone. It can be the interesting encounter on the phone with all of the people we have to call, no matter what they want. Joy can be having a sore throat; it can be getting laid off; it can be unexpectedly having to work overtime. It can be having to take a math exam or dealing with one's former spouse who wants more money. Usually we don't think that these things are joy.

Practice is about dealing with suffering. It's not that the suffering is important or valuable in itself, but that suffering is our teacher. It's the other side of life, and until we can see all of life, there's not going to be any joy. To be honest, sesshin is controlled suffering. We get a chance to face our suffering in a practice situation. As we sit, all the traditional attributes of a good Zen student come under fire: endurance, humility, patience, compassion. These things sound great in books, but they're not so attractive when we're hurting. That's why sesshin ought not to be easy: we need to learn to be with our suffering and still act appropriately. When we learn to be with our experience, whatever it is, we are more aware of the joy that is our life. Sesshin is a good chance to learn this lesson. When we're prepared to practice, suffering can be a fortunate thing. None of us wants to recognize this fact. I certainly try to avoid suffering; there are lots of things I don't want happening in my life. Still, if we can't learn to be our experience even when it hurts, we'll never know joy. Joy is being the circumstances of our life just as they are. If someone's been unfair to us, that's it. If someone's telling lies about us, that's it also.

The material wealth of this country in some ways makes it more difficult for us to experience the basic joy that we are. Travelers to India sometimes report that along with the enormous poverty, there is an extraordinary joy. Faced with life and death all the time, the people have learned something that is hard for most of us: they have learned to appreciate each moment. We don't do very well with that. Our very prosperity—all of the things we take for granted and all of the things we want more of—is in a way a barrier. There are other barriers, more basic ones. But our wealth is certainly part of the problem.

In practice, we return over and over again to perception, to just sitting. Practice is just hearing, just seeing, just feeling. This is what Christians call the face of God: simply taking in this world as it manifests. We feel our body; we hear the cars and birds. That's all there is. But we are unwilling to stay in that space for more than a few seconds. We go shooting off, remembering what happened to us last week or thinking about what's going to happen next week. We obsess about persons that we're having trouble with or about our work or whatever. There's nothing wrong with these ideas popping up, but if we get stuck in them, we're into the world of evaluation from our self-centered viewpoint. Most of us spend most of our lives in this viewpoint.

It's natural to think, "If I didn't have such a difficult partner (or difficult roommate or difficult something else), then I know my life would be much calmer. I would be much better able to appreciate my life." That might be true for a short time. Life would feel better for a time, of course. But such comfort is not as valuable as facing what upsets us, because it's this very upset (our tendency to get attached to our dramas, to get involved in them and get our mind racing and our emotions fired up) that is the barrier. There is no real joy in such a life, no joy at all. So we run from difficulties; we try to eliminate something—our partner, our roommate, our whatever—so that we can find a perfect place where nothing can upset us. Does anybody have a place like that? Where could it be? What could even approximate it? Years ago I used to allow myself ten minutes a day to daydream about a tropical island, and every day I would furnish my little hut. My fantasy life got better and better. Finally, I had all of the conveniences. Wonderful food just showed up, and there was the gentle ocean and a lagoon, just right for swimming, next to the hut. It's fine to daydream consciously if there is a time limit. But my dream couldn't exist, except in my mind. There is no place on earth where we can be free of ourselves. If we were sitting in a cave meditating, we'd still be thinking about something: "How noble of me it is to sit in this cave!" And after a while: "What excuse can I invent to get out of here and not look bad?" If we stop ourselves and find out what we're really feeling or thinking, we'll notice—

even if we're working hard—a thin veil of self-concern over our activity. Enlightenment is simply not doing this. Enlightenment is simply doing what we're doing totally, responding to things as they come up. The modern term is "being in the flow." Joy is just this: something comes up; I perceive it. Something is needed, and I do it, and then the next thing, and the next. I take some time out for a walk or to talk to my friends. There is no problem in a life lived in this way. The joy would never stop, unless I interrupt it with evaluation: reacting to events as problems, blaming, rejecting, straining. "I don't want to do that." When what comes up doesn't fit my idea of what I want to do, I have a problem. If the activity is one I enjoy, I may also drain it of joy. Can you think of examples?

STUDENT: I try to be perfect at it.

STUDENT: I think that doing it makes me important.

STUDENT: I stop paying attention to it and just think about getting it done.

STUDENT: I start to compare myself with others and get competitive.

STUDENT: I worry about whether I'm doing it right.

STUDENT: I start to worry that it will come to an end.

JOKO: Good. And below the conscious level, there is our deep-seated conditioning, the unconscious motives that drive us to do what we do. All that stuff floats up in time. Even when we have an activity that we like in life, even if we have a partner whom we basically like, the nature of being human is to keep trying to fix things, which takes away the joy. Any self-centered evaluation of a situation will obscure the pure perception which is joy itself. When such thoughts arise, we just see the thoughts and let them go, see the thoughts and let them go, see the thoughts and let them go. We return to the experience of whatever's going on. That is what brings joy into view.

Good sitting doesn't mean that we suddenly have some clear space in which nothing's happening. That may happen occasionally, but it's not important. What is necessary for good sitting is that more and more we are willing to be aware of whatever is happening. We're willing to be aware that, "Yes, I do nothing but think about Tahiti. Isn't that interesting." Or "I broke up with my boyfriend six months ago and what am I doing? All of my thoughts are stuck there. How interesting!" Emotions build out of this kind of thinking—depression, worry, anxiety—and we're stuck in our obsessions. Where's the joy?

For most of us, to stay in the present moment and to keep reminding ourselves that that's what we're here to do, is suffering. We have to be willing to do this practice not just when we're sitting, but for the rest of our lives. If we do, then we increase the percentage of our lives in which we experience joy. In order to do this, we have to pay a price, however. Some people will pay it; some people won't. People sometimes imagine that I can produce joy for them; they think I have some magic. But I can't do anything for others except to tell them what to do. I can't do it for anybody except myself. That's why, if practice is made too easy and there's no price to be paid, we don't ever turn the key in the lock to that door. If we keep running in our life from everything that displeases us, the key never turns.

We should not push ourselves excessively. Depending on our capacity, we may need to back off, to withdraw. But if we withdraw, we can be sure that our problems stay right with us. When we "run away" from our problems, the problems stay right with us. They like us, and they'll stay right with us until we pay some real attention to them. We say we want to be one with the world, when what we really want is for the world to please us. If we are to be "one with the world," we must go through years of meticulous practice, of hacking away. There is no shortcut, no way to a life of relative ease and joy, without paying a price. We must see that we get embroiled in our personal stuff, just notice it, and return to this world of pure perception, which doesn't interest us at all, for the most part.

Suzuki Roshi once said, "From the ordinary point of view, to be enlightened would seem pretty dull." There's no drama in it whatsoever; there's just simply being here.

We differ in our ability to be with our perception. But we all have the capacity. It may manifest at a slightly different rate, but we all have the capacity. Since we're human, we can be awake, and we can always increase the amount of time we are awake. When we're awake, the moment transforms: it begins to feel good; it gives us power to do the next thing. This capacity can always increase. We must be aware of what we are this second. If we're angry, we have to know this. We have to feel it. We have to see what thoughts are involved. If we're bored, this is definitely something to investigate. If we're discouraged, we need to notice this. If we're caught up in judgment or self-righteousness, we need to notice this. If we don't see these things, they rule the roost.

To sum up: as we sit, two activities are occurring: One is pure perception, just sitting here. The content of that perception can be anything. The other activity is evaluation: jumping out of pure perception into our self-centered judgments about everything. In sitting, we deal with this tension, this strain, and this repetitive thinking. We have to deal with our residual conditioning; it's the only way to joy. We deal with what's happening right here, right now.

Chaos and Wonder

As I talk with students, I hear many things about why they sit: "I want to know myself better." "I want my life to be more integrated." "I want to be healthier." "I want to know the universe." "I want to know what life is." "I'm lonely." "I want a relationship." "I want my relationship to go better." There are endless variations on these and other motivations for practice. They are all absolutely fine; there's nothing wrong with them. But if we think that the point of sitting is to accomplish these things, then we misunderstand what we are doing. It's true, we have to begin to know ourselves and our emotions and how they work. We need to sense the relationship of our emotions to our physical health. We have to look at our lack of integration and all that this lack implies. Sitting touches every aspect of our lives; yet when we forget one thing, we have forgotten everything. Without it, nothing else works. It's hard to give it a name. We might call it wonder. When we forget the wonder of that which we encounter, then we're in trouble; our lives don't work.

It's true that through our practice, we need to make good contact with the things I've mentioned above: emotions, tension, health—these and other factors. Until we have become used to making these connections, the wonder doesn't appear. Our connection does not have to be complete, but only when we're not fussing around with all of these factors do we see the wonder. For example: if I am with someone who simply irritates me, I have forgotten the wonder of the person. Another example: the wonder of doing a job that I don't want to do. Yesterday, I decided to clean the space under the sink. That's one job we tend to forget. Yet there was wonder in that, too: just wondering at the little bits of dirt and other stuff I found.

The wonder isn't something else, different from what we do. We think of wonder as an ecstatic state, and wonder can be ecstatic. Driving across the Rockies, viewing the Grand Canyon—such scenes are so spectacular that for a moment we see the wonder in them. Such experiences may have a strong emotional dimension. But wonder isn't always emotional, nor could we spend all of our time in such an emotional state.

We may suppose that wonder is found only in certain special activities. "Maybe artists and musicians find it easy to see the wonder. But I'm an accountant. Where's the wonder in that?" Even if artists and musicians do contact the wonder in their specific areas, they may not see it elsewhere. It might seem, for example, that physicists and other scientists are far from the wonder of life. Yet I've been around physicists a lot, and I have discovered that it's very important to physicists that a solution be elegant. That's an interesting word to pop up in the middle of a lot of mathematics and computers. I once asked a physicist why he used the word. He said simply, "Any good solution has to be elegant." When I asked him what that meant, he said that elegance meant stripping down to the essence so that one doesn't have a lot of extras. There is wonder in that. The solution may not even be true; physicists deal in theory. In a sense, no formula is true. There's nothing "true" about any relationship, either. But at this moment, a relationship can be—just the wonder. If we don't realize this, we don't realize our practice.

Practice isn't simply being integrated or being healthy or being a good person, though all of these things are part of practice. Practice is about the wonder. If you want to check your own practice, the next time something comes up in your life that you can't stand, ask yourself, "Where's the wonder here?" That's what increases as we practice. We gain ability to see the wonder of life no matter what it is and regardless of whether we like it or don't like it. For example, when we approach a relationship in this way, we can say, "I love you for what you are and I love you for what you are not." Instead of faultfinding—

"You talk too much. You never talk. You leave your clothes everywhere. You never clean off the kitchen counter. You pick on me all the time"—the wonder shines through. "I love you for what you are, and I love you for what you are not."

How do we know if our practice is a real practice? Only by one thing: more and more, we just see the wonder. What is the wonder? I don't know. We can't know such things through thinking. But we always know it when it's there.

Sometimes I can't see the wonder at all, though I see it much more than I did five years ago. A real practice moves us along a continuum toward more and more awareness of the wonder. I don't mean being in some blissful state; it may be just the wonder of seeing a person we don't like. "How wonderful—she's just as she is!" Or we may see it in someone who has a serious illness. Such a person may have such a powerful presence that it lights up the whole space around them.

As you go through your day, through your little upsets and difficulties, ask yourself, "Where is the wonder?" It's always there. Wonder is the nature of life itself. If we don't feel it, we just keep doing our practice; we can't force ourselves to feel it. We can only work with the barrier we are facing. The barrier is created by ourselves; it's not caused by what has happened to us. That's part of the wonder, too. If you know what I'm talking about, fine. If you don't know what I'm talking about, that's also fine. Both are part of the wonder: to know or not to know; either way, it's all fine.

STUDENT: I've been thinking a lot about the conflict with Iraq. I can't see any wonder in that at all.

STUDENT: I can't help but feel that the conflict is horrible. Under that feeling, I feel fear. We don't want to see the wonder because we're stuck in the fear.

JOKO: Yes, that's generally true.

STUDENT: When I think of the conflict, I sense some wonder in the prospects of greater world unification.

JOKO: Yes. As a person, I look at the conflict with horror. But the chaos is itself interesting. In the discipline of physics, there is a relatively new field called chaos theory. The war is producing chaos. With the chaos comes new possibilities. Everything is being shaken up, and from now on, the whole Middle East is going to be different. Our relationships to everybody involved are going to be different. Their relationships to everything are going to be different. We can't see the order in the chaos because we're human. It's not necessarily bad; even in horror there is wonder. Wonder is that which is happening. And we can't judge or assess that. Of course, if I could prevent the killing, I would. None of it makes sense; it's just chaos, and yet the chaos is not chaos—it's wonder. From chaos comes new order, which in turn becomes chaos. That's what life is. Peace for us is being willing to be with the chaos. That doesn't mean we don't take action. But even our action is part of the chaos. We always have two points of view: our personal point of view and that which develops through sitting, which is the wonder. For example: it's terrible that so many millions of people were killed in the last war; yet from the point of view of the welfare of the earth, fewer people are better. The earth has too many people already. If I'm one of the people who was killed or if someone I know was killed, of course to me personally it was a disaster. Yet life on earth cannot be kept in a fixed position. Saddam Hussein is the next piece on the chessboard; as he moves, everybody moves and there's going to be chaos. Is that good or bad? Neither. It's just what it is.

STUDENT: It's like a cancer cell: we want to reduce the cancer cell because it's trying to harm the whole body.

JOKO: But the cancer cell doesn't view it that way. It's just doing what it's doing.

STUDENT: We want to take steps to do something about the cancer; yet at a certain point we can also realize it is wonder.

JOKO: We can be fighting the cancer, doing everything we can to survive, and at the same time we can sense the wonder of this process that we are. If I had cancer, I'd fight it right down the line. I'm a fighter. At the same time, the wonder is always present.

STUDENT: It seems as though the last thing I want to see is the wonder.

JOKO: You're right. The last thing we want to see is the wonder because it's humbling; we always feel insulted to some degree. Everything in life is the wonder, but since life as it is almost never suits us, we can't see the wonder. Then we puzzle over why we're so miserable. What we're banishing from our life is what we truly want and need.

STUDENT: Thinking about the new balance in the Middle East reminds me of the extra tensions in my relationship recently. We're going through our own little battles and changes, and we're working out new balancing. It's like a microcosm of what's going on in various parts of the world. And by watching the Middle East conflict, I can see a bit more clearly what's happening to me right now at home.

STUDENT: When I lived in the Middle East for three years, a point of view that many Arabs hold came through clearly to me. In this country we get much of our oil from that area; yet we waste much of what we use. We have a greedy need for oil. Our greed is out of control, and we're taking someone else's resources to satisfy our own greed. It's part of the chaos. There is an Arab perspective on these questions that is really quite valid.

STUDENT: Recently I returned from a trip to Africa. While traveling in Africa, I would sometimes encounter Arab men in their flowing robes. I noticed my reaction to them, based upon things I had been told about how oppressive some Arab cultures are to women. I felt my body getting tight. One day as I was walking down the aisle on a plane and brushing past one of these Arab men, he said, "Excuse me," and he looked into my eyes and smiled. At that moment something opened to me, and I saw him simply as a person and not as an Arab.

STUDENT: I'm often fascinated by all the chaos around me. I watch the conflict in my own mind, and other people tell me of the things that they're going through, and then I see the people going to work in Los Angeles county. It's a huge confusion, and almost everybody gets to work. It's almost unbelievable! If I imagine someone out there trying to choreograph it all—"Move, move, move!"—it would be totally impossible. Everything seems pressed to the breaking point. Yet because of the pressure, people back off a bit and let others in, and the whole thing flows. It's fascinating that it works at all.

JOKO: Once while flying to Los Angeles, I was talking with a fellow passenger who was a city planner. He looked out the window, down at the freeways and buildings, and said, "It can't hold together much longer!" But things do hold together because there's an adjustment that takes place. Somehow people adapt.

STUDENT: I notice that I relax because of the inevitability of the chaos—and perhaps others do, too. Maybe that's what keeps the city from being more insane than it is. Anyone who drives any distance on a freeway or a crowded street actually has to let go, in order to cope. It's a time in the frenetic city when people have to let it be, and let go to what's happening. It's a sort of spiritual play.

JOKO: In the fighting in the Middle East and elsewhere, we see the end result of the inner violence in all of us. We imagine that we can solve our problems by external fighting and war. We spend unbelievable amounts on armaments; yet our child mortality rate is one of the highest in the industrialized world. That's part of the chaos, too. It's fine to take a personal point of view, and try to change these things. But our personal point of view needs to be balanced by a recognition that millions of things—far more than we can ever comprehend—are coming together, shifting, and changing, all the time.

Until we face our own situation, with all the chaos in our lives, we can't do much else in any effective way. There's going to be chaos in any case, but when we face it, we see it differently. We don't want to face it, however. We want to live inside the boxes we have created and just keep redecorating the walls rather than breaking out the door. We really like our prisons; that's one reason that practice is so difficult. Resistance is the very nature of being human.

A person like Saddam Hussein does not appear out of a vacuum, for no reason; he is the result of many, many circumstances, just as Hitler was. We shouldn't think, however, that if the whole world did zazen, there would be no chaos. That's not it either. The chaos will continue. We don't need to worry about that. But if we practice, in time we are more willing for things to be the way they are. We'll continue to have personal preferences about how things should go, but not personal demands. Preferences and demands are very different. When things don't go the way we prefer, we adjust much more quickly to how they are. That's what happens after years of sitting. If you're looking for something else—well, sorry. . . .

Paradoxically, learning to be with the chaos brings a deep kind of peace. But it's not what we usually picture to ourselves.

STUDENT: Is that the wonder?

JOKO: That's the wonder.

VIII

NOTHING SPECIAL

From Drama to No Drama

In Zen practice we move from a life of drama—a kind of soap opera—to a life of no drama. Despite what we may say, we all like our personal dramas very much. The reason? No matter what our particular drama is, we are always at the center of it—which is where we want to be. And through practice, we gradually shift away from that self-preoccupation. Thus, to move from a life of drama to a life of no drama, though it sounds extremely dull, is what Zen practice is about. Let's look at this process more closely.

When we begin sitting, it's good to begin with several big breaths, filling up the abdominal area, the middle chest, and the upper chest until we're full of air, and then just letting it out and holding the exhalation for a moment. Do this three or four times. In a sense, it's artificial, but it helps to create a certain balance and forms a good basis for sitting. Once we've done this, the next step is to forget it: forget controlling our breath. We won't entirely forget, of course, but it's useless to control the breath. Instead, just experience it, which is very different. We're not trying to make the breath long, slow, and even, as many books suggest. Instead, what we want is to let the breath be the boss, so that the breath is breathing us. If the breath is shallow, let it be that. As we become our breathing, the breath of its own accord starts to slow down. The breath stays shallow because we want to think rather than experience our lives. When we do this, everything becomes more shallow and controlled. The word *uptight* is very apt; it describes this condition well. We're drawn up into our head, throat, shoulders; we're scared, and our breath comes up, too. A breath that stays down (as it tends to do after years of sitting) is one where the mind has given up hope. All that we hope for, we slowly give up, and the breath stays down. It's not something we have to try to do. The practice is simply to experience the breath as it is.

We also think we should have a quiet mind. Many books say this: that to become enlightened is to have a quiet mind. It's true: when we have no hope, our mind quiets. As long as we have hope, our mind is trying to figure out how to fulfill those wonderful things that we want to happen to us, or trying to protect ourselves from all the terrible things that shouldn't happen. And so the mind is anything but quiet. Now, instead of forcing the mind to become quiet, what can we do? We can be conscious of what it's doing. That's what labeling our thoughts is about. Instead of being caught up in hope, we begin to see, "Oh, yeah, for the twentieth time today, I'm hoping for relief." After a good sesshin, we may have said it five hundred times: "I hope he'll call me when sesshin is over." And so we label: "Having a hope he'll call me when sesshin is over." "Having a hope he'll call me when sesshin is over." When we've said that five hundred times, what happens to it? We see it for what it is: nonsense. After all, the truth is that he either will or won't call. As we watch the mind over the years, the hopes slowly wear out. And we're left with what? It may seem gruesome, I know: we're left with life *as it is*.

It's useful to go about this process with an attitude of investigation. Instead of viewing our sitting as good or bad, something that should steadily improve, we should simply investigate, watch what we're really doing. There is no good or bad sitting; there is only awareness or unawareness of what is going on in our life. And when we maintain more awareness, the questions we have about our life are seen in a new light. We're left not with another viewpoint, but with a different way of seeing things. As this process develops over time, very slowly the mind quiets—not completely, and what quiets is not the thoughts. (We can be sitting twenty years, and have thoughts rushing through our minds.) What quiets is our *attachment* to our thoughts. We see them more and more as just a show, like watching children at play. (My mind thinks practically all the time. Let it think, if it wants.) It's our *attachment* to the thoughts that blocks samadhi. We can have lots of thoughts, yet be in deep samadhi, so long as we're not attaching to them and are just experiencing. It is true that the longer we sit, the less we tend to think, because we tend to obsess less. So, the mind does become quieter, though certainly not because we say to ourselves, "I *have* to have a quiet mind!"

As we sit, from time to time we gain different insights about our lives. Insights themselves are neither good nor bad, and from the point of Zen practice, they're not even particularly important. Though they may have some usefulness, zazen is not about gaining insights. They do occur; we suddenly see, "Oh, yeah—that's what I do. Interesting." Yet even grasping the insight is just stuff that's coming and going, coming and going through our minds. We become scientists living this experiment called our lives. Our selves and our thinking are spread out in front of us; we look at the show with interest, but not as our own personal drama. The more of this perspective we develop, the better our lives are. For example: if we're doing an experiment on salt and sugar, we don't say, "That's terrible! The salt and the sugar are fighting!" We don't care what the salt and the sugar are doing, we just watch them and observe their interaction. In contrast, we usually *do* care about what our thoughts are doing. We don't just watch them with interest, as scientists just watch to see what happens. "If I mix this and this—interesting. If I mix in different proportions—interesting." The scientist simply watches and observes.

When this quality of watching, observing, and experiencing our lives gets stronger, reality (which is just awareness) encounters unreality, our little drama of thoughts. And we see more clearly what is real and what is unreal, as light illumines the darkness. But when we bring more reality (awareness) into our lives, what had been dark and troublesome seems to change. When we bring more awareness into our lives, we begin to eliminate our personal dramas. And we don't really want to do this. We *like* our personal dramas, and we like to maintain them. Each of us has his or her own pet story; for example, we may believe, "My circumstances are particularly bad. My childhood was worse than most." Or, "That one experience has really wrecked things for me." It's true, these events happened, and they have created our conditioning. But so long as we maintain our beliefs that the stories we tell are the truth of our lives, genuine practice will not take place. The beliefs block practice.

Unless there is some willingness to abandon these personal life beliefs, there's nothing that I or anyone else can do. Sometimes enough suffering will itself create that little chink into which awareness can enter. But until that little gap occurs, there's nothing anyone can do. And people who are really stubborn can maintain their personal stories until they're dead. Such persons have hard lives. A personal belief of this kind— "I am a victim"—is like a dark closet. If we want to sit in this closet with the door shut tightly, nothing can get in. Unfortunately, so long as we insist upon sitting in this closet (and we all do, sometimes), we find that no one really wants to come in and sit with us. Frankly, nobody is particularly interested in someone else's drama. What we're interested in is our own. I may want to shut myself in my own closet, but I'm certainly not going to sit in yours.

We all get in our particular closets. The closet is our personal drama, and we want to be alone in it, to sense ourselves at the very center of it. It's a juicy misery. And whether we realize it or not, we love it. But when we've had the experience of opening the door and letting the light in, once we've seen what it's like to have some genuine light in the closet, we never can stay in the closet indefinitely again. It may take us years, but eventually we'll open the door. One way of looking at sesshin is that it forces that door open for some of us. That's why sesshin can be uncomfortable.

At some point, we begin to see that what happens in our life is not the issue; there will always be something happening. What happens will always be a mix of what we like and what we don't like. There's no time when that ceases. As we become more of the scientist, however, we are less caught up in what's happening and more able simply to observe what's happening. The ability and willingness to do this kind of observing increases over years of practice. At first it may be minimal. Our job is to increase this willingness and this ability.

In the end, it doesn't matter how we feel. It's not important whether we feel depressed, jittery, scattered, happy. The job of the student is to look, experience, be aware. For example, depression, completely experienced, ceases to be depression and becomes samadhi. Jitteriness can also be experienced, and as we experience it, a shift occurs, and we don't have to worry about being jittery. No circumstance, no feeling, is the point. The point is the opportunity to experience.

We often suppose that we have to dredge up submerged psychological "stuff" and work on it. That's not quite true. After all, where is this stuff hidden? It's not really accurate to suppose that there is some stuff underneath consciousness that will work its way out, though it may feel that way to us. During sesshins we may become emotional, sad, desperate, but these emotions are not hidden mysteries that suddenly appear. This is just who we are, and we're experiencing who we are. When we try to work this stuff out, it's just another form of self-improvement that doesn't work. Practice is not a matter of sitting so that our stuff can come up in order that we can work on it and make ourselves better. The fact is, we're already fine. It's not a question of going somewhere.

We block our awareness by our guilt and by our ideals. For example, suppose I've told someone, "I'm just not a good teacher. I don't handle every situation perfectly." By becoming attached to that thought, I have blocked any capability of learning. Guilt and ideals of how I *should be* block the only thing that matters, a clear awareness: "I see what's happening, I did goof up, didn't I? Well, what can I learn?" Another example might be a cook worried about dinner. Suppose the dinner *is* burned. The cook doesn't have to go into "Oh! it's the end of the world! What will people think of me, I just burnt everything!" At that point, what can be done? Simply look for every loaf of bread in the house and pass it out. It's not the end of the world if the dinner burns. But guilt blocks learning.

The only thing that matters is awareness of what's going on. When we get into ideals and guilt, decisions themselves become difficult, because we don't see how we're caught in our worries: "Is it going to benefit me? What will happen? Is it really a good move? Is my life going to be more secure, more wonderful, more perfect?" Those are the wrong questions. What are the right questions? And what are the right decisions? We can't say in advance, but at some point, we will know, if we don't get caught up in the guilt, the ideals, and the perfectionism we usually bring to our decisions. Sitting is about this kind of clarification.

All techniques are useful, and all are limited. Whatever technique we bring into our practice will serve us for a while— until we start not really using it or drifting with it or dreaming. So the important thing with any technique is our intent. We must intend to be present, to be aware, to be practicing. And nobody has that intent all the time. We have it intermittently. We also want to find a teacher who is going to take care of all of this for us; we all want to be saved and taken care of. The intent to practice is the most important thing. There's no technique that will save us, no teacher who will save us, no center that will save us. There's no *anything* that will save us. That's the cruelest blow of all.

Turning our lives of drama to lives of no drama means turning a life where we're constantly seeking, analyzing, hoping, and dreaming into one of just experiencing life as it appears, right now. The key factor is awareness, just experiencing the pain as it is. Paradoxically, this is joy. There is no other joy on this earth except this.

This kind of practice has a deadly effect: it will take away our drama. It doesn't take away our personality. We're all different, and we will remain different. But the drama is not real. It is the blockage to a functioning, caring life.

Simple Mind

The only mind that can sense life in a transformed way is a simple mind. The dictionary defines *simple* as "having or composed of one part only." Awareness can take in a multiplicity of things, just as an eye can take in many details at once. But awareness itself is one thing only. It remains unchanged, without additions or modifications. Awareness is completely simple; we don't have to add anything to it or change it. It is unassuming or unpretentious; it can't help but be that way. Awareness is not a thing, to be affected by this or that. When we live from pure awareness, we are not affected by our past, our present, or our future. Because awareness has nothing it can pretend to, it's humble. It is lowly. Simple.

Practice is about developing or uncovering a simple mind. For example, I often hear people complain that they feel overwhelmed by their lives. To be overwhelmed is to be caught by all the objects, the thoughts, the events of life, and to be affected emotionally by them, so that we feel angry and upset. When we feel like that, we may do and say things that hurt ourselves or other people. Unlike the simple mind of pure awareness, we are confused by the multiplicity of the external environment. Then we can't see that everything external is us. We can't see that everything exists in us until we can live eighty or ninety percent out of a simple mind. Practice is about developing this kind of mind. It is not easy. It takes endless patience, diligence, and determination.

Within this simplicity, this awareness, we understand past, present, and future, and we begin to be less affected by the barrage of experiences. We can live our life with appreciation and some compassion. No longer does our life revolve around judgments, such as: "Oh, he's so hard on me. I'm such a victim." "You hurt my feelings." "You're not the way I want you to be."

People sometimes tell me that after sesshin, life just flows, without any problem. The same issues are there, but they present less difficulty. That happens because in sesshin, mind becomes more simple. Unfortunately, we tend to lose this simplicity, because we again become caught in what appears to be a very complex life around us. We feel that things aren't the way we want them to be, and we begin to struggle and to be at the mercy of our emotions. When this happens, we often behave in destructive ways.

The longer we sit, the more we have periods—at first brief, then longer—when we sense that we don't need to be opposed to others, even when they are difficult. Instead of seeing them as problems, we begin to enjoy their foibles, without having to fix them. For example, we can enjoy the fact that they're too silent, or they talk too much, or they put on too much makeup. To enjoy the world without judgment is what a realized life is like. It takes years and years and years of practice. Even then, I don't mean that every problem can be experienced without reaction; still, a shift occurs, and we move away from a purely reactive life, in which everything that happens can trigger our favorite defense.

A simple mind is not mysterious. In a simple mind, awareness just is. It's open, transparent. There's nothing complicated about it. For most of us most of the time, however, it is largely unavailable. But the more we have contact with a simple mind, the more we sense that everything is ourselves, and the more we feel responsibility for everything. When we sense our connectedness, we have to act differently.

When we get caught in our own thinking, we're not doing our work—feeling the past and the future, all in the present. We even imagine that if we're isolated in a room by ourselves, just being upset, it's okay. The truth is, however, that when we indulge ourselves in this way, we're not doing our work, and the whole of our life is affected. When we maintain awareness, whether we know it or not, healing is taking place. If we practice long enough we begin to sense the truth: we come to understand that the "now" embraces the past and future and the present. When we can sit with a simple mind, not being caught by our own thoughts, something slowly dawns, and a door that has been shut begins to open. For that to occur, we have to work with our anger, our upset, our judgments, our self-pity, our ideas that the past determines the present. As the door opens, we see that the present is absolute and that, in a sense, the whole universe begins right now, in each second. And the healing of life is in that second of simple awareness.

Healing is always just being here, with a simple mind.

Dorothy and the Locked Door

We're all looking for something. Most human beings feel a kind of incompleteness and are looking for something that will fill up the hole they feel. Even those who say, "I'm not looking; I'm content with my life," are looking also, in their own way. And so people come to this or that church, to Zen centers or yoga centers, to personal growth workshops—with the hope of finding this missing piece.

Let me tell you about a little girl named Dorothy. Dorothy did not live in Kansas, but in San Diego, in an enormous old Victorian house. Her family had lived there for generations. Everybody had his or her own room, and there were extra rooms and cubbyholes everywhere, as well as an attic and a basement. When Dorothy was still a tiny girl, she learned that there was something odd about the house: up on the top floor of that old Victorian mansion there was a locked room. As far back as people could remember, the room had always been locked. There was a rumor that once it had been unlocked, but no one knew what was in the room. The lock on the door to the room was strange, and no one had ever been able to find a way to open it. The windows to the room were blocked somehow, too. Once Dorothy had climbed up a ladder on the outside of the house and tried to peer inside. But she could see nothing.

Most of the family just got used to the room with its locked door. They knew it was there, but they didn't want to concern themselves. So it was just not mentioned. Dorothy was different, however. From the time that she was small, she was obsessed with that room and what was in there. She felt that she *had* to get it unlocked.

In most ways, Dorothy lived her life like a normal little girl. She grew; she had pigtails; she became a teenager; she got the latest hairdo; she had her best girlfriend, her best boyfriend; she got excited about the newest makeup and the latest hit song. She was pretty normal. But she never lost her obsession with the locked room. In a way, it dominated her life. Sometimes she would go up and sit in front of the room and just look at that door and wonder about it.

As Dorothy got a bit older, she sensed that the room had some connection with what was missing in her life. So she began various trainings and practices in the hope of finding the secret to opening the door. She tried out lots of different things: she went to this and that center, and this and that teacher, searching for the formula to unlock the door. She went to workshops; she got herself rebirthed; she tried hypnosis. She did everything; yet nothing unlocked the door for her. Her searching went on for years, all through college and into graduate school. She developed techniques to put herself into various mental states, but she was still unable to open the door.

Then one day when she came home, the house was deserted. She went upstairs to the top floor and sat in front of the locked door. Using one of her esoteric practices, she went into a deep state of meditation. On an impulse, she reached out a hand and pushed on the door—and it began to open. She was terrified. In all the long years of trying to unlock the door, nothing like this had ever happened. Dorothy was frightened and excited at the same time. Trembling, she made herself go through the door. And found. . . .

Disappointment and confusion. Dorothy found herself not in a strange, new, wonderful space in the mysterious room, but right back on the first floor of that old Victorian house, in the midst of all the old, familiar things. She had the same view, she was in the same location with the usual furniture; everything was just as it always had been. Disappointed and puzzled at the same time, some hours later she climbed the stairs to the top floor and went to the mysterious room. The door was still locked. Dorothy had opened the door—and she hadn't opened it.

Life went on. Dorothy got married. She had a couple of children. She still lived in the Victorian house, with her family. She was a good wife and mother. Still, she never gave up her obsession. In fact, her one experience of opening the door motivated her even more. She spent a lot of time on the top floor in front of the locked door, sitting cross-legged, trying to open the door. She'd done it once before, she could do it again. And sure enough, after years of trying, it happened again: she pushed on the door, and it opened. She thought excitedly to herself, "This will be the time!" She went through the door—and again found herself back on the first floor of that same old Victorian house, living with her husband and children. She raced up the stairs to the mysterious room, and what did she find? The door was locked.

What can you do? A locked door is a locked door. Dorothy continued her life. The kids grew. She acquired a few gray hairs. Dorothy still spent a lot of time sitting in front of the locked door, however. She was a fairly good wife and mother, but her attention was still mostly on the locked room. And she was a persistent, diligent person; she didn't give up easily. From time to time, she would manage to open the door and move through it, but always she ended up on the first floor, right back where she lived.

All the while, the house was slowly filling up with stuff. The family members seemed to accumulate more and more things, and the extra rooms became storerooms for junk. The house became so stuffed that there was no room for guests at all and hardly enough space for the family themselves. There was no room in the house for anything but Dorothy, her husband, and her children—which was just as well, because they were all so concerned about themselves that they could hardly think about taking care of anything else.

Gradually, Dorothy's obsession wore down. Her struggle to open that door began to get a bit old. Instead of spending so much time up in front of the door, she spent a bit more time with her children and her grandchildren, and taking care of the house: getting the floors refinished, redoing the drapes, and so on. The house was not in bad shape, but it had been a little neglected, because Dorothy had been busy sitting in front of the door. Her attention slowly shifted back into taking care of the everyday things that needed to be taken care of. It was a slow process. Occasionally she would go up to the top floor and look at the door, but if she opened it, she knew what she'd find. Very slowly, discouragement and disappointment settled in. More and more, she forgot about anything except just living her life, taking care of things, moment to moment. And then one day she was up on the top floor and she happened to look over at the door that was locked. Wow! It was wide open! Inside, in plain sight, was a comfortable guest room. There was a fine bed and a dresser and all of the small items that would make a guest comfortable.

Seeing this wonderful, spacious guest room, Dorothy realized what had become of the rest of the house. She saw how crowded and cramped everything was and how difficult it was to move around freely in the house. With that realization, change began. Without her doing much of anything, the rooms in that old Victorian mansion began to unstuff themselves. There began to be room for more and more things and people in the house. Space appeared. It was as if all the stuff was insubstantial, ghostly junk. It wasn't really there, after all. The house returned to what it had been all along. In fact, there had always been plenty of space for guests, and Dorothy now realized that the door had never been locked in the first place; it was always open. Only her rigid pushing had kept it shut.

This is our basic illusion about practice: that the door is locked. The illusion is inevitable: we all have it, to some degree. As long as we think the door is shut, it *is* shut. To try to open it, we do everything. We go to this or that center; we do workshops; we try this or that. Ultimately we find that the door was never shut.

Yet Dorothy's life of vain effort was perfect for her. That's what she had to do. In fact, that's what we all have to do. We have to give our practice everything we have, in order to realize that from the very beginning, there's nothing but perfection. The room is open, the house is open, if we don't clutter it with our phantom junk. But there's no way to know this until we know it.

A form of Christian spiritual discipline is the practice of the presence of God. As Christians, we are looking for that radiance in all things that mystics call the face of God. That radiance is not hidden in some far-off place, but is here and now, right under our noses. Likewise, Dorothy realized that what she had been seeking all her life was simply her life itself: the people, the house, the rooms. All were the face of God.

But we don't see that. If we really saw it, we wouldn't torture ourselves and each other as we do. We're unkind; we're manipulative; we're dishonest. If we saw that this very life we lead is the face of God itself, we would not be able to behave in such ways—not because of any commandment or prohibition, but just because we see what life is.

It's not that practice—sitting in front of the door—is useless. But much of what we call practice—chasing after ideals or enlightenment—is illusion. It doesn't open the door. Until we see this fact as clearly as the taste of our oatmeal in the morning, we will have to go through many byways and twistings, disappointments and illnesses—the teachers of our lives. All of these struggles are part of learning about the door. If we practice well, sooner or later the puzzle gets clearer, and the door is more often open.

STUDENT: It seems that Dorothy could have wasted less time if she had done her sitting in the kitchen, in the middle of her family and daily tasks, instead of retreating to the top floor of the house, away from everything.

JOKO: We always search where we *think* the answer is, until we're ready to see. We do what we do until we don't do it anymore. That's neither bad nor good; it's just how things are. We have to wear out our illusions. If we tell ourselves, "The way to open that door is to spend more time with my kids," this, too, becomes just another obsessive idea. Spending time with our kids in order to become enlightened will probably not make us better parents, in any case.

STUDENT: Isn't practice about opening the heart? Isn't that what Dorothy was trying to do, really?

JOKO: Yes, that's one way to describe it. And she discovered that . . . ?

STUDENT: Her heart was always open.

JOKO: Right. The parents we can't stand, the partner who wounded us, the irritating friend: there's nothing wrong with them, unless we think so. Until we're ready to see this, however, we won't see it.

STUDENT: If the story is about a guest room, then Dorothy never even thought about having guests over.

JOKO: That's right. She wouldn't even think about it.
We think, "I should be nicer, kinder, more hospitable." But if we're caught within our illusions, we can't be truly hospitable. We may go through the motions, but being truly hospitable means simply being ourselves, as we are. We can't welcome someone else if we haven't welcomed ourselves first.

STUDENT: When we're caught up in our personal melodrama as Dorothy was, we're not truly available to others. When we see through our personal melodrama, we are able to see others' needs more objectively, and respond to them.

JOKO: Yes. We've all had the experience of being so upset that we're simply unable to hear about someone else's troubles. We don't have room for that; all of our space is taken up with our own stuff. We haven't got any "guest room."
Yet we can't simply say, "I won't be obsessed," and will it to happen. Then, we still think there's a hole in our life, that we've got to unlock the door and discover what's on the other side.

STUDENT: My practice has been a series of disappointments. I imagine, "This workshop will do it for me." I attend the workshop, and while it may be useful in some way, ultimately it's disillusioning. I find it very difficult simply to stay with my disappointment, to feel my vulnerability. Instead, I cover it over in some way, and tell myself, "I'll just try harder. I'll find another workshop."

STUDENT: I feel that I have wasted much time and energy, precious moments of my life—complaining about my parents or the conditions of my life—all in the effort to unlock the door.

JOKO: It's of no use to look back and say, "I should have been different." At any given moment, we are the way we are, and we see what we're able to see. For that reason, guilt is always inappropriate.

STUDENT: It seems as though we have to go through a certain amount of suffering. We have to be crucified before we'll surrender.

JOKO: Without overdramatizing the point, that's true. We are very stubborn. That's okay, too.

STUDENT: Was Dorothy able to enjoy her life? It bothers me that one has to struggle for so long.

JOKO: Yes, I imagine that she sometimes enjoyed her life, even before she saw what it was. We all enjoy our lives at times. But beneath the enjoyment and gratification is anxiety. We're still looking for something behind that door, and we're afraid we'll never find it. We think, "If I had this or that, I'd be happy." Momentary enjoyment does not eliminate this underlying unease. There's no shortcut. We must finally see who we are and what that room is, behind the door.

STUDENT: With me, the underlying feeling is fear. It's a faint undercurrent to everything I do. Most of my life I haven't been fully conscious of it; it was just there, running my life.

JOKO: In sitting, we bring our attention to that faint undercurrent. That means to notice our thoughts and the subtle contractions in our body. For Dorothy, this happened when her obsession with the locked door began to weaken, and she began to pay more attention to the condition of the rest of the house. Her hopes began to die.

STUDENT: We just have to take care of our immediate tasks.

JOKO: Right. And taking care of what needs to be taken care of brings us back to what we are at this moment.

In the story about Dorothy, what do you make of the cluttered rooms in the house?

STUDENT: Attachments. Thoughts about lots of things. Memories.

JOKO: Memories, fantasies, hopes.

STUDENT: It seems that when we have immediate tasks to do, we tend to focus instead on the fear or anxiety or whatever— the locked door—and forget to pay attention to the task at hand. In a way, the fear (or whatever) is irrelevant. There's the task to do, and we just need to do it, fear or no fear. I struggle with my life because instead of just doing what needs to be done, I fight the underlying fear; I try to unlock the door.

JOKO: Right. Paradoxically, the only way to unlock the door is to forget the door.

Students often complain to me that when they sit, something interferes with their awareness: "I get spacey." "I get so nervous. I just can't sit still." Underlying these complaints is the thought that in order to sit effectively, we have to get rid of all unpleasantness; the locked door has to be unlocked, so we can get to the good stuff.

If we're spacey, we're spacey. If we're nervous, we're nervous. That's the reality of our life at the moment. Good sitting means simply to be present to that: to *be* the spaciness or the nervousness.

People go to great lengths to eliminate troublesome feelings. "I'm tense; I have to do a workshop to relax." So they do the workshop, and it makes them relaxed—but for how long? Wanting the tension relieved is like looking at the locked door, trying to figure out how to open it. If we're obsessed with opening the door, we may find techniques to open it momentarily; but then we find ourselves right back in our lives, just as they were, living in the same old house. Instead of obsessing about the locked door, we need to be going about our lives, which means cleaning up the house, taking care of the baby, going to work, whatever.

STUDENT: A friend and I were just talking about how hard a year we have both had. Throughout our twenties and thirties, we both had hope that things were going to get better for us. Now, in our forties, we've come to the sinking realization that that's not going to happen: our lives are not going to get better!

JOKO: Paradoxically, this painful disillusionment with the future helps us to appreciate life as it is. Only when we give up the hope that things will get fixed can we come to the realization that things are fine as they are.

STUDENT: Recently I've had a similar realization. For years I have been telling myself that my life will be better when I have saved up enough money to go into semiretirement. I'll have more time for volunteer work; I'll be able to sit more consistently, do more reading, and so on. Now I'm beginning to realize that what I need to do is right here at work. If I'm trying to get something finished, and someone comes in and distracts me, that's just what I need to do at that moment. What I ought to be doing is just what I'm doing.

JOKO: In closing, let's ask ourselves, "How am I trying to unlock the door as opposed to simply living my life?" We're all trying to unlock the door, to find the key or formula. We're looking for the perfect teacher, the perfect partner, the perfect job, and so on. To notice that we're trying to unlock the door is immensely valuable; it helps us to see what our lives really are.

Wandering in the Desert

Wandering in the desert, looking for the Promised Land: this is our life. The discipline of sesshin intensifies this impression of wandering; sesshin feels confusing, discouraging, disappointing. We may have read books that paint a pretty picture of the Promised Land, what it's like to achieve awareness of buddha nature, enlightenment, and so on. Yet we find ourselves wandering. All we can do is simply to be the wandering itself. To be the wandering means to be each moment of sesshin, no matter what it is. As we survive, living through the dryness and thirst, we may come to a discovery: wandering in the desert *is* the Promised Land.

That's very hard for us to comprehend. We know our pain and suffering. We want the suffering to end. We want to reach a Promised Land where the suffering doesn't exist anymore.

In working with those who are dying or severely troubled, Stephen Levine observes that true healing happens when we go into our own pain so deeply that we see it is not just *our* pain, but *everyone's* pain. It's immensely moving and supportive to discover that my pain is not private to me. Practice helps us to see that the whole universe is in pain.

A similar point can be made about relationships. We tend to think of relationships as discrete in time: they begin, they last for a time, and they end. Yet we are always in relationship, always connected to one another. At a certain point in time, a relationship may manifest itself in a particular way, but before that manifestation, it already existed, and after it "ends," it continues. We continue in some sort of relationship even with those who have died. Former friends, former lovers, former relatives continue on in our lives and are part of who we are. It may be necessary for the visible manifestation to end, but the actual relationship never ends. We are not truly separate from one another. Our lives are joined; there is just one pain, just one joy, and it is ours. Once we face our pain and are willing to experience it, instead of covering it up, avoiding it, or rationalizing it, a shift occurs in our views of others and of our life.

As Stephen Levine states, each moment of persevering with our difficulties and suffering is a small victory. In staying with pain and irritability, we open up our relationship to life and to others. The process is slow; our pattern does not reverse itself overnight. We fight a constant battle between what we want and what is, what the universe presents to us. In sesshin, we see that battle joined more clearly. We see our fantasies, our efforts to figure things out and pursue our pet theories; we see our hopes of finding a door into the Promised Land, where all struggle and suffering will cease. We want, want, want: a certain person, a certain kind of relationship, a certain kind of work. Because no want like that can ever be completely fulfilled, we have ceaseless tension and anxiety that go right along with our wanting. They are inseparable twins.

Sometimes it's helpful to accentuate the anxiety, to reach a point where we just can't stand it. Then, we may be willing to back up and take another look at what's going on. Instead of endlessly concerning ourselves with what's wrong out there—with our partner, with our job, or whatever—we may begin to shift our relationship to what is. We learn to be what we are at this moment in this relationship or in a tedious aspect of our job. We begin to see the connection between ourselves and others. We see that our pain is also their pain, and their pain is also our pain. For example, a doctor who makes no connection between herself and her patients will see patients simply as one problem after another, to be forgotten when they walk out the door. A doctor who sees that her own discomfort and annoyance are her patients' discomfort and annoyance will be sustained by this sense of connection and will work more precisely and effectively.

The everyday tedium of our lives is the desert we wander, looking for the Promised Land. Our relationships, our work, and all the little necessary tasks we don't want to do are all the gift. We have to brush our teeth, we have to buy groceries, we have to do the laundry, we have to balance our checkbook. This tedium—this wandering in the desert—is in fact the face of God. Our struggles, the partner who drives us crazy, the report we don't want to write—these are the Promised Land.

We're experts at producing thoughts about our lives. We're not experts, however, at just *being* our lives, our pain and pleasure, our defeats and victories. Even happiness can be painful, because we know that we may lose it.

Life is very short. The moments that we now experience are quickly gone forever; we'll never see them again. Each day that passes takes with it thousands upon thousands of such moments. How will we spend the little interval that's left to us? Will we spend it spinning out thoughts about how terrible life is? Such thoughts are not even real. We will have such thoughts, but we can know that we're thinking them and not get caught in them. When we can sit with the bodily sensations and thoughts that are the pain, the suffering transforms into the universal, which is joy.

The point of our lives, as Stephen Levine says, is to fulfill that which we were born for, to heal into life. That means to heal out of the pain of our personal, separate, constricted "I want," into openness. The point of our lives is to be openness itself, which is joy. Joy includes suffering, happiness, everything that is. This kind of healing is what our lives are about. When I heal my pain, without any thought at all I heal yours, too. Practice is about discovering that *my* pain is *our* pain.

So we can't end our relationships. We can walk out, get divorced, but we can't end them. When we think we can end them, everybody suffers. We can't end our relationship to our children; we can't even end a relationship with someone we don't like. Such an ending would require us to be something we're not and never will be, which is separate from others. When we try to be separate, the suffering begins all over again.

As Stephen Levine says, we are born to heal into life. That means healing into our pain, and healing into the pain of the world. For each of us, that healing is different, but the basic purpose is the same. We need to hear this truth and remember it over and over and over, a thousand times. To do the work, we have to go against the current in our society, which tells us to look out for number one: everyone for himself or herself. Daily practice, doing sesshins, maintaining contact when we live at a distance, all are helpful if we are to do this work, the work of healing into life, and come to see that we have even now reached the Promised Land.

Practice Is Giving

Practice is truly about giving, but that can be easily misunderstood, so we must be careful. Recently I read a book by a woman who was called "Peace Pilgrim." In three decades she walked more than twenty-five thousand miles, carrying her only possessions with her, witnessing for peace. Her book shows that she really understood practice, which she describes very simply. She says that if we want to be happy, we have to give and give and give. Instead, most of us want to get and get and get. That's the nature of being human.

It took Peace Pilgrim many years of hard training to transform her life. For her, that training was totally to give. That's wonderful—if we understand it correctly. Beginning students typically have self-centered ideas about practice: "I'm going to practice so I can be thoroughly integrated." "I'm going to practice so I can be enlightened." "I'm going to practice in order to be calm." Instead, practice is about giving, giving, giving. But we make a mistake if we simply adopt that as a new ideal. Giving is not about thinking. Nor should we give in order to get some results for ourselves. For most of us, however, giving is confused with self-centered motivations, and this remains true until our practice is very solid.

We must ask ourselves, "What is giving?" This can keep us busy for many years. For example, should we give others whatever they want? Sometimes—and sometimes not. Sometimes we need to say no, or simply stay out of the way.

There is no formula, so we're bound to make mistakes—and that's fine. We practice with the results of our actions, and this will take time. Perhaps after many years we begin to grasp the real nature of giving. A Zen teacher in Japan requires new students to practice for ten years without working with him personally. When the students return to him after ten years, he tells them to sit another ten years. Though that's not my way of teaching, he has a point. It takes time to discover what our life is.

Last week I received two calls from persons looking for advice about practice. One caller said that her friend had a spiritual realization that was a bit off, and she needed the right book to set her friend straight. Another called at 1:30 A.M. to say that he had read a wonderful book about enlightenment and felt that his own practice wasn't quite enlightened. He wanted help in figuring it out. I told him that it wasn't a good idea to call people in the middle of the night. He said, "Oh, is it the middle of the night?" I said, "Enlightenment is about awakening; and if you're going to be awake, you need to know what time it is." He said, "I never thought of that."

Enlightenment is the ability to give totally in every second. It's not about having some great experience. Such moments may occur, but they don't make an enlightened life. We need to ask, "What does it mean for me to give in this moment?" For example, when the phone rings, how can we give? When doing physical work—cleaning, painting, cooking—what does it mean to give totally?

Though we can't make ourselves into totally giving persons just by thinking, we can notice when we don't totally give. We hide our self-centered motivations from ourselves; practice helps us to realize just how self-centered we are. The truth is that at any moment, we are as we are. We need to experience this, to know our thoughts and bodily feelings, and then slowly our experience can turn itself over. *We* don't have to do it. It just turns itself over. We can't make ourselves be a certain way. To imagine otherwise is one of the biggest traps in practice. But we can notice our intolerance and unkindness, our laziness and the other games we play. As we notice how we really are, things slowly begin to turn—as they are with many of my students. It is wonderful to see. When the turnover happens, the kindness or givingness spreads. That's what practice is about. Instead of a new ideal—"I don't want to visit him this afternoon, but I *should* be giving"—we act, and experience what goes on with us.

So please: give, give, give—and practice, practice, practice. It is the Way.

Notes

Preface

vii   **As Lenore Friedman** *Meetings with Remarkable Women: Buddhist Teachers in America* (Boston: Shambhala, 1987), p. 112.

Whirlpools and Stagnant Waters

5   **Caught in a self-centered dream** The vows are as follows: "Caught in a self-centered dream: only suffering. / Holding to self-centered thoughts: exactly the dream. / Each moment, life as it is: the only teacher. / Being just this moment: compassion's way."

9   **"boundless field of benefaction"** Francis Dojun Cook, *How to Raise an Ox: Zen Master Dogen's Shobogenzo, Including Ten Newly Translated Essays* (Los Angeles: Center Publications, 1978), pp. 24f.

Responding to Pressure

24   **The verse of the Kesa** Francis Dojun Cook, *How to Raise an Ox*, pp. 24f.

24   **Gurdjieff called our strategy** For an elaboration of the concept of a "chief feature" see Don Richard Riso, *Personality Types: Using the Enneagram for Self-Discovery* (Boston: Houghton Mifflin, 1987).

The Baseboard

38   **The Supreme Doctrine** Hubert Benoit, *The Supreme Doctrine: Psychological Studies in Zen Thought* (New York: Viking, 1955), p. 145.

The Eye of the Hurricane

67 **Kyogun's Man up a Tree** *Gateless Gate, Newly Translated With Commentary by Zen Master Koun Yamada* (Los Angeles: Center Publications, 1979), p. 35.

Integration

93 **There is a traditional Zen story** See Paul Reps, compiler, *Zen Flesh, Zen Bones: A Collection of Zen and Pre-Zen Writings* (Garden City, NY: Anchor, Doubleday, no date), "The Thief Who Became a Disciple," p. 41.

The Tomato Fighters

98 **"The best athlete wants** *Tao Te Ching: A New English Version, with Foreword and Notes,* by Stephen Mitchell (New York: Harper & Row, 1988), chap. 68.

Experiences and Experiencing

121 **We would rather be ruined** W. H. Auden, from "The Age of Anxiety," in *Collected Poems,* ed. by Edward Mendelson (New York: Random House, 1976), p. 407.

The Icy Couch

125 **"that this spasm, which** Hubert Benoit, *The Supreme Doctrine: Psychological Studies in Zen Thought* (New York: Viking, 1955), p. 140.

125 **"One can indeed say** Benoit, *The Supreme Doctrine,* p. 145.

Attention Means Attention

168 **There's an old Zen story** Philip Kapleau, ed., *The Three Pillars of Zen: Teaching, Practice, Enlightenment* (Boston: Beacon, 1967), pp. 10–11.

Transformation

205 **As Carlos Castaneda writes** Carlos Castaneda, *Journey to Ixtlan: The Lessons of Don Juan* (New York: Simon and Schuster, 1972).

Wandering in the Desert

267 **Stephen Levine observes** Stephen Levine, *Healing into Life and Death* (New York: Doubleday, 1987).

Practice Is Giving

271 **"Peace Pilgrim"** *Peace Pilgrim: Her Life and Work in Her Own Words, Compiled by Some of Her Friends* (Santa Fe, NM: Ocean Tree, 1991). Also *Steps Toward Inner Peace— A Discourse by Peace Pilgrim: Suggested Uses of Harmonious Principles for Human Living.* Friends of Peace Pilgrim, 43480 Cedar Avenue, Hemet, CA 92343.